The World and Yugoslavia's Wars

The World and Yugoslavia's Wars

Edited by
Richard H. Ullman

A COUNCIL ON FOREIGN RELATIONS BOOK

COUNCIL ON FOREIGN RELATIONS BOOKS

If you would like more information on Council publications, please write the Council on Foreign Relations, 58 East 68th Street, New York, NY 10021, or call the Publications Office at (212) 734-0400.

Library of Congress Cataloging-in-Publication Data

The World and Yugoslavia's Wars / Richard H. Ullman, editor.
    220 pps. cm.
    Includes index.
    ISBN 0-87609-191-5
    1. Yugoslav War, 1991– —Diplomatic history. 2. Yugoslavia—Foreign relations—1980–1992. 3. Yugoslavia—Foreign relations—1992– I. Ullman, Richard H. (Richard Henry) DR1313.7.D58W67 1996
327.497—dc20
                                              96-14890
                                                  CIP

96   97   98   99   PB   10   9   8   7   6   5   4   3   2   1

Cover Design: Dorothy Wachtenheim

Contents

Introduction: The World and Yugoslavia's Wars

Richard H. Ullman

O N NOVEMBER 21, 1995, in the improbable setting of an air force base in the industrial rust belt of the United States, representatives of the three major ethnic groups of the former Socialist Federal Republic of Yugoslavia put their initials on an agreement that, if faithfully carried out, would bring to an end the most ferocious war fought on the continent of Europe since 1945.

Indeed, for sheer horror, especially for the savagery of crimes against noncombatants, the only apt comparison with the Yugoslav conflict is World War II itself. The similarity is not coincidental: many of the murderous hatreds that burned like an acid through the territory of the former Yugoslavia during the four-plus years from June 1991 through November 1995 had their origins in the same ideological-cum-religious-cum-ethnic conflicts that made the Balkans a killing field half a century before. The human toll of the recent conflict, like that of the earlier one, is mind-numbingly large. As many as 300,000 persons may have lost their lives since 1991—many of them willfully slaughtered, others the victims of starvation, disease, or exposure. And as many as two million persons may have been forcibly displaced from their homes or have otherwise become refugees.[1] Such privations were inflicted for the most part in fulfillment of a policy whose euphemistic label, "ethnic cleansing," would have been a credit to the propagandists of Hitler's Reich or Stalin's Soviet Union.

For the moment, perhaps longer, Yugoslavia's wars are in abeyance. The plural, wars, is appropriate: since 1991 there have been four. First was the brief and successful struggle for independence waged against

1

the federal army (the so-called Yugoslav People's Army, or YPA) by the republic of Slovenia. Next was Croatia's much more protracted but ultimately successful effort to achieve the same objective, which, like Slovenia's, began with a declaration of independence on June 25, 1991. Third was the attempt by the Serbs of the Croatian district known as the Krajina, where they were locally a majority, to join their lands to Serbia. They failed: in August 1995 the Croatian army overran the Krajina in a lightning invasion and forced most of the Serbs—some 170,000 of them—to flee for their lives.[2]

The fourth—and the largest and bloodiest—war ravaged the republic of Bosnia and Herzegovina. The complicated origins of that conflict might without undue distortion be said to lie in the insistence of the Bosnian Serbs, who made up 31 percent of the prewar population, on breaking up the republic and attaching the districts in which they lived to Serbia. They rejected the alternative: becoming part of a unified independent state whose government might be dominated by the 44 percent who were Muslims. In turn, the Muslims feared that they themselves would be dominated by Serbia if they were to remain in a rump Yugoslavia whose ethnic balance had been upset by the secession of Slovenia and Croatia. They chose instead to move toward independence—for a more or less unified Bosnian state that would include the increasingly unwilling Serbs, not one divided on ethnic lines. That sequence of impulses and actions, in March–April 1992, triggered the outbreak of Bosnia's horrifying war.[3]

Although they differed drastically in scope and intensity, all four of these wars were real ones. There remain, as well, two wars-in-waiting. At the core of the flames if either were to ignite would be ethnic Albanians, another national element of the former Yugoslavia. They were a presence in two republics. In Serbia, Albanians form 90 percent of the population of the province of Kosovo, which constitutionally enjoys formal autonomy. But during the last decade what once was Kosovo's substantial real autonomy has been reduced to an empty shell by the Serbian government of Slobodan Milosevic. Recently there have been not-so-veiled Serb threats that the Kosovars (as the Albanians are called) will be expelled to make room for Serb refugees from the Krajina and elsewhere. The second republic in which ethnic Albanians were an important part was Macedonia, whose own choice in 1992 of independence was unopposed by Serbia: as in Slovenia, the local Serb population was too small and too scattered to be grist for Belgrade's demagogic mill. A fifth of Macedonia's population is Albanian. An upheaval in Kosovo that resulted in international recognition of the right of Albanian Kosovars to self-determination might lead Macedonia's Albanians to seek substantial autonomy or even the incorporation into Albania of those areas of Macedonia in which they are a majority.[4]

If Yugoslavia's wars were to widen, expansion of the zone of conflict probably would come through the involvement of Kosovo's or Macedonia's ethnic Albanians. Such an event would raise the prospect of having Albania itself becoming involved, which might, in turn, call forth a military response on the part of a Greece fearful not merely of the spread of unrest to the ethnic Macedonian population of its northern provinces, but also that Macedonia would seek to annex them. And hostilities between Greece and Albania would raise the prospect of some sort of intervention by Greece's ancient enemy, Turkey, and therefore of additional ripples spreading outward.

The purpose of this book is to explore, from different perspectives, the implications of Yugoslavia's wars and would-be wars for the international system as a whole and for the principal powers within that system. Those implications would differ considerably depending on whether the violence were confined to the territory of the former Yugoslavia or whether it spread to, and engulfed, other states in the region. There has, in fact, never been a high probability that any of these scenarios for a wider war would become actual, and the wider the hypothesized circle of expanded conflict, the lower the probability has been. Indeed, as chapter 1 argues at length, a striking aspect of Yugoslavia's wars is not how likely they were to spread but how resistant to their enlargement the international system has been. That chapter argues explicitly, and most of the other chapters argue by implication, that since the beginnings of Yugoslavia's wars in 1991 none of the great powers has concluded that any plausible outcome of those wars would so jeopardize its interests as to impel its military intervention to defend them.

On the contrary, the major powers today perceive their interests in terms sharply different from those that made the Balkans the vortex of earlier great power conflicts. Europe's peace today is a divisible peace: violent conflicts will be sufficiently confined so that they will be very unlikely to escalate across the threshold of war among the major European powers. There will certainly be quarrels and animosities, more often within states than between them. Their locus will be predominantly in eastern Europe—on the territory of the satellites and republics of the former Soviet Union. The Balkans, obviously, will be a zone of some instability. Some of these quarrels and animosities—a very few of them—will escalate to serious levels of violence. Yet outsiders will have every incentive to remain outside rather than to escalate the level of conflict through competitive interventions. Most Europeans—indeed, an overwhelming majority of them—will live their entire lives without firsthand experience of the flames of war. Given Europe's history of wars that have not been contained, that is a revolutionary development. It is small consolation, however, to the peoples who will be involved in the conflicts that do take place. Indeed, for them its implication is grim. It means that rescue, in the form of an intervention by outside actors that smothers the flames, will be late in coming—if it comes at all.[5]

The war in Bosnia and Herzegovina exemplifies this point. It raged for nearly four years before the leaders of the Western powers acknowledged what had long been apparent to any newspaper reader or television viewer: that the U.N. presence under the limited rules of engagement that Thomas Weiss describes in his contribution to this volume had the effect only of prolonging the violence rather than damping it. With the somewhat ambivalent acquiescence of their Russian counterparts—an ambivalence combined with a growing hostility, both chronicled in these pages by Paul Goble—Western governments, at the insistence of U.S. President Bill Clinton, decided at long last to bring to bear enough military force to induce the contending parties to reach a settlement. In deciding to act, they were motivated not so much by interest as by embarrassment. "We've known for years of the devastation," U.S. Secretary of Defense William Perry told journalists in early January 1996 when he flew into Sarajevo with detachments of the North Atlantic Treaty Organization (NATO) Implementation Force. Nevertheless, he said, it was still "unspeakably saddening" to see it firsthand. "It's just appalling," he continued, "that this could happen in Europe in the 1990s, that the world would let this happen." And he noted in conclusion: "it does give me a very good, warm feeling, though, that the world is taking an action now."[6]

"The world," of course, did not let Yugoslavia happen. Governments did. The indecision, vacillation, confusion, and dissimulation that characterized the approach to the problem of Yugoslavia by both the United States and its major European allies are treated at length in chapter 5 by David Gompert (himself a senior policymaker in the administration he discusses at length, that of President George Bush) and by Stanley Hoffmann in chapter 4. Nor did "the world" initiate the actions that gave Secretary Perry his warm feeling. Again, a few governments did, his own among them. Their newfound consensus in the wake of particularly atrocious Bosnian Serb behavior—overrunning the "safe areas" of Srebrenica and Zepa and executing thousands of Muslims, then firing a mortar shell into the main Sarajevo market—gave rise to the NATO bombing campaign of August–September 1995 that made it possible for Perry to land at Sarajevo airport five months later.[7] There is a point, of course, when interest and embarrassment merge. When television sets worldwide nightly show pictures of massacred civilians, governments that previously have not perceived an important interest at stake in any specific outcome of a conflict discover that they have a real interest in ceasing to appear—to their own publics and to the world—as not only callous but impotent.

Students and practitioners of international relations can only applaud the fact that the statesmen of today assess their stakes in the Balkans as quite different and very much less weighty than their predecessors as recently as two decades before had assessed them as being. Those earlier assessments made the region the vortex of great power rivalries and, therefore, a tinderbox for wider wars. But most of these analysts would then deplore one obvious consequence of these changed assessments: that for more than four years the governments of the world, and of Europe in particular, stood by and took no effective action to put an end to the horrors that were consuming a once-tranquil and "civilized" land.

Reluctance to get involved is reinforced by another characteristic of the post–Cold War era: the governments of liberal democracies are extremely reluctant to place members of their armed forces in situations where their lives may be at risk. This is true even in the instance of all-volunteer armed forces, such as those of the United States and the United Kingdom. For the United States it is a peculiarly constricting condition. Two administrations in Washington refused to contribute U.S. ground forces to U.N. peacekeeping activities for fear of potential casualties. By the time of the Dayton agreement, 54 French soldiers had been killed in peacekeeping efforts in the former Yugoslavia (the French, as Hoffmann makes clear, had been the most aggressive peacekeepers, especially under the presidency of Jacques Chirac); had they been Americans, the pressure on the president to withdraw any remaining personnel would probably have been enormous. In chapter 3, Thomas Weiss points out the anomaly of this situation: "Ironically, the only country to project military power worldwide is timid while lesser powers with considerably less capacity are far more willing to sustain the deaths and casualties that are often concomitants of the present generation of U.N. peacekeeping."

A particularly striking aspect of the world's relationship to Yugoslavia's wars is that throughout the West, but especially in Europe, publics consistently favored stronger actions to bring the fighting to a close than governments did. As Richard Sobel makes clear in chapter 6, the publics in the United States and western Europe had been appalled for some time by the images from the former Yugoslavia. Public opinion in the West was increasingly united in demanding that governments do something to end the bloodletting. Especially in Europe, but at many junctures also in the United States, publics favored robust measures of military intervention. Sobel reports that there was in Europe nearly always at least a plurality in favor of such measures even when they were posited to be unilateral. Once the poll takers posited international sharing of the burden, under either NATO's banner or that of the United Nations, a plurality became a majority. That was also the case in the United States, so long as only air and naval forces, and not ground combat forces, would be involved. The data indicate that the public favored internationalization not only because it meant that the burden would be shared but because it conferred a legitimacy that unilateral actions lacked.

Legitimacy is a central issue in two other chapters of this volume. In chapter 8 Abram and Antonia Chayes analyze the myriad things that must be done to make it more likely that the Dayton agreement will not merely be a temporary cease-fire but will form the basis of a lasting peace. Among the many documents that were endorsed at Dayton as if almost in passing was a constitution for the new state of Bosnia and Herzegovina. The Chayes make clear how problematic such efforts at state-building often are. Most of all, the various centers and layers of authority need to be accepted as legitimate rather than as imposed by either domestic or foreign forces.

Legitimacy is also at stake in the issue of war crimes. The U.N. Security Council decided early in 1993 to establish an international tribunal for the prosecution of persons responsible for "serious violations of international humanitarian law." By the end of 1995 the tribunal, presided over by a distinguished South African jurist, had indicted 56 men—49 Serbs and 7 Croats. It had held only one trial, however—of a Bosnian Serb who was arrested while visiting Germany. The continuation of the project, and especially any attempt to bring to justice leaders of any of the warring factions, raises squarely the question: What, if anything, can be done to assure that the process seems legitimate to the members of all the region's peoples, particularly the Serbs?[8]

The issue of legitimacy is also at the core of what Jean Manas finds in chapter 2 to be the trade-off between the goals of peace and justice. In contexts like those of the former Yugoslavia, he asserts, it is impossible to seek both peace and justice at the same time. War can be brought to a close if the aggressed-upon side is willing to make sufficiently large concessions to the aggressor. But the concessions make a mockery of the ideal of justice. By the same token, one can rigorously pursue the goal of justice if one is prepared to forgo peace. Outside actors who have tried to influence the course of events in the former Yugoslavia—for example, by proposing the terms of a settlement—usually demonstrate that they have failed to recognize the immutability of this trade-off. By trying to achieve both, they end up achieving neither. The pages of this book contain many examples that demonstrate how apposite are Manas's observations.

The chapters that follow had their origins in a study group sponsored by the Council on Foreign Relations during 1993–94. All have been revised and brought up to date many times as their authors struggled to keep up with events. The Dayton agreement of November 21, 1995, supplied the natural break the editor was seeking to enable him to bring the volume forward to publication. For that watershed he wishes to thank the tireless master of the Dayton process, Ambassador Richard C. Holbrooke. He is grateful also to Leslie H. Gelb, president of the Council on Foreign Relations, for pushing him to convene the study group and then insisting that its products be of publishable quality; to Nicholas X. Rizopoulos, senior studies editor of the Council and authority on Balkan politics, for his provocative contributions to the group's discussions and then for his searching critiques of early drafts of the papers that eventually became the chapters of this book; and to Linda Wrigley, who brought her impeccable sense of relevance and of style to the line editing of penultimate drafts.

Notes

1. For a discussion of the human and demographic consequences of the conflict, see Milorad Pipovác, "Piecing Together the Balkan Puzzle," in Payam Akhavan and Robert Howse, eds., *Yugoslavia the Former and Future: Reflections by Scholars from the Region* (Geneva: United Nations Research Institute for Social Development, 1995), pp. 145–46. Correspondent Roger Cohen, in his valedictory article following 21 months in Bosnia, stated that the death toll in Bosnia alone was more than 200,000. "Spent Bosnia Now Tries to Make Its Peace," *New York Times*, December 31, 1995, p. 1.

2. See, among many, the following interpretive articles by Roger Cohen in *New York Times*, written in the wake of the Croat occupation of the Krajina: "From 'Greater Serbia' to Lesser Serbs: A War Turns," August 20, 1995, p. E1; "Finally Torn Apart, the Balkans Can Hope," September 3, 1995, p. E6; "Calling History to Arms: Serbs Invoke Their Past," September 7, 1995, p. A1; "Serbs of 'Greater Serbia' Find Suffering and Decay," September 17, 1995, p. 1.

3. For these events, see Susan L. Woodward, *Balkan Tragedy: Chaos and Dissolution after the Cold War* (Washington, DC: Brookings Institution, 1995).

4. Ibid., pp. 215–16. See also the very useful map on p. 217.

5. For an extended statement of the argument that Europe's peace today is a "divisible peace," see Richard H. Ullman, *Securing Europe* (Princeton, NJ: Princeton University Press, 1991).

6. Office of the Assistant Secretary of Defense for Public Affairs, "Secretary of Defense William J. Perry Departure Interview, Sarajevo, Bosnia," January 3, 1996, p. 1. See also Ian Fisher, "Pentagon Boss Walks in Footsteps of Peace-keepers," *New York Times,* January 4, 1996, p. A8.

7. The shelling of the Mrkale market, killing 38 civilians, was the main factor that gave rise to the NATO air strikes. The mass executions after the fall of Srebrenica were then still only rumors, regarded as well founded but still unconfirmed. For a definitive account, see "Bosnia-Hercegovina: The Fall of Srebrenica and the Failure of U.N. Peacekeeping," *Human Rights Watch/Helsinki,* vol. 7, no. 13 (October 1995).

8. The resolution creating the tribunal was U.N. S.C. Res. 808, February 22, 1993. For a summary table listing the name, ethnicity, rank, or position and location of crime(s) of all those indicted during the period 1993–95, and the tribunal's charges against each, see "The Accused, the Allegations," *Washington Post,* December 18, 1995, p. A17.

Chapter 1

The Wars in Yugoslavia and the International System after the Cold War

Richard H. Ullman

URING the first half of the 1990s, the admixture of lands and peoples once known as Yugoslavia gave grim evidence that some of Europe's fondest hopes were only illusions. One such hope—the one from which all the others flowed—was that Europe would be a zone of peace. The last decade of the Cold War had seen the maturation of a number of institutions designed to bring about the peaceful resolution of European conflicts; with the end of the Cold War, it was confidently assumed, these institutions would come into their own.

Yugoslavia was a living laboratory for experiments in conflict resolution. Indeed, the Yugoslav state itself was built upon a hypothesis: that not only could its eight main ethnic groups coexist within the federal structure forged by Josip Broz Tito at the end of World War II but that, with the passage of time, they would increasingly submerge their differences in a common Yugoslav identity. The hypothesis was one of Europe's central hopes-turned-illusion: the experiment failed.

As it turned out, the hope at the core of the experiment depended to a remarkable degree on Tito himself—on both his moral authority and his authoritarian mode of governance. After his death in 1980, control gradually shifted into the hands of provincial demagogues who styled themselves as democrats and who quickly discovered that beating the drum of ethnic nationalism was the surest way to accumulate more personal power.

The old multicultural order did not merely collapse, however. In 1991–92 it shattered amid warfare of the most brutal kind. Outsiders looked on in disbelief that a relatively modern, organized, peaceful polity, fully part of Europe, could sink so far into the abyss that the most bestial and arbitrary violence against members of other ethnic groups not only became routine but in many instances was sanctioned by whatever passed for governmental authority. (More desirable, even, than killing an adult was killing a child, especially a male child, for that would kill the future.) The extraordinary thing was how effective the demagogues were, and how weak and ineffective were the efforts of the moderates who made up the bulk of the population and who presumably ordinarily would have called for a halt to the insanity. Anecdotal accounts are overwhelming in their quotidian horror. Families that had lived for decades as friendly and cooperative neighbors suddenly faced one another—some moved by fear, others by greed—as murderous enemies. The tidal wave of bloodshed swept right over those who labeled it madness.[1]

Nothing exemplified this conflation of hope and illusion more than the city of Sarajevo, whose skyline had become so familiar worldwide to television viewers of the 1984 Winter Olympic Games: for centuries its mosques, churches, and synagogues had coexisted peacefully side by side, a proud symbol of tolerance and cultural harmony among the diverse peoples of the republic of Bosnia and Herzegovina. There, more than anywhere, people took pride in identifying themselves simply as Yugoslavs. But as so often occurs, under war's influence tolerance and trust gave way to suspicion and hatred. In 1992 Bosnian Serbs, seeking to secede from the republic while taking most of its territory with them, placed Sarajevo under almost constant siege. With each harsh passing year of war, the ruling Muslim faction of the republic's leadership and the city made Sarajevo an ever stronger symbol of its own increasingly militant Islamic sectarianism.

Another hope that proved to be illusory was that the Yugoslav People's Army (YPA), formed from the partisan brigades and the National Liberation Army of World War II, would remain the embodiment of Tito's multicultural ideal. When Yugoslavia's crisis came, however, the YPA was well on its way to becoming an instrument of the nationalism of the most numerous ethnic group within the old federation, the Serbs. On June 27, 1991, when the YPA went into battle for the first time, it trained its guns not on invading Soviet forces seeking to force Yugoslavia to return to communist orthodoxy—the contingency that for so long had guided its planning and its exercises—but on Slovene fellow citizens of the Yugoslav federation. The Slovenes had committed the unpardonable sin of seceding from the increasingly Serb-dominated federation and declaring their republic a separate, fully sovereign state.

For those who still live within what once was Yugoslavia, and who survive its wars, these illusions and many others like them will be costly. As chapter 8, by Abram and Antonia Chayes, makes clear, the process of healing the wounds of war and restoring some semblance of economic prosperity will be lengthy and arduous. The conflict already has imposed significant costs not only on the neighbors of the former Yugoslavia but on the wider international community.

Yugoslavia's Wars and International Anarchy

For many analysts, Yugoslavia's wars have become a metaphor for the international system itself, a system that is more turbulent and anarchic today than it was at any time during the last several centuries, and that is likely to become more so. That is not to say that the international system of the Cold War was not anarchic, in the sense that it lacked an overarching supranational authority able to assure order either in the interactions of states or in the relations of groups and individuals within them. Yet it was also a relatively organized system in which order was maintained by each of the two superpowers taking on the role of disciplinarian within its own bloc.

The techniques the superpowers employed for keeping errants and dissidents in line differed according to the ideological precepts and accepted practices of East and West. Within each bloc, the patron superpower employed combinations of carrots and sticks to assure that there was relative order rather than anarchy. The result was that the international system of the Cold War years was in important respects clearly more stable than today's. However, one should not forget that there were very few days during the four-plus decades of Cold War when a fairly robust hot war (often more than one) was not going on somewhere—always in the Third World, mostly in Asia, and usually costly in terms of lives.

Might the dissolution of Yugoslavia have occurred in the international system of the early 1980s or, indeed, at any other period of tension between the two Cold War blocs? Such a question raises two others. The first views a hypothetical Yugoslav crisis from the outside in: Would the Cold War blocs have regarded the breakup of Yugoslavia as sufficiently *un*threatening to their larger interests so that either or both might have been able to forgo intervention, even if it appeared that the other bloc *was* intervening? The second question looks from the inside out: When Cold War tensions ebbed, as they did during the period of détente between Washington and Moscow during the early 1970s, might the leaders of Slovenia and Croatia ever have felt that they could get away with a unilateral push for independence without precipitating outside intervention?

Obviously there can never be definitive answers to such counterfactual questions. But the likelihood of a wider and more dangerous conflagration arising from a crisis in Yugoslavia surely must be judged to have been quite high, at least through the 1960s, and not negligible later, especially when that judgment is reinforced by the experience of two world wars. The breakup of post-Tito Yugoslavia was a staple ingredient in Western war game scenarios. Searching for a plausible train of events to trigger a hypothetical war between East and West, scenario writers in the Pentagon or at the War Colleges could always safely posit a Yugoslav crisis. They frequently did so. No doubt mirror images of the same scenarios figured in Soviet and Warsaw Pact war games. Western scenarios usually began with the death of Tito. However, in 1980, when Tito died, there was no conflagration. In fact, the breakup and then the crisis that the scenarios assumed really did occur, but in slow motion rather than as a cataclysm. Indeed, so slow was the motion that many observers missed it. The 1980s, they thought, would bring rising prosperity to a united Yugoslavia. Real life, of course, was not so kind: the 1980s saw the opening of cleavages among the nations that made up Yugoslavia and an economic downturn that made the cleavages irreparable.[2]

War games inform policy; they do not govern it. But they may create expectations. And they shape war plans. The two great alliances, the North Atlantic Treaty Organization (NATO) and the Warsaw Treaty Organization, never came close to hot war. So the plans remained on the shelves. Had real war ever appeared likely, leaders of both alliances would have found that their standard military repertoires included responses to the contingency of the breakup of Yugoslavia either caused or followed by the intervention of the other alliance. In an escalating crisis, large, complex organizations do not like to improvise; they prefer to follow standard, well-rehearsed routines. If one side had intervened in a Cold War Yugoslav crisis, competitive intervention by the other side is as easy to imagine as abstention.

During the Cold War, when both sides knew that such risks were ever present, along with knowledge came caution. When potential costs are high, far less than certainty of having to incur them is sufficient to deter. Thus, it seems unlikely that the leaders of either Slovenia or Croatia would have made a break for independence had they thought that one consequence of their doing so could well have been East-West war. Similarly, the Muslim leadership of Bosnia and Herzegovina has consistently reiterated that it would not have chosen independence had the earlier departure of Slovenia and Croatia not given Serbia even more disproportionate weight in the rump Yugoslavia in which the Bosnians would have found themselves.[3] Thus, the international politics of the Cold War contributed significantly to holding Yugoslavia together.

Before 1989 another factor had the same effect—the declining but still lingering prestige of Titoist ideology. Tito's vision of a multinational, socialist Yugoslavia still retained some of its power. By 1989 that power had largely dissipated, owing first to the campaign by Serbia to alter to its advantage the federation's delicate system of internal balances and, second, to the discrediting of communist socialism that was occurring all over eastern Europe and even within the Soviet Union.[4]

Thus far we have been dealing with speculations—indeed, with speculations about the past: What would have happened *if . . . ?* What we *know* happened is that in the climate of 1989–91 the leaders of Slovenia and Croatia believed (the Croats with less confidence) that they could break free of the bonds of the federation without serious penalty. The Slovenes—ordinary citizens as well as the leaders—correctly perceived that the price for their unilateral declaration would be paid by others, not themselves. But most Croats accurately saw the danger that awaited them and therefore wanted the Slovenes to back down, lest Croatia's president, Franjo Tudjman, and the militant nationalists whom he led felt forced into complete secession rather than some variant of autonomy.[5]

In the case of Croatia, Tudjman and his colleagues felt strong enough to give to the Serb minority in the Krajina only the flimsiest of guarantees of their civil and political rights—guarantees that the Croats proceeded to violate. And the Serbs, in their turn, felt able to resort to measures of hideous violence against civilian populations, measures not dissimilar to those employed by the Nazis in wartime occupied Europe—or to those of the Croatian movement known as the Ustashi, Germany's allies, during the same period.[6]

Some of these speculations were built on the assumption of a continuation of some form of bipolarity and of the Cold War. Their purpose was to emphasize that by the time of the Slovene and Croatian secession, the bipolar world was gone, scarcely likely to return. There is another set of speculations worth making, however, ones that are future-oriented and focused on post–Cold War institutions. How might the threat of secession and war in Yugoslavia have been handled by a European Union (EU) whose members were more clearly of one mind than they are today and more able to pursue their oft-stated goal of a "common foreign and security policy," or by an Organization for Security and Cooperation in Europe (OSCE) with more developed aptitudes for conflict resolution and enforcement of settlements? And what roles might NATO have played?

Any problem can be "solved" with verbal formulations that gloss over the very aspects that make it intractable. One can imagine, for example, a European Union armed with a combination of sticks and (mostly) carrots that might have made it more likely that the Yugoslav federation would have held together in some form or another, or at least have dissolved in a manner that largely precluded resort to violence. Such a combination might have included extensive credits at favorable rates, assured entry into the EU, immediate trade concessions and perhaps investment credits to fill the gap in the interim, and a variety of similar measures all designed to persuade Yugoslav voters that moderate politicians, rather than nationalist demagogues, could deliver a better future.

Thus, if the EU had been able to speak with one voice in dealing with nonmember states, if the goal of a common foreign and security policy had become reality, and above all if that policy were one that diverted large quantities of resources into an economic program for Yugoslavia, dissolution and disaster might have been averted. Even if it were not averted, however, its flames might have been contained and then snuffed out had the leading Western powers, operating through the Western European Union (WEU) if the Americans declined or through NATO if Washington agreed, intervened in August and September 1991 with sufficient strength to prevent the Serb-controlled YPA from leveling the Croatian city of Vukovar. In effect, that would have meant the West's drawing a line in the sand and being clearly willing to prevent the Serbs from crossing it.

To assume such behavior on the part of the west Europeans or the Americans is to underline just how improbable anything like it would have been. This is especially true regarding measures that might have averted the disintegration of the Yugoslav federation. Given all the other demands on the separate European governments and publics, and on the common institutions of the European Community (EC)—as it then was—why should they have made significant concessions to Yugoslavia? The EC had a long line of would-be members. What justification could there possibly have been for moving Yugoslavia from the rear of the line to the front? Or for voting in international financial institutions for credits for Yugoslavia large enough (and that would have been very large) to make a difference?[7]

There was, of course, one justification: to prevent not merely one calamitous war but several. Yet not until the wars were raging was the scenario sufficiently plausible to justify extraordinary measures. Even then, calamity induced inaction and indecision. Here was a paradigmatic illustration of Hegel's adage that Minerva's owl flies at dusk. We achieve wisdom only when it is too late for effective action.[8] In hindsight, just about any price would have been worth paying to avert the Balkan tragedy. If only we had known then what we know now: thus runs the lament. But to what sphere of human activity does it not apply?

Confronted first by the Slovene and Croat secession from the Yugoslav federation, then by the siege and systematic destruction by the Serbs of the Croatian city of Vukovar and the attempted siege of Dubrovnik, and next by the brutal effort of the Bosnian Serbs to "cleanse" much of Bosnia and Herzegovina of its Muslim population, the governments of the major powers could agree on only a minimalist program of using small, lightly armed contingents of military forces under U.N. auspices to protect agencies providing humanitarian assistance. The United Nations Protection Force (UNPROFOR) would adhere to a position of formal neutrality among the contending parties. As chapters later in this volume make clear, not for four years could the major powers and the international organizations that substantially reflected their policies—the United Nations, the EC, and NATO—summon the political will to take action remotely adequate to stop the slaughter and ethnic cleansing of which all parties were guilty (the Serbs, however, most of all) or to roll back the concomitant Serb efforts to redraw by force the boundaries of Yugoslavia's successor republics. Only with the intensive but limited bombing campaign of late August and September 1995 did Western powers intervene with anything like sufficient force to coerce the Bosnian Serbs to agree to a territorial settlement, even one that gave the Serbs considerably more land than would be commensurate with their numerical weight in the Bosnia of Tito's time.

It is easy to conclude from this record of near impotence on the part of the international community that the post–Cold War world is one safe for aggressors and that crimes against humanity as repugnant as ethnic cleansing will go unpunished.[9] Sometimes—alas, it goes without saying—that will be the case. What determines whether the international community is moved to take decisive action, however, is less the magnitude of the crimes than the identity of the victims and the victims' friends. Help is much more likely if the victims have behind them a powerful protector state prepared to act because it sees its own security interests affected, such as the United States in the instance of Iraq's invasion of Kuwait, or a regional organization with whose populations they share ethnic or religious roots. Although the Bosnian Muslims have aroused much sympathy and not insubstantial support, they have not found a powerful patron unambiguously committed to their cause. Nor did the coincidence of shared Islam prove sufficient. It brought the Muslims arms in discrete but growing quantities from Iran, Saudi

Arabia, and other Middle Eastern states, and some of these, it is said, "volunteer" military personnel as well.[10]

Two events in rapid succession turned the tide for the Muslims, however. First was the sudden, dramatic, and total victory of the Croatians over the Krajina Serbs in early August 1995. In this campaign the Croats were the beneficiaries of an extensive buildup of arms, mostly surplus equipment from former Warsaw Pact countries, imported in violation of the U.N.-mandated arms embargo, almost certainly with the help of Western intelligence agencies. Along with the arms came training supervised by 15 retired senior American officers operating as a private company, Military Professional Resources, Inc., who clearly enjoyed a close, continuing relationship with the Pentagon.[11] The second event was the American-led NATO bombing campaign of August–September 1995. Although Bosnian Serb military forces were not targeted as such, their ammunition depots and communications facilities were, and the Muslim-Croat alliance (a fragile structure based on what was, at best, only a partial coincidence of interests) was quick to take advantage of the disarray among its enemies. Western diplomats found themselves facing a new task: reining in the Muslims and the Croats to prevent them from trying to take the Bosnian Serb stronghold of Banja Luka, an event that seemed likely to lead to an escalation of the conflict through overt and large-scale intervention of YPA forces from Serbia itself.[12]

Yugoslavia's Wars and Western Stakes

In the weeks leading up to the outbreak of World War II, newspaper billboards and kiosks in Paris bore the legend *Mourir pour Danzig?* (To die for Danzig?). On more than a few occasions during the long siege of Bosnia's capital there were echoes (*Mourir pour Sarajevo?*) of that question from 1939. Not surprisingly, very few outsiders—even from Islamic states—were willing to take mortal risks to bring about any particular outcome in the former Yugoslavia. That proved especially true of Western governments; none concluded that its interests were commensurate with such risks, not even Germany, the major power that once had been most deeply involved in southeastern Europe. Before both world wars, Germany sought and achieved economic domination over the region. In the middle and late 1930s, Nazi strategists preparing for aggressive war used German capital to develop assured supplies of cheap raw materials, foodstuffs, and some industrial goods. Neither the United Kingdom nor France made a serious effort to counter this spread of German hegemony.[13]

In the autumn and winter of 1991–92 the coalition government led by Chancellor Helmut Kohl and Foreign Minister Hans Dietrich Genscher relentlessly lobbied Bonn's European Community partners to recognize the secessionist regimes in Slovenia and Croatia. This démarche raised questions about German motives: Was the Bonn government seeking to recapture the leading role its predecessors once had? For the government and, indeed, for all except perhaps some fringe elements in German society, the answer is negative. The nature of Germany's interest in the Balkans today contrasts sharply with that of the past. "Preventive recognition," as the Germans called it, would make a conflict that many still saw as a civil war into an unambiguously international war, thereby creating a legal basis for outside powers to come to the aid of victims of aggression. As Bonn saw it, Serbia would then have no alternative but to obey the rulings of international authority or become an international outlaw.[14]

Kohl and Genscher were successful in promoting widespread recognition of the Yugoslav succession states, but recognition does not seem to have been the silver bullet, solving all problems, that its advocates forecast. Since early 1992 Germany has maintained the lowest of profiles regarding the former Yugoslavia. With some embarrassment, Foreign Ministry officials in Bonn—who almost uniformly opposed their chiefs' policies—have explained the absence of German military personnel in UNPROFOR by pointing to what, until the Federal Republic's constitutional court ruled otherwise in July 1994, was commonly held to be a binding prohibition against the use of German troops outside the traditional NATO area. To any mention of this formal prohibition they usually add the observation that, after the atrocious behavior of Nazi forces in the Balkans during World War II, any presence on the ground today of uniformed Germans would be anathema.[15]

Only in mid-1995 did these strictures begin to bend. At that time Bonn announced that it would contribute transport and strike/reconnaissance aircraft to U.N. and NATO operations in Bosnia, and staff and medical personnel to U.N. headquarters in Croatia. And in late August and September 1995, when NATO mounted its large-scale bombing raids on Bosnian Serb military installations, the 270 aircraft from nine countries that took part included 14 German Tornado fighter bombers armed with antiradar missiles. Perhaps in deference to lingering German sensibilities, NATO commanders used the German Tornados for reconnaissance missions in which the aircraft and their crews were themselves in harm's way but did not directly inflict harm.[16]

Even more than in other countries, in Germany the politics of Yugoslavia has been primarily a politics of gesture, aimed at seeming to "do the right thing" for the Croatians and Slovenians (many of them former "guest workers")—and, incidentally, at satisfying the country's ample population of Croatian immigrants and the German Catholic hierarchy—rather than at maximizing any German national interest. The most persuasive argument in German politics seems to have been that, since the reunification of Germany had come about through the international community's willingness to take seriously the principle of national self-determination, the breakaway Yugoslav republics should enjoy no less an opportunity. That argument, however, is an expression of a principle, not of an interest.

Germany did have one particular interest at stake in Yugoslavia's wars: stemming the flow of persons fleeing them. The refugees were victims of ethnic cleansing or simply of the general upheaval. For them the Federal Republic, with its robust economy and the presence already of communities of most of the former Yugoslavia's ethnic groups, was a powerful magnet. Their eagerness for refuge in Germany, however, was matched by Bonn's desire to bar the door. The refugee problem meant that Bonn's interest in peace was both generalized and stronger than its interest in any particular outcome to the Yugoslav conflict. All things being equal, Helmut Kohl's government would like to see a strong Croatia emerge from the ruins. But Bonn would gladly settle for a stable peace. What matters most is the region's future stability, for instability creates refugees. Yet—and here is the conundrum—at least equally important is the need to keep German casualties to an absolute minimum, preferably to none at all. Faced with a choice between instability and stability purchased at a significant cost in German lives, Bonn would unhesitatingly choose instability.[17]

What is true of Germany today is true of the other major powers of the West, and of Russia too. No government has behaved as if it had vital interests at stake in the former Yugoslavia. Indeed, it is quite apparent that the absence of any perceptions of substantial interests (other than preventing the conflict from escalating into a much wider war) has made it so difficult for outside actors to frame effective policies. Policymaking was especially difficult for governments with troops on the ground as members of UNPROFOR. That is because, almost invariably, the safety of these troops soon became far more important in the domestic politics of the sending country than any possible outcome in the former Yugoslavia itself.[18]

In the summer of 1995, as part of NATO's response to the Bosnian Serbs' refusal to respect the status of Sarajevo and five smaller cities as U.N.-protected "safe areas," Britain and France deployed to Sarajevo their newly created joint mobile rapid reaction force (RRF), with 12,000 men and much more potent armaments (heavier guns, tanks, and attack helicopters) than those of their UNPROFOR detachments. The two European powers were already the largest troop contributors to UNPROFOR, with nearly 4,000 troops each, and their contingents had suffered the most casualties. While sufficient in number for traditional peacekeeping missions, UNPROFOR was obviously undermanned and underarmed for more aggressive peace enforcement ("robust peace maintenance," in the new argot of the trade) or the still more aggressive "peacemaking" that would characterize any really serious attempt to pursue national objectives on Yugoslav territory.[19] Even the addition of the RRF would not have been sufficient to change this condition.

Nearly all of the national elements of UNPROFOR sustained casualties. All the troop-supplying governments, but especially the Western ones, have found—in Bosnia and elsewhere—that even a few casualties are difficult to justify before parliaments at home unless there is something approaching societal consensus that the interests at stake are vital. Such consensus is deeper than mere approval. Thus, the prospect of a small number of casualties often is enough to cause a government to draw back from participating in a military operation whose purpose would otherwise receive widespread approval from government and society alike.

Moreover, it seems to have made no difference that UNPROFOR soldiers were nearly all volunteer, professional "regulars," not conscripts. The proposition that men and women who freely enlist in armed forces do so with the knowledge that they are electing to place themselves in harm's way from time to time seems to make no impact upon democratic electorates.[20] Public attitudes are significantly influenced by mass media that graphically play up the circumstances surrounding each casualty. That has been particularly the case with operations such as those in Bosnia, where the troop-sending states failed to identify in any persuasive way the national interests that their operations served. Thus, just when the end of the Cold War has made it relatively easy to secure a consensus within the U.N. Security Council, the perceived domestic political costs of loss of life among a nation's armed forces have made it difficult—often prohibitively so—to mount even a peacekeeping operation to monitor compliance with a settlement to which the contending parties have agreed, let alone a peacemaking operation in which outside forces are called upon to impose a cease-fire through coercion.

Because of this sensitivity to casualties, not only London and Paris but nearly all the troop-supplying governments repeatedly threatened to withdraw their personnel in the event of any developments that would notably increase the danger to which they are exposed. Among these possible developments, two were mentioned most often. One was a NATO air attack that would cause one or another of the parties to the conflict to strike out against the peacekeepers, as the Bosnian Serbs did when they took peacekeepers hostage in May 1995. Another was the lifting of the embargo, whose main effect has been to prevent the Bosnian

government from acquiring heavy weapons matching those of its enemies. The supposition was that, if the embargo were lifted, Serb forces
might retaliate, long before new arms could reach the Muslims, by
attacking U.N. peacekeepers.

The involvement of one or more great powers in a regional conflict
may sometimes result in a wider war. Yet in other circumstances it may
keep a war from spreading. That no government of a major outside
power thinks that its vital interests will be either substantially enhanced
or diminished by just about any reasonably plausible outcome of the
Yugoslav wars does not mean that warfare will be confined to the territorial space of the republics carved from the former Yugoslavia. Both
in the former Yugoslav republic of Macedonia, which also had opted
for independence, and in the Kosovo region of Serbia there are large
areas inhabited mostly by ethnic Albanians. Indeed, 90 percent of
the population of Kosovo is Albanian. In both regions, but especially in
Kosovo, tensions between Albanians and Serbs have been high for years,
and there is a real danger of violent conflicts, particularly if militant
Serb nationalists—perhaps even operating without the approval of the
Milosevic regime in Belgrade—attempt to expel any part of Kosovo's
Albanian population.[21]

Wider Wars: The Balkans as Tinderbox

Any pogrom-like attack by Serbs on Albanians would, of course, inflame
Albania itself and open the door to a still-wider conflict. There are Greek
communities in both Macedonia and Albania, and Bulgarians in Macedonia. Both Greece and Bulgaria, but especially Greece, might be drawn
in by the political need to be seen at home to be protecting ethnic
brethren. From there, the holding of a plebescite in the affected border-
lands, followed by their actual annexation, is but a relatively short step.

It is conceivable, although barely likely, that Turkey might be drawn
into the maelstrom, especially if Greece should become involved and attempt to seize territory now part of Macedonia or of Albania itself. It
should be noted, however, that Turkey was a major troop contributor
to UNPROFOR; in late May 1995 its contingent numbered 1,474.[22] Even
if Turkey's Islamic parties were to win a more decisive victory than they
did in the parliamentary elections of December 1995, they would be unlikely to embark upon a large-scale intervention that would be both lo-
gistically difficult and potentially quite costly. That would especially be
the case if Turkey were still embroiled in its seemingly endless war
against Kurdish separatists.

Any government in Ankara would feel some pressure from public
opinion to get involved. But it would be likely to do its best to resist

pressures to do much more than take a strong pro-Muslim rhetorical stand on a new Balkan war. Moreover, the fact that Turkey is still an applicant for membership in the EU might cause even moderate Islamists in Ankara to be wary of placing too much emphasis on Islam as a focus of Turkey's identity. In the unlikely event that militant Islamists were to take over the reins of government, incentives for greater involvement in the Balkans would undoubtedly be higher. So too, however, would be the resistance of other states, including the Western powers, to any leading role for Turkey.[23]

Turkey is not a great power today. At best it is a power to be reckoned with within its region. The other states mentioned here are not even that, although the YPA, in the days when it was more than merely a Serbian force, might have made a Soviet invasion prohibitively costly. A wider Balkan war today would be a true catastrophe, for it would likely be fought with the barbarous ferocity, fueled by ethnic hatreds, that has characterized all the fighting in the former Yugoslavia until now and, indeed, that characterized previous Balkan wars. Whether such a war would amount to more than a *local* catastrophe, however, depends on the extent to which the great powers became involved and on the regional effects of their involvement.

Thus far, with the exception of a few incidents, such as the dropping of bombs from YPA aircraft on Hungarian territory, the direct impact of the wars in the Balkans has not been felt beyond the territory of the former Yugoslavia. Of course, the war's economic impact, particularly in the form of disrupted trade and forgone investments, and its human impact in the form of massive flows of refugees, has been felt throughout the region and beyond. Yet, despite all the attention the war has received in national capitals, at the United Nations, by NATO, and by the organs of the EU, the actual involvement of the great powers was minimal up to the bombing campaign of August–September 1995 and the subsequent successful effort by the United States to force the contending factions to negotiate an end to the fighting. Even then, as Secretary of State Warren Christopher, chief negotiator Richard Holbrooke, and the other American officials who staged and managed the marathon-like Dayton negotiations made clear, they always were prepared to walk away if the parties could not reach agreement. That was, of course, a negotiating tactic. But it was also more: for them and for their European counterparts, being seen by their own publics at last to be working on forging a peace that would bring an end to the bloodletting—and yet not putting many of their own military personnel at serious risk—was at least as important as the peace agreement itself.[24]

That the major powers do not see vital interests at stake now is an indication of how much European international politics in the post–Cold

War era differ from those of previous eras. For much of the present century, any change in the alignment of one of the Balkan nations—especially Yugoslavia (or, before Yugoslavia existed, Serbia)—was regarded as the potential cause of a larger European war. During most of the Cold War, however, it often seemed that Yugoslavia mattered not so much for economic or geopolitical reasons but for the abstract reason of which camp it was in. The shaping event came in 1948, when Stalin expelled Yugoslavia from the Cominform (and therefore from the Socialist camp) under the mistaken assumption that the move would bring about Tito's downfall and his replacement by a more pliable regime willing to follow Moscow's lead. Instead, Tito emerged more secure in his power than ever, and even though Stalin's successors worked hard to erase the damage that his hard-line tactics had done, Western influence was never again eclipsed by that of the Soviet Union.[25]

Yugoslavia's Wars and International Institutions: What Roles for NATO?

For the international community, the greatest impact of Yugoslavia's wars may stem from another hope they have proved to be illusory: that the web of international security institutions constructed during the last half century would function as a safety net and would not permit European peoples to descend into barbarism. In particular, that was the assumption widely shared in Europe and North America about NATO, primary among those institutions, symbol of and vehicle for the commitment of Western governments—North American and European—to pursue common security goals though common policies. Yugoslavia's wars saw the first shots ever fired in anger by the alliance. But they also occasioned NATO's most serious division since the Suez crisis of 1956. That division and its resulting restraints on any but the most limited military action demonstrated that NATO's supposed power was highly contingent upon circumstances and that the alliance could seem—indeed, for many months was—largely impotent.

The targets of NATO's first shots were not Warsaw Pact armies flooding into the north German plain, the scenario that dominated the alliance's planning and training throughout four and a half decades of the Cold War, but four overage YPA warplanes that, like many others previously, had flagrantly violated the U.N. Security Council resolution prohibiting Yugoslav belligerents from using aircraft within a stipulated exclusion zone. In a second action a month later, in February 1994, local U.N. authorities, to whom NATO commanders were subordinated, permitted the destruction only of an empty, rusted, and obsolete YPA tank. In November 1994 NATO aircraft struck once more, damaging the runways of an airport in the Krajina from which Croatian Serbs had been flying in support of the Bosnian Serbs. But because Lieutenant General Bertrand de Lapresle, the French commander of UNPROFOR in the former Yugoslavia, feared that the Serbs would retaliate against his peacekeepers, he insisted that air strikes should avoid hitting 15 parked *Bosnian* Serb warplanes.

Then, in late May 1995, came the events that most starkly underlined the absurdity of NATO's situation. Responding to a series of local offensives by the Bosnian government, Bosnian Serb forces fired hundreds of artillery and mortar rounds into Sarajevo and other towns where Muslims were concentrated, towns previously declared "safe areas" by the U.N. Security Council. Many civilians were killed or wounded. This time the U.N. civilian and military commanders in the field decided that a more robust reaction was justified. At their request, NATO fighter-bombers destroyed an ammunition depot adjacent to the Bosnian Serb headquarters at Pale.

The Bosnian Serbs' response seemed to catch the alliance by surprise. It should have surprised no one. They made hostages of all the UNPROFOR soldiers they could reach, some 350 in all. Many they chained to structures thought to be likely targets of future NATO attacks, correctly assuming that NATO governments, constrained by public opinion in their own countries, would cease the air attacks rather than risk the hostages' lives.

Now, however, the Bosnian Serb leaders erred. They seem to have assumed that NATO would not be able to cobble together the two agreements necessary to pose a serious threat: an internal agreement among its member governments and then an external agreement with the U.N. secretary-general and his representatives in the field, each permitting the use of much larger quantums of violence. And, in particular, the Bosnian Serbs seem not to have calculated that their own behavior might be so grossly offensive as to cause NATO to ratchet up its response by much more than an order of magnitude. Yet just that train of escalation was set in motion on August 28, 1995, when a 120-mm mortar round, fired from territory controlled by the Bosnian Serbs, exploded in the midst of Sarajevo's main market, killing 37 civilians and seriously injuring 85 others.[26]

A year and a half earlier, on February 5, 1994, another shell exploding in the same market had killed 68 persons and injured 200 others. Images of maimed bodies had filled television screens around the world. NATO's response then was to demand that the Serbs hand over to UNPROFOR their heavy weapons—large-caliber guns and tanks—but then to take no other retaliatory action. (The same demand was made of the Muslims, who readily complied: they possessed far fewer such weapons and they welcomed the prospect of a more level playing field.) However, Serb compliance was short-lived. Within months—as soon as they realized that the West would do little to stop them—they forcibly entered the various UNPROFOR depots where the weapons were stored and demanded their return. Outgunned, the U.N. forces had no alternative but to comply. These and many other past humiliations were cumulative. The August 1995 massacre brought even more gruesome television images, which, in turn, still further amplified the mood among Western electorates that, this time, *something* must be done.

NATO's response was a minutely planned NATO bombing campaign aimed at military targets, especially ammunition stocks, weapons, and communications nodes. The campaign began August 30 and ran, with some pauses, until September 17. By then NATO warplanes had flown 3,515 sorties—roughly one good flying day in the Gulf War. Alliance planners were determined to avoid targets where there might be even a small chance of "collateral damage" to nearby civilians. That goal was achieved. So were the larger objectives of the air campaign: the Bosnian Serbs agreed to pull back their heavy weapons. Even more important, they agreed to take part with the Bosnian Muslims and Croats in peace talks that, from the outset, were premised upon the condition that they would emerge with only 49 percent of Bosnian territory, not the 70 percent that only weeks before had been in their grasp.[27]

For NATO, these moves into the Balkan quagmire were, in General Omar Bradley's memorable phrase about the Korean War, "the wrong war, at the wrong place, at the wrong time."[28] Indeed, the Yugoslav case was the hardest that Europe could offer. Nowhere else on the continent can there be found the multifold ethnic antagonisms within a relatively small geographic space that were all too apparent in the Yugoslavia of the late 1980s. Moreover, during these early post–Cold War years, NATO was faced with the problem of redefining itself. The great enemy that had provided its raison d'être had suddenly ceased to exist. Flushed with success, NATO suddenly faced becoming irrelevant. The understandable reaction of national governments and Brussels bureaucrats alike was to use rhetoric to stake out new territory. Meeting in Rome in November 1991, less than five months after Slovenia and Croatia declared independence and five months before the start of the war in Bosnia, the alliance's heads of state and government adopted what they called NATO's "new strategic concept." The danger the alliance faced was no longer "calculated aggression" from Moscow but "instabilities that may arise from the serious economic, social and political difficulties, including ethnic rivalries and territorial disputes, which are faced by many countries in central and eastern Europe."[29]

The final communiqués for this meeting and the Oslo meeting of NATO foreign ministers the following June asserted that the new role of the alliance was to assure the stability of Europe. It would perform European crisis management and peacekeeping, and do so in collaboration with other regional institutions—the Conference on (now renamed "Organization for") Security and Cooperation in Europe (CSCE/OSCE), the European Community (now Union) and the expression of its military identity, the Western European Union, and the Council of Europe. Effectively deployed, the representatives and resources of these institutions might have a moderating effect on future conflicts like those that sundered Yugoslavia.[30]

Optimists might apologize for what appears to have been three years of opportunity wasted by observing that the trial came too early: NATO's and Europe's facilities for conflict resolution were still in their infancy during the years of Yugoslavia's breakup. Pessimists would not reach for excuses. Nor would they emphasize the singularity of the Yugoslav example. Far from being characteristic merely of one state, they would say, Yugoslavia's traumas carry obvious implications for states everywhere whose existence depends on the likely viability of multicultural politics. Such states are all too vulnerable to the disruptive efforts of demagogic politicians skilled in the uses of modern means of mass communication. And as for the likelihood of a prompt and effective response by the "international community" even when there is a relatively well defined aggressor, Kuwait was the exception: states in trouble would be advised to have other remedies at hand.

The Fruits of Dayton

The chapters in this volume offer few grounds for optimism that the agreement initialed at Dayton on November 21, 1995, and signed at Paris on December 14, will bring lasting peace to Bosnia and Herzegovina. That does not mean there will be renewed war in the near future. In the four and a half years since Slovenia and Croatia declared their independence, there have been a number of cease-fires and even formal truce agreements. Some seemed quite promising precursors of peace. But with the exception of general recognition of the independence of Slovenia and Macedonia (although Greek opposition complicated the case of the latter), they all have been premised on exhaustion with war, not on satisfaction with the particular peace terms on offer at the moment. And they always have broken down as one party or another reached the conclusion that conditions were such that it could gain more through renewed fighting than through talking.

The Dayton agreement brings together a trio of antagonistic odd couples. First are the Muslims and the Bosnian Serbs. It is difficult to imagine a political settlement that would sufficiently satisfy them both, over a decade or so, to the extent that even relatively minor frictions between them would not lead to new outbursts of violence. The same is true of the second couple, the Muslims and the Herzegovina Croats, partners in a jerry-built federation called an "entity" in the Dayton agreement—a second entity being the so-called Bosnian Serb Republic. A firefight between Croat and Muslim patrols in the city of Mostar early in 1996 was damped by EU observers before lives were lost, but the event was scarcely reassuring about the federation's future. Finally, it is difficult to imagine a lasting accord between Croatia and Serbia, the third odd couple. The 170,000 or so Serbs who fled from the enclave of the Krajina in early August 1995, driven out by Croatia's unexpectedly powerful offensive, are not likely to allow any leadership in Belgrade to forget their plight or to accept with equanimity the results of this new round of ethnic cleansing.

Two other factors serve to undermine the chances that the Dayton agreement will bring peace to Yugoslavia. One is the year's limit placed by President Clinton on the participation of the 20,000-strong U.S. contingent in the 60,000-person force sent to Bosnia to implement the agreement (hence its NATO acronym, IFOR, or Implementation Force). It is possible that substantial numbers of allied troops will remain, even if the Americans leave. But it is more likely that the congressional pressures that caused Clinton to agree to a time limit will generate similar domestic pressures on the governments of other major troop-contributing states, especially if they suffer significant numbers of casualties early in their stay. The one-year limit establishes parameters for wrecking the peace. One can hear those who want to rekindle the war saying, "Keep cool until the Yanks leave."

The second problematic factor is the contrast between IFOR's well-financed and robust peacekeeping operation and the fund-starved civil program that was also part of the Dayton agreement. In the words of two specialists, the civil program is "arguably the most ambitious multidimensional peace operation ever undertaken."[31] It provides for the return and resettlement of refugees, adjudication of property claims, guarantees for human rights, formation of an international civilian police force, reconstruction of highways and other civil infrastructure, and (thorniest of all issues, as Abram and Antonia Chayes make clear in chapter 8) the arrest and trial of war criminals. All these and many more concerns are to be met within the framework of a new Bosnian constitution, on which the negotiators at Dayton also agreed. But the civil arrangements read more like a wish list than an agenda for action. In particular, their implementation assumes—and depends on—the active participation of a dozen international organizations, from the United Nations High Commissioner for Refugees to the OSCE to the European Court of Human Rights. Even the United Nations Educational, Scientific and Cultural Organization (UNESCO) is given a role—the preservation of "national monuments." Yet all of these agencies are short of funds. All of them have their own agendas, on which Bosnia may well not have primacy of place. The documents initialed at Dayton are silent regarding how the needed resources might be obtained.[32]

All these worries may be premature. Although a year is not a long time for peacekeeping operations, nevertheless it may be long enough for new political structures to grow. Yugoslavia descended into tribal warfare because the moderate politicians who might have prevented it could not prevail against the militant demagogues. But four and a half years of war have produced few clear winners and many obvious losers. Much of the economy of all the former republics but Slovenia is moribund. Now that the horrors of war are so familiar, playing soldier in the mountains as a change from everyday life may not have the same appeal for young men, not to mention their fathers, as it did in 1991 and 1992. In short, rather than a failure, Dayton may prove a success, what was needed to wake the peoples of the former Yugoslavia from a bad dream, and a framework for reconstruction. That may indeed be the case. But what we know about the Dayton agreement and the military and civilian resources needed to make it more than paper promises do not logically support an optimistic conclusion.

Serbia and the Russian Connection

The perception on the part of the great powers that they have no vital interests at stake in the Balkans is a product of the momentous changes in international relations that were partly a cause but mainly a consequence of the end of the Cold War. In particular, these were changes in the value that the major powers placed on geopolitical alignments within the international system. Especially during periods of great tension, but even during periods of détente, American and Soviet leaders tended to assess any changes in the political alignment of territorial units as either strengthening or weakening the alliances they led—a calculation augmented by their sense that their personal political standing often rose or fell likewise. The climactic events that began with the (mostly) peaceful east European revolutions of 1989 marked the sharp decline of the utility—indeed, the credibility—of zero-sum thinking about international alignments.[33]

The tide that washed away Russia's Soviet empire did not, of course, stop with the liberation of Moscow's post-1945 satellites in central and eastern Europe; it went on to dissolve the Soviet Union itself. Where once all ethnic Russians were included within the Soviet Union, there were now fragments of a Russian community in nearly all of the newly independent states formed on the territory of the old Soviet Union. The largest of these states, the Russian Republic, is very unlikely to seek the full reunification of the Russian people. As contrasted with the situation of Germany, where the ethnicity of the German Democratic Republic was monolithically German, making merger with the Federal Republic an easy matter, ethnic Russians are far from constituting a majority even in those former Soviet republics where they are present in large numbers. However, their status and the rights they enjoy as a minority are of obvious concern within Russia, where, as chapter 7 by Paul Goble points out, their complaints of mistreatment are amplified by the media and by nationalist politicians.

The parallel with events in the former Yugoslav Federation is striking. Serbia also faced a situation in which the dissolution of the old federal structure left hundreds of thousands of Serbs living either in Croatia, where the Croats were the dominant ethnic group, or in Bosnia and Herzegovina, where the Muslims and the Croats would have been able to combine to outvote the Serbs. To Serb leaders these were untenable situations that could be put right only by the use of force. The wars that have raged since Croatia declared its independence in mid-1991 were thus the product of Serb fear and Serb greed—fear of living in a polity in which other ethnic groups could prevail by the weight of numbers and greed to acquire some of the land owned by members of those other groups, perhaps adjacent to land owned by Serbs or to Serbia itself. The fear expressed itself immediately; the greed grew as Serb strategists and fighters began to realize the full extent of the opportunities for aggrandizement opening before them.

If the parallels between the situations of Serbia and Russia are striking, so are the differences. The role that Russia seems to be seeking in relation to the other former Soviet republics differs significantly from the role that Serbia sought in relation to the fragments of the former Yugoslavia. By virtue of its geographic expanse, the size of its population, the relatively advanced state of its economy, and even its imperial status during the era preceding the revolutions of 1917, Russia could plausibly aspire to something like a hegemonic role in what was once its undisputed domain. Serbia could not. Its claims to hegemony among the republics of the former Yugoslavia were never accepted. Nor would they have been accepted had the federation not disintegrated: Serbia lacked the advantages of size and of undisputed past hegemony that Russia enjoyed as the legal successor to the Soviet Union. To achieve their aims—initially to hold the Yugoslav federation together, later to assert a claim for leadership among the fragments—Serb leaders, in Belgrade and beyond Serbia's borders in Croatia and Bosnia-Herzegovina, had to resort to arms because persuasion and conciliation were not in their repertoire.

Thus, Belgrade's ambitions and methods made the Serbs, wherever they were, into pariahs, the subject of stringent U.N.-mandated economic sanctions that were lifted only with the Dayton agreement. By contrast, the "international community," in the form of the U.N. Security Council, has gone a long way toward recognizing Moscow's claim to something like a hegemonial role among the members of the so-called Commonwealth of Independent States (CIS).[34] In good measure, this seems to be the result of expediency. No other power has been prepared to play even a peacekeeping role, much less one of peace enforcement, in the vast reaches that once were the Soviet Union. Although Western publics were deeply disturbed by the crude, harsh methods employed by Russia's armed forces in putting down Chechnya's bid for independence in December 1994 and January 1995, Western governments are well aware that those same publics will not support any operations on the territory of the former Soviet Union that will place their own military personnel in jeopardy. If "peace operations" (to use the U.N. term) are to be carried out in the "near abroad," Russia's armed forces are almost certain to be the dominant—probably the only—participants.

The same Western governments and publics that still seem willing to allow Russia substantial leeway within the territory of the former Soviet Union are likely to be less complacent should Russia begin to play a much more assertive role in support of Serbia in the Yugoslav cauldron. There is little likelihood that it will do so, however. Russian diplomacy in the Balkan crisis has been extremely prudent. American journalistic reporting tends to play up instances when Russia has cast a vote in the U.N. Security Council opposed to actions or policies that Washington prefers. Yet in every such instance but one (and that one a relatively unimportant instance), the United Kingdom and France have been on the same side as Russia.[35]

Moscow's motivation in staying close to the British and French positions may be a desire not to jeopardize the financial assistance it receives from the United States. (Washington would not retaliate against London or Paris; therefore, it could not do so against Moscow.) However, an equally persuasive explanation is that Russia—like the United States or the other major Western powers—has no vital interests at stake in the former Yugoslavia. While the Russian government may sympathize with the Serbs as being unfairly singled out to bear the bulk of the blame for the Yugoslav debacle, and while that sympathy may have its roots in a common Slavic, Orthodox heritage, it is easy to overestimate the strength of any bonds created by that sympathy. Neither Kosovo, the site of the the fourteenth-century battle that even today is so important in Serb mythology, nor Kosovo, the scene in recent years of an intense struggle between Serbs and Albanians, has any resonances in Moscow. The vast majority of Russians would feel revulsion if the Serbs were to move to push out the Albanians in order to seize more land for themselves.

Indeed, in its involvement with Yugoslavia, Russia has behaved less like a state seeking primacy than like one that wants to be seen to be consulted, a member of the innermost circle. Thus, Russia was eager for a seat along with the United States, Britain, France, and Germany on the self-styled "contact group" of mediators aiming to negotiate an end to the war in Bosnia and Herzegovina. Indeed, on several occasions senior Russian diplomats attempted through bilateral talks with Belgrade to cut through the impasse between Serbia and the Western allies. Deputy Foreign Minister Vitaly Churkin achieved something of a breakthrough in February 1994 when he reached an eleventh-hour agreement with the Bosnian Serbs that helped to lift the siege of Sarajevo and averted planned NATO air strikes.[36] In this and in other instances, the Russians acted unilaterally; yet, while their negotiating tactics differed from those of the Western allies, and while they clearly sought to steal some flattering limelight for themselves, there is no indication that they were seeking to undermine Western positions or policies.[37]

Russia was also an early contributor to the ranks of UNPROFOR, sending a battalion of peacekeeping troops while the war was still confined to Croatian territory and later allowing the U.N. command to shift them to Bosnia. By all reports, however, neither their training nor their equipment was that of first-line troops—in contrast with the quality of the more numerous British and French detachments contributed to UNPROFOR. Russian parents have made clear by widespread demonstrations that they will accept casualties from military adventures no more readily than their counterparts in the West. As with membership in the "contact group," however, the government of Boris Yeltsin in Moscow seemed to want at least some Russian military presence in the former Yugoslavia not because it had its own well-defined Balkan agenda but simply for the purpose of "being there."

Russia's tortuous behavior over its participation in the multinational force that will enforce the peace in Bosnia graphically reflects the complex impulses that motivate Moscow's diplomacy. IFOR owes its existence and international legitimacy to a vote of the U.N. Security Council. But to avoid the conflicts that surrounded and often paralyzed

UNPROFOR, it falls entirely under, and is responsive only to, NATO command. For domestic political reasons, however, the Yeltsin government decided that Russian troops cannot be permitted to obey the commands of what many Russians still perceive to be a Cold War institution. Yet American command was somehow acceptable. Ever since NATO's founding nearly half a century ago, its supreme allied commander in Europe (SACEUR) has been an American who has simultaneously been commander in chief of U.S. forces in Europe (CINCEUR). So it was arranged that Russian troops in Bosnia would be under the command of General George Joulwan in his capacity as CINCEUR while the troops of all the other participating states (including American troops) will be under General Joulwan as SACEUR. Again, the motivation seems to be a desire for "being there." With a polity in disarray, an economy riddled by inefficiency, a population made fearful by burgeoning crime, an army in disgrace after Chechnya, Russia draws some reassurance from the fact that it may nevertheless still claim a seat at the table alongside the world's other principal powers.[38]

The United States, Bosnia, and the Leadership of the West

By contrast, the "other superpower" (in fact, the only superpower) cannot escape from the table even when it tries to relinquish its seat. America's absence from international collective action unbalances the scales, and there is no state or combination of states that can be an effective substitute. Chapter 5 by David Gompert makes clear just how reluctant the Bush administration was to get involved in any way in Yugoslavia's wars. That reluctance had far-reaching consequences. It meant that U.N. forces were present in far smaller numbers than those initially proposed.[39] UNPROFOR was never large enough or heavily enough armed to undertake offensive operations such as, for example, inserting a blocking force between the city of Vukovar and the YPA (in fact, Serb) divisions that besieged and destroyed it, or retaliating for the bombardment of Dubrovnik. Such an active role might have profoundly changed the course of events: there is considerable evidence suggesting that the Serbs were extremely worried about international action against them and that early intervention in Croatia by a sufficiently capable force would have led them to moderate their behavior.[40] Without a substantial American military presence, however, real pressure on the Serbs was most unlikely to be brought to bear.

Moreover, the United States was consistently inconsistent in its policies and actions. The problem was not merely that the Bush administration had decided to leave to the Europeans what it saw as almost cer-

tain to be a Yugoslav quagmire—a posture tacitly confirmed by the
Clinton administration when it came to office in 1993. Rather, the problem was that for two and a half years, until the summer of 1995, when
it concluded that the United States should take over leadership of what
might be called both the military and the negotiating tracks, the Clinton
administration kept altering its position.

Previous to this assertion of primacy, the administration limited itself
for much of the time to urging on its allies what came to be called "lift
and strike." Lift referred to the U.N.-mandated embargo on supplying
arms to the warring parties; Washington assumed that the Muslims
would benefit more than the others from its removal. Strike meant robust measures by NATO air forces against Bosnian Serb military forces
and their logistical bases. The administration always had to make clear,
mainly in deference to strongly negative congressional opinion, that it
would contribute no American ground forces to UNPROFOR. Yet everyone knew it would be ground forces that would take the brunt of any
Serb retaliation for air strikes. Other than participation in a true peacekeeping force whose presence was agreed to by all the belligerents, the
only circumstance in which the United States would depart from that
prohibition would be if the troop-providing governments were to decide
to withdraw their forces. U.S. ground force units might be available, as
President Clinton put it in June 1995, "if our allies decide they can no
longer continue the U.N. mission and decide to withdraw, but they cannot withdraw in safety. We should help them to get out."[41]

By the early summer of 1995, withdrawal of U.N. forces seemed a distinct possibility. The Bosnian Serbs' humiliation of the would-be peacekeepers in May and June had made it amply apparent that, under the
prevailing rules of engagement, the mission of the U.N. contingents had
become untenable. With some 350 of their number held hostage, the
U.N. commanders tacitly agreed to call off NATO air strikes on Bosnian
Serb targets and ordered their troops not to resist when the Serbs simply walked into scattered depots throughout Bosnia and "liberated" the
heavy weapons (tanks and artillery pieces) they had deposited there, in
response to NATO's threat of bombing, in February 1994.

It was in these unpromising circumstances that the German government altered its posture toward Yugoslavia's wars. As we have seen, in
late June 1995, after three years of the most intense reluctance to permit
more than a handful of German military personnel to carry out missions
anywhere near the former Yugoslavia, Bonn seemed to change its mind:
for the first time, a government spokesman announced, Germany would
send armed forces to the Balkans to support U.N. peacekeepers. There
would be no ground troops—sensitivities in the region were still too raw
for that—but units sent would include strike and transport aircraft and

headquarters and medical personnel. Asked to explain this policy change, a senior official of the Foreign Office responded with a revealing comment: "The Americans are clearly standing on the sidelines of developments. The decisive initiative is coming from the French and the English. If our most important European partners judge the situation in Yugoslavia this way, then Germany must show its solidarity."[42]

"My alliance right or wrong"—or so the German official seemed to be saying. Bonn's assessment of the policies that Paris and London had been pursuing in Bosnia was not the issue. Nurturing Bonn's relations with the other two governments was. Their contribution of large contingents of ground forces to UNPROFOR involved substantial political risk, and each had sustained losses. They had paid a human and political price that Germany had not. Chancellor Helmut Kohl and his colleagues were especially sensitive to such concerns: they knew that, as the most powerful state in Europe, with a problematic past, Germany was not fully trusted, and they feared a downward spiral of mistrust unless the Europeans tied themselves together in a way that made it increasingly costly to go separate ways. Therefore the importance of harmonizing policies with Paris and London.

The partnership in question was not NATO, however, but the European Union, with its own security organization, the WEU and its stated goal of a common foreign and security policy. The most salient characteristic of the WEU is a negative one: its membership does not include the United States. For that reason, successive French governments have tried to make of the WEU a favored instrument. In nearly every instance, however, reality has intruded in the form of general acknowledgment—now including the government of French President Jacques Chirac—that NATO was much more capable of managing integrated military forces.[43]

Just as the German government had concluded that providing tangible military support for its principal EU partners was more important than Bonn's assessment of the relative wisdom of their policies, so there were voices urging a comparable priority on the Clinton administration in Washington. Preserving NATO as an effective organization and as a vehicle for intimate collaboration between the United States and its European allies was of paramount value, according to this argument: European leaders and publics would in the future find it much more difficult to follow the U.S. lead if it did not share the risks involved in having troops on the ground with UNPROFOR or, at minimum, if it did not share the financial burden of supporting U.N. operations in the former Yugoslavia. Yet neither sending U.S. ground forces nor helping the allies pay the costs of their own forces had any appeal for the Republican majority in Congress, most of whose members were unmoved as well by arguments based on the assumption that preserving the unity of the alliance was a uniquely important value in itself.

The result was a dilemma. As *Financial Times* columnist Ian Davidson put it, "Washington has been prepared to get into an open conflict with Europe over Bosnia because it does not really feel concerned by this civil war." However, he continued, "if the Europeans are forced to fight their way out of Bosnia, and the United States leaves them to it, the Atlantic alliance will suffer a blow from which it may not easily recover."[44] Many assessments were even more dire, asserting that the alliance's failure for four years to frame a coherent policy and then take concerted measures in response to the wars in Yugoslavia had grievously undermined its credibility, a deficit made up only partially by the bombing campaign of August and September 1995 and the replacement three months later of UNPROFOR by the much more formidable IFOR.

These changes—the technical virtuosity of the bombing campaign in which the United States flew two thirds of the sorties, the robust nature of IFOR and its permissive, shoot-to-kill rules of engagement, and above all the negotiating hothouse at Dayton, Ohio, which resulted in the agreement of November 21, 1995—were all the products of forceful American leadership. Two crucial facts remain, however. First is that President Clinton's assertion of leadership enjoys only the most precarious support of the isolationist Republican-controlled Congress that was elected in November 1994. What little support he has could evaporate quickly if the Yugoslav settlement begins to unravel. Second is that American leadership was a long time coming, four and one half years. Just as the Bosnian Serbs during those years were so often able to call NATO's bluff, not to mention that of the United Nations, so other international bullies may be tempted to try the same. Thus a principal pillar of a new world order based on the rule of law has been tested by the Yugoslav debacle and found wanting.

The Many Scripts of World Order

This argument has obvious validity, but it is also somewhat beside the point. The ongoing drama that we call world order draws on a number of scripts. One script has been followed in Yugoslavia, another in the Gulf in response to Iraq's invasion of Kuwait, yet another in Somalia, and still another in Chechnya. Moreover, these labels scarcely exhaust the list. Rwanda, Haiti, Cambodia, Nagorno Karabakh, and many others could be added. Each connotes a particular combination of persons wanting more power over a given geographic space (often, but not always, exclusive power) and others who resist them; either or both are prepared to act violently, if only to catch the attention of the world outside. When one examines these episodes of violence and response, it is striking how different the various scripts seem to be. It is also striking that while each episode had about it some of the conditions that make for international war, all except Iraq's invasion of Kuwait are examples, primarily, of communal conflict internal to a recognized sovereign state.

It should come as no surprise that, among these episodes, the largest scale and, by many standards, most successful international action took place in 1990–91 in response to the Iraqi invasion of Kuwait. The script that was followed—deploying superior military force to stop and then reverse border-crossing aggression—was the one best known. As it happens, in none of the other episodes was anything resembling this script followed, but the absence of implementation cannot be attributed to any failure by governments and publics to reflect on the benefits and costs of responding in a given instance with military force. Rather, it is due to the fact that only in the instance of the Gulf crisis was there a perception within the governments of at least some major powers that they had vital interests at stake that only a forceful response could safeguard.[45] Fortunately for those who favored using force, the ranks of those governments included the British, French, and Saudi as well as the American. Notably, they included neither the Japanese nor the German governments, the latter then still in thrall to the widespread assumption that the Federal Republic's "Basic Law" forbade the deployment of German forces outside the NATO area.

In an era in which there no longer exists a large, powerful, obvious enemy, such as the one the Soviet Union provided for the West over so many years, it requires only a relatively small number of military casualties to induce doubts among the publics of modern democracies regarding the importance of any situation in which their governments have intervened. Somalia, like Lebanon in 1983, was such a case. Regarding the former Yugoslavia, two administrations in Washington have been quite clear in saying that, much as they would like to see an end to the warfare that has racked the country with such devastating effect for so long, the United States did not have at stake there anything that could be labeled "vital interests."

When governments speak in such terms, it is scarcely surprising that publics tend to agree: publics need constant persuasion that affecting a set of circumstances beyond their borders is worth the lives of their sons or daughters. In the case of Bosnia, moreover, another phenomenon has been at work: as the war goes on from year to year and shocking atrocity follows shocking atrocity, outsiders become numb to, and then bored with, the seemingly endless flow of accounts of violence and death. And as the military capabilities of the Bosnian Muslims grew, and with it the stridency of *their* demands, outsiders found it increasingly difficult to draw a clear distinction between the supposed aggressors and the supposedly aggressed-upon.

There is no question but that NATO has been damaged by the Yugoslav tragedy: would-be aggressors and local bullies everywhere are likely to assume that an effective Western response to their actions would come only slowly, perhaps (probably, some would say) not at all. As President Clinton put it, with both NATO and the United Nations in mind, "You can't go about the world saying you're going to do something and then not do it."[46]

It can be argued, however, that the view of NATO as a classical collective security organization, moving with near automaticity under its constitution (the 1949 Treaty of Washington) to take action in response to a challenge to the security of one or more of its members, is a theoretical construct that has never existed. Reality—even during the Cold War and certainly after—has been quite different. NATO will not act unless its members are in agreement that either very large stakes or very low risks are involved. As Saddam Hussein learned to his surprise, if a bully is not only nasty but potentially fearsome enough, he would be imprudent to base his planning on the assumption that NATO, either as an alliance or as a "coalition of the willing" (as the allies dubbed themselves in the Gulf War), will not react with effective force. A Russia that threatened to use military force against an eastern European neighbor would surely set off more alarms in the West and rouse a more robust and coordinated response from Western governments than the Bosnian Serbs did. So, in all probability, would those in the successor republics of the Soviet Union, or in eastern Europe, who choose to use force to press ethnic claims.

Moreover, any critique must take into account the fact that the dissolution of Yugoslavia occurred at the worst time possible. The dawning of the brave new world of world-order rhetoric took place before the nations that would have leading roles in the complex structure of post–Cold War European security had learned their parts—indeed, some would argue, before their actual lines had been written. That process of exploration and development is still going on, much affected by the experience of Yugoslavia's wars.

For the peoples and governments of Europe and North America, that experience has been searing. In the future they will undoubtedly give higher priority to preventive diplomacy (whether high enough really to affect outcomes, however, is an open question). They may even find the will and the means to offer contending parties substantial economic inducements to resolve their differences peacefully. However, only an optimist unencumbered by any knowledge of history would predict that when another Vukovar is being laid waste or a Srebrenica is about to fall, "the United Nations," "the West," or "Europe" will interpose a military force to prevent it. That is because, as I have argued elsewhere, Europe's peace is a divisible peace.[47] Violent conflicts will be sufficiently confined so that they will be very unlikely to escalate across the threshold of war among the major powers. As in the case of street crimes in today's cities, bystanders hesitate to get involved. That may be taken as good news for most of us: our noninvolvement will result in inconvenience for us in the form of enormous disruptions to economic processes and vast movements of refugees who would not have fled had the conflict been ended early enough, but at least we will be relatively safe in our homes and communities. It bodes much less well for those unfortunate enough to find themselves in the Vukovars and Srebrenicas of tomorrow.

Notes

1. For an authoritative account of the dissolution of the Yugoslav state, see Susan L. Woodward, *Balkan Tragedy: Chaos and Dissolution after the Cold War* (Washington, D.C.: Brookings Institution, 1995).

2. For these processes, see Susan L. Woodward, *Socialist Unemployment: The Political Economy of Yugoslavia 1945–1990* (Princeton, NJ: Princeton University Press, 1995).

3. See Woodward, *Balkan Tragedy*, pp. 172–73.

4. The Titoist vision continued to command strong support as late as May–June 1990, when a survey of more than 4,000 respondents asked whether their personal attachment was strongest to their immediate region, to the republic in which they lived, or to Yugoslavia. Large majorities of Muslims (84 percent), Montenegrins (80 percent), Serbs (71 percent), and Macedonians (68 percent) all said Yugoslavia; the proportion was lower for Croats (48 percent) and Albanians (49 percent). Only Slovenes strongly rejected the Yugoslav label (26 percent). See Misha Glenny, "Yugoslavia: The Great Fall," *New York Review of Books*, March 23, 1995, p. 58. These results were not surprising: those who voted in greater numbers for Yugoslavia were those who materially gained the most from the federation.

5. See Woodward, *Balkan Tragedy*, pp. 162–73.

6. Ibid., pp. 181–82, 189–92.

7. For a lucid discussion of the Yugoslav debt crisis and the efforts of the international financial institutions, see Harold James's history of the International Monetary Fund, *International Monetary Cooperations since Bretton Woods* (Washington, DC: International Monetary Fund and Oxford University Press, 1996), pp. 556–58.

8. From the introduction to *The Philosophy of Right*, translated and edited by T.N. Knox (Oxford: Oxford University Press, 1942), p. 13.

9. See, for example, the article considered the foundation stone of this genre: John J. Mearsheimer, "Back to the Future: Instability in Europe after the Cold War," *International Security*, vol. 15, no. 1 (Summer 1990), pp. 5–56.

10. According to a report ("Islamic Money Helps Muslims in Bosnia, but Not Enough to Win") from Sarajevo in *The Christian Science Monitor*, January 26, 1995, p. 1, U.N. officials said that while small quantities of smuggled arms had reached the Muslims, they had been insufficient to affect battle outcomes. Many Islamic countries sent cash—the most easily trans- portable and concealable item of assistance—which the Bosnian govern- ment used to buy industrial equipment, commodities of all sorts, and some weapons. All such efforts, it should be noted, were violations of the U.N.- mandated arms embargo, which remained in legal effect regardless of the fact that, although banning traffic to all of the former Yugoslavia, its actual effect was to penalize almost exclusively the Bosnian Muslims. The bulk of the Islamic volunteer forces was composed of some 3,000 to 4,000 mujahedeen, veterans of the war in Afghanistan, who became a source of concern for the NATO peacekeepers who deployed to Bosnia under the Dayton agreement. See Chris Hedges, "Foreign Islamic Fighters in Bosnia Pose a Potential Threat for G.I.'s," *New York Times*, December 3, 1995, p.1.

11. See Alan Cowell, "U.S. Builds Influence in Croatia," *New York Times*, August 1, 1995, p. A6; and "Croat Army Takes Rebel Stronghold in Rapid Advance: Serbs Routed in 2 Days," *New York Times*, August 1, 1995, p. 1.

12. See Stephen Kinzer, "Bosnia Vows Not to Attack Serb Town," *New York Times*, September 20, 1995, p. A14.

13. For a masterful account of these events, see Antonin Basch, *The Danube Basin and the German Economic Sphere* (London: Kegan Paul, 1944). See also David E. Kaiser, *Economic Diplomacy and the Origins of the Second World War: Germany, Britain, France, and Eastern Europe 1930–1939* (Princeton, NJ: Princeton University Press, 1980).

14. See Hanns W. Maull, "Germany in the Yugoslav Crisis," *Survival*, vol. 37, no. 4 (Winter 1995–96), esp. pp. 101–5. See also Woodward, *Balkan Tragedy*, pp. 183–89.

15. Interviews in Bonn, December 1993. For the effort by Serb propagandists to link today's Germany with the Nazi past, see also the editorial, "Bosnian Skies," *Financial Times*, June 29, 1995, p. 11. For the constitutional court's ruling, see Lothar Gutjahr, "Stability, Integration, and Global Respon- sibility: Germany's Changing Perspectives on National Interests," *Review of International Studies*, vol. 21, no. 3 (July 1995), pp. 311–12. See also Maull, "Germany in the Yugoslav Crisis," pp. 112–13.

16. For Bonn's decision to send units to Bosnia, see Stephen Kinzer, "Bosnian Muslim Troops Evade U.N. Force to Raid Serb Village," *New York Times*, June 27, 1995, p. A3; and Maull, "Germany in the Yugoslav Crisis," pp. 119–22. For the air operations of August–September 1995, see the Sep- tember 15 edition of the periodic NATO briefing paper, "Operation Deny Flight," and "Press Briefing (Update) NATO Operation Deliberate Force," Allied Forces Southern Europe, Naples, Italy 1700 09 September 95. Briefer: Group Captain Trevor Murray, Chief Air Operations, and a similarly

headed transcript for September 12, all available on-line from the NATO Integrated Data Service. See also *New York Times*, September 2, 1995, p. 2.

17. See Gutjahr, "Stability, Integration, and Global Responsibility," pp. 301–17; and Hanns W. Maull, "Germany's New Foreign Policy," in Hanns W. Maull and Philip H. Gordon, eds., *German Foreign Policy and the German National Interest*, seminar paper no. 5, American Institute for Contemporary German Studies (January 1993), pp. 11–14.

18. For a discussion of stakes and interests, see Philip H. Gordon, *France, Germany, and the Western Alliance* (Boulder, CO: Westview, 1995), pp. 53–66.

19. As of May 27, 1995, the day after the NATO air strikes that led to the mass hostage-taking by the Bosnian Serbs, Britain had 3,565 troops in the field, all in Bosnia, while France had 3,835 troops in Bosnia and 787 in Croatia. See the comprehensive table in Steven Greenhouse, "Quandry Over U.S. Bosnia Policy," *New York Times*, May 28, 1995, p. A12.

20. Nor does it move the personnel affected. During the winter of 1990–91, when it became clear that blockade alone would not be sufficient to cause Iraq to disgorge Kuwait and as military operations in the Persian Gulf seemed about to begin, there were many press reports of American non-commissioned men and women asserting that if they had known they would ever have to fight an actual war, they never would have enlisted.

21. It has been suggested that Slobodan Milosevic intends that the Serb refugees expelled by Croatia from the Krajina in August 1995 will settle in Kosovo rather than in Serbia proper. Given the explosive nature of communal relations in Kosovo, that would seem to be storing up trouble.

22. *The Military Balance 1995–1996* (London: Oxford University Press for the International Institute for Strategic Studies, 1995), p. 64. This authoritative publication specifies force levels for all the troop-contributing states.

23. See John Darnton's long survey article, "Discontent Seethes in Once-Stable Turkey," *New York Times*, March 2, 1995, p. 1.

24. Among many accounts of the end-game at Dayton, see those in *Financial Times*, November 22, 1995, p. 1; and *New York Times*, November 22, 1995, p. 1.

25. For these events, see, for example, John C. Campbell, *Tito's Separate Road: America and Yugoslavia in World Politics* (New York: Harper & Row, 1967).

26. All newspapers on August 29, 1995, carried accounts of the event. See, for example, Roger Cohen, "Shelling Kills Dozens in Sarajevo; U.S. Urges NATO to Strike Serbs," *New York Times*, p. A1.

27. For an excellent account of Operation Deliberate Force, see Rick Atkinson's two lengthy articles, "Air Assault Set Stage for Broader Role" and "In Almost Losing Its Resolve, NATO Alliance Found Itself," in the *Washington Post*, November 15 and 16, 1995; both begin on p. A1. An official account, "Operation Sharp Guard," is available from NATO's Public Affairs Office and on-line from the NATO gopher.

28. United States Congress, 82nd Congress, 1st Session, *1951, Military Situation in the Far East*, Hearings before the Joint Senate Committee on Armed Ser-

vices and Foreign Relations, p. 732. Bradley went on to say "and with the wrong enemy." For NATO in 1995, of course, there was no "right enemy"; the alliance was at peace.

29. See North Atlantic Treaty Organization, *NATO Handbook* (1993), appendix II, "The Alliance's Strategic Concept Agreed by the Heads of State and Government Participating in the Meeting of the North Atlantic Council in Rome on 7th–8th November 1991."

30. North Atlantic Treaty Organization, "Rome Declaration on Peace and Co-operation Issued by the Heads of State and Government Participating in the Meeting of the North Atlantic Council in Rome on 7th–8th November 1991," press communiqué S-1 (91) p. 86; ——— "Final Communiqué, Ministerial Meeting of the North Atlantic Council in Oslo, 4 June 1992."

31. From the detailed critique by Elizabeth Cousens and Michael Doyle, "Dayton Accord's Dangerous Dueling Missions," *Christian Science Monitor*, December 26, 1995, p. 23.

32. See, inter alia, Barbara Crossette, "Civilian Effort for Peace in Bosnia Seen Lagging," *New York Times*, January 3, 1996, p. A6. The text of the (Dayton) General Framework Agreement for Peace in Bosnia and Herzegovina and its 11 annexes and side letters is available on the World Wide Web by calling for http://dosfan.lib.uic.edu/www/current/bosnia/daytable.html. The constitution of Bosnia and Herzegovina is annex 4 (—dayann4.html).

33. For an extended discussion of these changes, see Richard H. Ullman, *Securing Europe* (Princeton, NJ: Princeton University Press, 1991), esp. chs. 1 and 2.

34. See, for example, "U.N. Endorses Russian Troops for Peacekeeping in Caucasus, Reuters," *New York Times*, July 22, 1994, p. A2.

35. On December 2, 1994, when Moscow used its Security Council veto to block a resolution sponsored by Muslim states proposing measures to prevent fuel from being shipped from Serbia to Serb-held areas of Bosnia and Croatia. Alessandra Stanley "Conflict in the Balkans: The Kremlin Asserts Itself by U.N. Veto," *New York Times*, December 4, 1994, p. A21.

36. *Washington Post*, July 27, 1994, p. A22.

37. See, for example, the *Washington Post*'s account (June 15, 1994, p. A31) of a Moscow meeting between Russian Foreign Minister Andrei Kozyrev and Bosnian Serb leader Radovan Karadzic in June 1994. Kozyrev, it said, stated bluntly that Russia found it unacceptable that the Serbs should control 70 percent of Bosnia's territory and that if the Serbs should choose to renew large-scale warfare, they could "forget about Russia's support."

38. "This strategy assures a certain place for Russia in the negotiating effort," Deputy Foreign Minister Vitaly Churkin told Lee Hockstader of the *Washington Post* ("Russia's Dapper No. 2 Diplomat Guides Crucial Policy on Bosnia," July 27, 1994, p. A22).

39. The British government—never enthusiastic about intervention in the Yugoslav crisis—estimated in late 1991 that 50,000 troops might be required

merely to keep the peace, a number confirmed by the Secretariat of the Western European Union. See James Gow and Lawrence Freedman, "Intervention in a Fragmenting State: The Case of Yugoslavia," in Nigel S. Rodney, ed., *To Loose the Bonds of Wickedness: International Intervention in Defence of Human Rights* (London: Brassey's, 1992), pp. 114–15.

40. James Gow of the Department of War Studies at King's College, London, has been particularly assiduous in gathering this evidence. See, inter alia, his "One Year of War in Bosnia and Herzegovina," *RFE/RL Research Report*, vol. 2, no. 23 (June 4, 1993), pp. 5–6.

41. From President Clinton's national radio address, June 3, 1995, as transcribed in *New York Times*, June 4, p. 16. Clinton first tried on May 29 to define the conditions under which U.S. ground forces might be introduced into the Bosnian conflict. See ibid., May 30, p. A1. However, only three days later, "moving [as reporter Todd S. Purdom put it] to quell a fire storm of congressional and public criticism," Clinton narrowed the list of conditions even more. See ibid., June 4, 1995, p. 1.

The ambivalence, inconsistency, and unilateralism in the official American stance was epitomized in the effusive adulation by the president, the Congress, and the media of U.S. Air Force Captain Scott F. O'Grady, whose F-16 fighter had been shot down in early June 1995 while on a routine patrol over Bosnian Serb territory. At a time when 43 U.N. peacekeepers on the ground had already been killed and hundreds more were in acute danger, Americans watching the nightly television reports from Bosnia seemed to need to know that even though none of their countrymen shared those particular risks, a few nevertheless faced threats of a different kind. For evading capture for six days while hiding in the forest awaiting his eventual rescue, the personable O'Grady was declared an "authentic national hero," an appellation that he himself found absurd. *New York Times*, June 11, 1995, p. 14.

42. Alan Cowell, "Germany to Send Forces to Balkans to Support U.N.," *New York Times*, June 27, 1995, A3. See also Gutjahr, "Stability, Integration, and Global Responsibility," pp. 308–12.

43. The WEU had played a minor role in the Yugoslav drama, one that consisted of monitoring ship traffic on the northern reaches of the Adriatic and along the Danube River to check for violations of the arms embargo. It was a role that came close to exceeding the organization's planning and coordinating capabilities, however.

44. Ian Davidson, "A Hollow Shell," *Financial Times*, June 28, 1995, p. 12.

45. Situations like Chechnya or Nagorno-Karabakh on the territory of the former Soviet Union present particular difficulties; in those instances, among the great powers, only Russia is likely to conclude that it has vital interests at stake.

46. From "Transcript of Press Conference by President Clinton and President Kim of South Korea," Washington, July 27, 1995, U.S. Newswire (on-line).

47. See Ullman, *Securing Europe*, esp. pp. 27–29, 244–46.

Chapter 2

The Impossible Trade-off: "Peace" versus "Justice" in Settling Yugoslavia's Wars

JEAN E. MANAS

A S SOON as Yugoslavia's wars began, numerous forceful demands were made for outside intervention. Yet the intensity of these calls to action masked the extent to which all interventions (or would-be interventions) are plagued by the tension between two competing and equally legitimate goals. While outside actors—governments, nongovernmental organizations, and private individuals—strive to stop the fighting and secure peace, they also strive to serve justice, which sometimes requires the prolongation of hostilities. Resolving this tension between peace and justice is even more difficult than it initially appears.

Unfortunately, most policy discussions avoid this issue. Presuming a certainty and clarity of purpose, they focus instead on problems of implementation. This disposition is perhaps most evident in the routine invocation of the label "failed" to characterize the involvement of outside actors in the region. Logically, it would be difficult to speak of failure if there is no certainty regarding or clarity on what would constitute "success."

Two Ideals: Peace and Justice

Outside interventions in the former Yugoslavia have been motivated consciously by two ideals: peace and justice. The great majority of observers believe that it is morally unacceptable to discard one goal in

42

favor of the other. Thus, both the singleminded pursuit of a utopian outcome and the acceptance of a patently unjust peace have been ruled out as a matter of course, and all proposed settlements have been appraised and graded according to the extent to which they promise to satisfy both ideals.

Although many outside intervenors (or would-be intervenors) pursued both peace and justice in the former Yugoslavia, they rarely faced up to the fact that, at any level of specificity, the two ideals are in tension: the pursuit of justice entails the prolongation of hostilities, whereas the pursuit of peace requires resigning oneself to some injustices.[1] Moreover, even those policy analysts who recognized this tension underestimated the challenge it poses. The tension cannot be resolved simply by engaging in an ad hoc "balancing" of peace and justice in order to determine what kind of arrangement maximizes both.

The problem with ad hoc balancing is that it creates a perverse incentive for the warring parties to embrace extremism and resort to violence. Since the international community will not agree to a settlement that does not promise to be peaceful, all a party needs to do is make it clear, by words and violent actions, that it will not settle for anything short of a complete capitulation to its demands. This very act moves the maximizing solution closer to the settlement desired by that party. In Yugoslavia the Bosnian Serbs pursued this strategy remarkably well: responding to every proposed settlement with continued fighting, they saw the internationally supported arrangement get closer and closer to their position.

Two principal approaches exist that hold out the promise of a principled rather than an ad hoc solution to this quandary. The first approach consists of drawing a line and sticking to it. But the difficult task arises of figuring out where the line ought to be. The second approach, by contrast, avoids this problem by adopting a position of neutrality with respect to the optimal arrangement: the "correct" arrangement is one to which the opposing parties agree. The next two sections discuss these approaches in turn and explore the difficulties associated with them.

A Framework for a Just Peace: International Law

In order to identify a "just peace," most observers turn to international law as the appropriate framework. International law takes the state as its foundational unit. It views the world as permissibly divided into a number of states with clearly delineated territories and is concerned primarily with regulating the interaction between these states. The law's first principle is that state borders are inviolable. This means, roughly, that states are prohibited from transgressing those borders, except in certain exceptional circumstances. Traditionally, the law also has declared states to be absolutely sovereign within their own territories. The post–World War II era, however, has witnessed the emergence of human rights norms that place certain limits on a state's power over its own population.

There is little question that human rights have been roundly violated in the former Yugoslavia. Hundreds of thousands of persons were forcibly expelled from their homes—and many thousands murdered—in an outrageous practice that has added a new expression to the English language, "ethnic cleansing." Clearly, for a settlement to uphold international legal norms, it would have to include a provision ensuring that all displaced persons be able to return to their homes. It also would require that the perpetrators of atrocities be punished.

International law thus imposes a number of important requirements on any potential solution. These requirements do not, however, shed much light on the core issue of Yugoslavia's wars—how the contemporary Yugoslav space ought to be reorganized in light of the competing claims to the identity of territory in that part of the world. The principle of the inviolability of borders is of no use: since the principle *presupposes* the location of borders, it does not purport to answer the question of where borders ought to be when a state is in the midst of a breakup.

The rest of the international legal corpus is not of much help either. At first blush, the principle of greatest applicability is that of the self-determination of peoples. This principle is presumed to help identify legitimate secessions. Moreover, if the principle is applicable, the central authorities are prohibited from trying to frustrate it, by force or otherwise. Under some interpretations of the principle, the seceding entity might even be entitled to make recourse to force in its effort to effect its secession. By contrast, if the principle is inapplicable, the central authorities are justified in using force to keep the state intact.

Naturally, the applicability of the principle depends wholly on how one defines the terms "self" and "people"; but surprisingly, international law provides little guidance as to how the terms are to be defined. There is consensus that the population of each territory considered to be colonial under the U.N. Charter constituted a distinct "people" or "self" for the purpose of the applicability of the principle of self-determination.[2] Little agreement exists, however, over whether the population of any substate unit other than a colony constitutes a distinct people for this purpose.[3] As Arnold Toynbee perceptively remarked in the wake of an earlier Balkan war, the self-determination principle "is merely the statement of a problem and not the solution of it."[4]

Yugoslavia's wars have given rise to efforts to give the principle some meaning in the context of the breakup of a state that is not a colonial empire. These efforts, however, have been plagued by serious conceptual difficulties.

The Principle that States Ought Not Be Defined Ethnically

Implicit in much of the discussion surrounding the Yugoslav quandary has been the novel principle that the term "people" ought not be defined "ethnically," on the grounds that an ethnic definition augurs a bottomless pit and, because it is inconsistent with humanist values, it is thoroughly obnoxious. During the earlier stages of Yugoslavia's wars (up through spring 1992), this principle was cited as an argument against the partitioning of the state. During the later stages of the conflict (from early 1993), the principle has been invoked as a self-evident universal truth in the condemnation of Serb nationalist efforts to create a Greater Serbia or to carve self-governing Serb states out of Bosnia and Croatia.

Both uses of the principle reveal two fatal flaws. The first is that the prohibition against ethnic-based secessionism overlooks the ethnic bias built into most, if not all, existing states, including Yugoslavia and its six constituent republics. France is a French, not a Breton, state. Turkey is a Turkish, not a Kurdish, state. Yugoslavia, at least in its waning days, came to be viewed as a Serb state. The newly independent Croatia is a Croat state, and the newly independent Bosnia promised to be a predominantly Muslim state, more "Muslim" in any event than the Yugoslavia that the rural Serbs of eastern Herzegovina had come to view as their state.

It is such ethnic bias that has historically fueled and ultimately justified secessions. Indeed, the idea of an independent and united Yugoslavia itself was the result of a reaction to biases inherent in the seemingly multiethnic Austro-Hungarian empire (in favor of Austrians and perhaps Hungarians and definitely against southern Slavs) and the Ottoman empire (in favor of Muslims, and later Turks, and definitely against Christians and Serbs). If southern Slavs could secede from the Austro-Hungarian and Ottoman empires, why could not Croats secede from Yugoslavia and Krajinan Serbs secede from Croatia?

Moreover, whether the bias in favor of one group translates into severe oppression of a minority or not has little to do with the question of whether secession is justified. Indeed, "minority" ethnic groups might be treated very well in countries with a "majority" bias. Nevertheless, they might still want to have their own state in their respective regions. What would be wrong with that request if those secessionist minorities agreed to treat members of the current majority (who would become minorities in the new state) as well as they (the present minorities) are being treated currently in the larger state? Such a request cannot be deemed any more ethnicist than the insistence on the preservation of the status quo.

There are two responses to this line of reasoning, although both are ultimately unsatisfying. One response is that ethnicism is a bottomless pit. Once one recognizes the right to ethnic self-determination, there is no end to how many states could come into existence. But that response is a red herring and is fundamentally unpersuasive as a means of laying down a principled defense of a particular map. The problem with line-drawing is that today's line is as arbitrary as any.

Another response concedes that existing entities might have an ethnic *bias*, but that the right course of action is to correct the bias rather than destroy that entity. While it is difficult to argue with the aim of this response—"ethnic neutrality"—it appears to be unattainable. So long as citizens of a polity define themselves ethnically, that polity will, a fortiori, have an ethnic bias, if for no other reason than the existence and effects of bloc voting. Minority rights and other political arrangements protective of minorities might take the edge off this bias (and they are certainly welcome so long as they are universally applicable and not relevant only to certain parts of the world), but they cannot ever get rid of it completely.[5] No amount of protection for minorities will put the Breton speakers and the French speakers on an "equal" footing in France. The same holds true for the succession states of Yugoslavia. In any case, regardless of whether ethnic neutrality is ever attainable, there is no basis on which to reject secessionist demands if the seceding entity agrees to treat members of the majority as well as it currently is being treated in the larger state. If it is acceptable for Slovenes to be a minority in Yugoslavia, why is it unacceptable for Serbs to be a minority in Croatia, or for Croats to be minority in a Krajinan Serb republic?

There is a second, more subtle, reason why the effort to divide up Yugoslavia (or Bosnia) is no more ethnically motivated than the effort to preserve it. That reason is to be found in the definition of the term "ethnic group." If an ethnic group is defined by reference to certain characteristics, then clearly it is ethnicist to be for Croatia, for a Greater Serbia (or for Corsica, Kurdistan, or Quebec), but it is not ethnicist to be for Yugoslavia, for Bosnia (or for France, Turkey, or Canada). But by simply focusing on different characteristics, one can view Yugoslavia, Bosnia, France, Turkey, and Canada all as ethnically defined. One way to highlight these characteristics is to view these countries through the prism of their citizenship policies. If there were no such thing as a French or Canadian "ethnicity," there would be no automatic grant of citizenship to children born to French or Canadian parents. Nor would one be denied either citizenship on the basis of being born, say, to Chinese parents in Uruguay. Another way to highlight these characteristics is to reach back into history. Yugoslavia itself was the product of the efforts of southern Slavs to carve a southern Slavic nation-state out of two multiethnic empires: the Ottoman and the Austro-Hungarian. Viewed this way, the distinction between Yugoslavism and Croatianism (and in the later stage of the conflict between Bosnianism and Serbism) boils down to the fact that Yugoslavism (or Bosnianism) had, at the time, attained its ideal of a state while its adversary had not. This is hardly a ground on which to declare the latter's quest for a sovereign state impermissible.

Some might argue that Yugoslavia, as a mosaic of southern Slavs and other assorted Balkan peoples, ranked higher on the multiethnicity scale than Slovenia. However, that is hardly a basis on which to require Slovenia to remain part of Serb-dominated Yugoslavia, especially since Slovenia's avowed purpose in seeking independence was rapid incorporation into the European Union (EU), a development that would, at a minimum, be neutral from the perspective of multiculturalism, since any loss to pluralism in Yugoslavia would be offset by a gain in the EU.

Defending Secession along Republic Lines

Although in the initial stages of Yugoslavia's wars some outside actors (particularly the United States and the Soviet Union) argued against the partition of the country, for a long time thereafter there was quasi-unanimity in international circles that the "correct" map of Yugoslavia was one that divided the country along the lines of the Yugoslav republics. Slovenia, Croatia, Bosnia, Macedonia, and the rump Yugoslavia (Serbia, Montenegro, Kosovo, and Vojvodina) were each viewed as a distinct unit. Most international, and in particular Western, actors would not even consider the alternatives to this arrangement. "Yugoslavia" itself was relegated to the dustbin of history, while any efforts to change the republics' borders and to effectuate further secessions were pushed into the realm of illegality, if not immorality. Accordingly, Yugoslav troops trying to save the union and Serb troops trying to establish a rump Yugoslavia that included parts of Bosnia-Herzegovina and Croatia were labeled as aggressors. Likewise, Bosnian Serbs and Krajinan Serbs trying to create their own independent republics were dismissed as "warlords" or "thugs."

Certainly, had the international community insisted on maintaining the republics' borders and brought its considerable resources to bear on the various actors, "peace"—defined as a cessation of gunfire—might have been achieved. But then again, the cessation of gunfire would have been no less likely had the international community thrown its full weight behind the preservation of Yugoslavia or the creation of a Greater Serbia. Hence the central question: Why this particular map?

In an effort to explain their preferred map, international analysts came up with various justifications. They distinguished the first wave of secessions (Croatia, Slovenia, Bosnia, and Macedonia) from the later ones (those of the Krajinan Serbs, the Bosnian Croats, and the Bosnian Serbs) in a number of ways. But on closer examination, these distinctions are not as sharp as they have been made out to be.

One justification has been discussed already. Under this first rationale, the second wave of secessions were illegitimate because they were motivated by ethnicism, or the desire to improve the linkage between existing states and ethnic groups. But as indicated earlier, this argument is specious, more so as a way to distinguish the two waves of secessions. In Yugoslavia, the first wave of secessions was as ethnicist as the second. Croats and Slovenes wanted Croat and Slovene states; they did not wish to remain part of a multiethnic, federated Yugoslavia. On what principle can Krajinan Serbs be denied the same wish?

Under a second rationale, the first wave of secessions was legitimate because those secessions took place along administrative borders ("republic borders") that were recognized as such under Yugoslav law.[6] This is a curious argument. It is difficult to see why one would want the right to secession to depend on the preexistence of internal municipal borders. Did Algeria have a weaker claim to secession than Senegal because, under French municipal law, the former was part of France while the latter was a distinct colonial territory? Paris obviously thought so, but the U.N. General Assembly respectfully disagreed.[7] It also is difficult to see the equity in treating internal municipal borders as sacrosanct: Why should Crimea forever remain a part of Ukraine simply because an impulsive tyrant decided to redraw the Soviet Union's internal borders? Giving internal municipal borders the same weight as international borders also promises to frustrate efforts to deal with ethnonational tensions through regional autonomy and federalism arrangements. Fearful that an internal border, once drawn, would take a life of its own, a state would be reluctant to create a legal arrangement that would set an internal border. Turkey, for instance, would never recognize a Kurdish region in light of the precedent set by the Yugoslavia example. Indeed, this danger has even found an illustration in the Yugoslav context. Serbia has abolished the status of Kosovo as a distinct autonomous region. Although the international community has been unhappy about this act, it certainly was a logical step. The radical extension, in international discourse, of the prohibition on aggression to acts committed to prevent secession along internal municipal borders has made federal authorities wary of leaving those borders in place. Presumably this is a consequence that many international observers, particularly advocates of creative means of diffusing ethnonational tension, would consider undesirable.

Moreover, even if municipal borders were given a state-constitutive status, this would not necessarily help distinguish the first wave of secession from the second (although it may help render illegitimate inter-unit border struggles or federal efforts to keep the federation intact). The administrative border argument fails to provide guidance in identifying which administrative borders are state-constitutive and which are not. If republics could become states, what about "autonomous regions," such as Kosovo? If Bosnia-Herzegovina could become a state, why not Herzegovina or even Sarajevo or Bihac? These are not mere hypotheticals. For a time, Bihac did strive for statehood under the leadership of a Bosnian Muslim businessman who had no sympathy for the official Bosnian government in Sarajevo.[8]

A third related, and particularly compelling, rationale for the legitimacy of secessions along republic lines is that they were permissible under the Yugoslav constitution.[9] Those who advance this contractarian argument maintain that it is only fair to hold the antisecessionists to a provision in their own laws.[10] This argument contains two flaws. First, it is unclear whether the Yugoslav constitution in effect at the time of the secessions did in fact provide for secession. Moreover, although some constitutional scholars have read that right into the constitution, one could legitimately respond that, in the absence of a mechanism for effectuating that right, the secessions were impermissible as they were actually carried out.[11] Second, and more important from the perspective of the larger international framework, this argument concedes that the legitimacy of a secession depends on the vagaries of a domestic document. Thus, regions of a nation-state with a particularly oppressive central authority that makes clear that the regions do not have the right to secede are placed in a comparatively worse position than regions of a nation-state governed by a central authority that experiments with decentralization. Again, this is likely not a consequence intended by those who wish to encourage different ways of letting different people coexist.

A fourth rationale grounds the state-constitutive stature of the republic borders not in their status under Yugoslav municipal law but in their recognition by the international community. Under this argument, a border, even if drawn for the first time internationally, becomes inviolable once the international community recognizes it as legitimate. This invocation of international "process" to legitimize a border holds some appeal, but it raises questions about the legitimacy of the process that led to the recognition of the borders in the first place. That a secession from a nation-state could be considered legitimate simply because a group of states decided to recognize a border running through that nation-state has significant consequences for the very concept of sovereignty. This invocation of process might have been less worrisome if the international community had in place a legitimate mechanism for the recognition of internal borders. But no such mechanism exists. The ad hoc mechanism set in place by the European Union, which mandated that only breakaway republics respectful of minority rights be recognized as independent states, might have filled the void (although this is highly debatable insofar as there existed no basis for requiring the warring parties to accept EU arbitration). But even that mechanism represents a lost opportunity, since the EU states, ignoring their own recognition criteria, elected to recognize Croatia despite the contrary recommendation of the Arbitral Commission established to apply those criteria.

In sum, no principled basis exists under international law to distinguish the two waves of secession. Naturally, the opposition to the later wave is understandable, driven as it was by reactions to the means (forcible expulsion of populations, mass killings) associated with efforts to actualize those secessions. But opposition to the means should be decoupled from opposition to the goal. Mass killings and forced expulsions would be objectionable even if the goal they were intended to serve was noble. Alternatively, a goal might be noble (or at least acceptable) even if the means utilized to effectuate it was illegitimate. Thus, a right to statehood cannot be extinguished (assuming it is applicable) simply because some of its advocates and beneficiaries have committed wrongs in an effort to vindicate that right.

Map-Neutrality and Intermediation: An Alternative Framework?

As we have seen from the preceding discussion, international law provides no basis for declaring that Yugoslavia's division along "republic" lines constitutes a superior response to the strife in the region. This is not meant to suggest, however, that any one of the alternate solutions (such as the preservation of Yugoslavia as a unified nation-state or its division along other lines) would have constituted a superior response. The discussion of the international legal framework was intended solely to demonstrate the difficulty of declaring any one map superior to another or announcing any one identity to have a greater claim to sovereignty than another, as the international community has rushed to do.

To some international observers, the implications of this line of reasoning are clear (and welcome). If no settlement is *more* just than another, then clearly no settlement is *less* just than another. If this is so, then one ought to choose the option that is most likely to secure the peace.

At first blush, this peace-oriented perspective makes the task appear easy. Obviously, the settlement that is *certain* to secure the peace is a settlement to which all the parties accede. From this perspective, whatever arrangement the parties agree upon constitutes a "just peace." And no arrangement would be deemed to constitute a "just peace" in the absence of such an agreement. In the search for a settlement, the international community should be steadfastly map-neutral and limit its role to helping the parties reach an agreement.

This particular approach to the search for a "settlement"—one that appears to be result-neutral and based on negotiation—is appealing in light of the difficulties of articulating a "correct" resolution to Yugoslavia's wars. Accordingly, the approach has gained adherents steadily as the conflict has dragged on. However, the approach is not as neutral as it is said to be. Substantive bias is built in to the very identification of the "parties" for purposes of negotiation, the choice of which is certain to affect the outcome.

This difficulty is rarely acknowledged because the definition of parties appears so natural and uncontroversial: Are there not three parties in Bosnia—the Bosnian Croats, the Bosnian Serbs, and the Bosnian Muslims? On closer examination, however, the process of fixing parties turns out to be as contestable as the process of determining a correct map. It requires not the fixing of "territorial" borders but the fixing of "communal" borders. Yet the problems inherent in fixing borders are the same across the board. In Bosnia, as elsewhere, there are competing identities, and most individuals feel the pull of more than one. Borders—any borders—will by definition do violence to some of these pulls just as they confer privilege and honor others. A Serb-dominated Yugoslavia disadvantaged the Croat identity. The creation of Croatia disadvantaged the Serb identity.

Similarly, the recognition that there are three legitimate parties in Bosnia is certain to disadvantage those who do not belong to any of these three communities and those who do not conceive of their identity as communally constructed. Some might feel Bosnian, pure and simple. Others might conceive of themselves as Serbo-Croat; still others as Yugoslav, Slav, or European, or more locally as Sarajevan. Some might even be agnostic with respect to ethnonational referents and conceive of their identity in gender or class terms. If there is no basis for declaring one particular territorial division of the Yugoslav space superior to another, how can there be a basis for declaring a particular communal division of Yugoslav society superior to another? If the carving up of Yugoslavia into six pieces cannot be justified, how can the division of Bosnians into three groups (or, as the Dayton accords will have it, two "entities") be justified?

Just as the central question earlier was "What map?" the central question here ought to be "What parties?" The answer to this question is not all that easy to determine, even if one were steadfastly fixated on peace. The pragmatic answer—that an entity would be deemed a party to negotiations if it had access to means of violence in sufficient quantities to affect adversely the peace—is unsatisfactory, even on its own terms. An international process that limits the seats around the negotiating table to entities with access to the means of violence renders access to means of violence an important goal for all entities. Such a process promises to undermine the very goal (peace) that it is designed to serve.

The Vindication of Fundamental Norms

Two conclusions emerge from the preceding discussion. First, international law, the one universally accepted framework for determining a principled settlement, is indeterminate on the salient issues associated with ethnonational strife and the accompanying struggle over the identity of territory. Second, the alternative of seeking peace, any peace, through intermediation also is plagued by conceptual difficulties. The implications of these conclusions are clear. Ideally, until the international community can find a basis for articulating what would constitute a "just peace" in the former Yugoslavia, it ought to have adopted a position of complete neutrality with respect to issues over which there is little certainty, such as the location of borders or the organization of contemporary Yugoslav space. As for mediation, in light of the substantive bias built into it and the problem of privileging parties with access to violence, the international community also should have considered abandoning that task. It goes without saying, of course, that the international community did not follow these precepts. One striking deficiency in the Dayton accords—at least on the conceptual level—is their failure to articulate the principles upon which they are based.

This is not to suggest that the international community would have had nothing left to do in the former Yugoslavia. Although it is formidably difficult to articulate what a "just" resolution of Yugoslavia's wars would entail, the ideal of justice is not wholly indeterminate. There are issues over which there is little uncertainty. The violation of fundamental norms (ethnic cleansing, mass killings) is unequivocally wrong. As the international community struggles over the challenge of coming up with a just settlement, it can (and should), in the interim, commit itself fully to the vindication of these fundamental norms.

This course of action might appear modest, but it is still a big job. First, those norms that are truly fundamental must be determined. All would agree that the prohibition on genocide is one such norm, but how far can the list be extended? Should, for instance, the prohibition on mass expulsion also be considered a fundamental norm, even though recent history is replete with examples of internationally sanctioned mass expulsions?[12]

Second, the effort to vindicate fundamental norms does not necessarily provide clear guidance on the correct course of action. Just because we know that what *they* do is wrong does not mean that we know what *we* ought to do. Even as we focus on the most egregious acts, we cannot escape acute dilemmas. If we had insisted on the vindication of fundamental norms, we might have had to reject a settlement that will alleviate the immediate human suffering and minimize the probability that atrocities will take place in Yugoslavia in the future.

With respect to issues like these, there appear to be two options: the "realist/pragmatist" option and the "idealist" option. For the realists/pragmatists, purity is unattainable, even with respect to fundamental norms. A human rights crusade is a costly affair. What we need to do is balance justice against peace. As the Bosnian crisis reminded us, however, such balancing might change from day to day. What is an ideal balance today might not be so tomorrow. Allowing the "superior" solution to be determined by the specificities of time and place carries with it a high price tag. It encourages those who are unhappy with a particular solution to make sure that the solution no longer maximizes the competing values of peace and justice. For a Serb unhappy with the repatriation of the Muslim victims of ethnic cleansing, for instance, a rational alternative would have been to do whatever it takes to convince the international community that returning displaced persons to their homes will not maximize peace and justice. For a Bosnian unhappy with the results of ethnic cleansing, the rational alternative is to convince the international community of the exact opposite. Embracing "realism," then, risks depriving us of an ability to protect the realist solution, as marginalized actors will do all they can, and by any means necessary, to sabotage that solution.

In light of this cost, it might be tempting to go to the other extreme, to reject the realist position fully and to adopt the idealist position that the vindication of fundamental rights is not negotiable. Any settlement is unacceptable that does not provide that all war criminals will be punished and that all Yugoslavs will have the right to return to their homes. To the idealist, this is important, not simply with respect to the people affected but also to demonstrate to others that wrongdoing does not pay. But this purism comes with a price tag too. And the principal problem is that those costs are unlikely to be borne by the same people who would reap the benefits of a purist course of action. How is one to weigh the immediate suffering that a sustained war effort against Serbia would inflict on Bosnian (*and* Serb) civilians, as well as on U.N. troops, against the benefit that some victims will reap from that effort and the establishment of a desirable general precedent?

Coping with the Challenge

This close examination of the issues presented by Yugoslavia's wars leaves us in a quandary. The issues are not unique to this conflict, of course, but are to be found in all instances of ethnonational strife. As noted, one way out of the impasse generated by the struggle over borders, both territorial and communal, is to abandon altogether the effort to resolve the issues at stake in these struggles and to try instead to vindicate certain fundamental norms over which there is little uncertainty. Thus, outside actors had no basis in principle for declaring to the participants in Yugoslavia's wars what the "correct" borders of the reorganized Yugoslav space were. Nor did the outside actors have a basis for requiring that the parties abide by their (the outsiders') sense of an acceptable peace. They did not even have a basis for demanding an immediate end to hostilities. The outside actors have been on solid ground of principle only when requiring that the parties respect certain universal norms.

But as the argument thus far suggests, this alternative is not a perfect guide for action. Just because it is clear that some of what *they* did was unequivocally wrong does not mean that the moral calculus, as it applies to *our* actions, is crystal clear. What is the correct response to the violation of universal norms? What balance ought a response strike between the desire for justice and the yearning for peace? The basic tension reemerges even as we anchor ourselves in the paradigm of fundamental norms.

In the end, this leaves us with a call for reflection: reflection over the cost (to peace) we are willing to incur as we try to vindicate fundamental rights and the cost (to justice) we are willing to incur as we embrace peace. Some might characterize this call for reflection as an escapist retreat into the ivory tower: since we do not have the courage to fight evil and are reluctant to look the horror in the face, we pretend that things are more complex than they actually are to justify our inaction. While it is true that the raising of moral difficulties could be an excuse for inaction, that need not be the case. In any event, the possibility of paralysis is no justification for jumping on whatever bandwagon is traveling down Main Street on any given day.

This leaves us with a few suggestions that, while they may no longer be useful for settling Yugoslavia's wars, may help us to deal with similar conflicts elsewhere:

1. Outside actors (governments, international organizations, and non-governmental organizations) should steadfastly avoid declaring any one set of borders superior to others. Similarly, they should not embrace one type of political settlement (say, the preservation of existing state borders with political rights granted to the minority as a group) at the expense of another (say, secessionism). Instead, outside actors should adopt a position of result-neutrality on the salient issues underlying this type of conflict. By way of illustration, Western policymakers were wrong in declaring the territorial integrity of Bosnia-Herzegovina sacroscant, and the United States erred in announcing that the war in Chechnya was solely an internal Russian affair.

2. Outside actors also should avoid preconditioning border changes on peaceful means to effectuate them. This position still presupposes that the maintenance of current borders is somewhat less suspect than the effort to alter them. For groups striving to alter borders, this position is inherently biased because it creates a presumption in favor of existing borders. These groups would be quite justified in proposing that the presumption be reversed, particularly when certain conditions are applicable. Under such a revision, it would be impermissible to resort to force in order to *preserve* existing borders. The reverse presumption is not a wild hypothetical. In the Yugoslav context, it was applied to the Belgrade government, which was roundly condemned for resorting to force in order to preserve the integrity of the federation. The general rule has been, however, that states may resort to force to preserve their territorial integrity. Both the official Bosnian government and Russia benefited from this conservative position.

3. Outside actors should focus all their energies on vindicating fundamental norms, which provide us with the firmest ethical grounding. In certain rare instances, the vindication of fundamental norms *might* require the protection of certain borders. If there are grounds to believe, for instance, that the transgressor of a particular border will be disrespectful of fundamental norms, outside actors might rally behind maintaining that border. They should, however, painstakingly clarify the reasons for their actions. There ought to be no opposition to the territorial ambitions of the would-be expansionist; the opposition ought to be limited to the egregious actions that are considered likely to accompany that expansion.

4. Some international observers might be tempted to defend an across-the-board commitment to territorial borders on the ground that such an indiscriminate commitment constitutes a proxy for an effort

to vindicate fundamental norms. This position has no conceptual basis and is empirically unsupported. Fundamental norms have been violated with equal frequency behind the security of territorial borders and in the course of altering those borders.

5. Outside actors should realize that even an attempt to vindicate fundamental norms will be plagued by a fundamental tension between the desire for peace and the desire for justice. Although in some instances the two might coincide (as, for instance, when peace requires the arrest and prosecution of a criminal), it is simply wrong to believe that peace is never attainable without justice. History is replete with examples of unjust settlements. The tension between peace and justice means that vindicating fundamental norms can never take the form of a crusade but always must involve reflection and deliberation.

Notes

1. Admittedly, not all international observers have pursued these two ideals, and some who have pursued peace and justice have also pursued other goals, such as containment. Yet it is safe to assume that the twin ideals of peace and justice have structured much of the policy thinking and discussion with regard to the former Yugoslavia. Many actors have embraced both ideals, in part, if not in whole. The remaining actors have, at a minimum, invoked them if for no other reason than to score rhetorical points. Hence, a careful examination of the two ideals and their interrelatedness is justified.

2. See, for example, Lee Buchheit, *Secession: The Legitimacy of Self-Determination* (New Haven, CT: Yale University Press, 1978), pp. 17–20.

3. At the height of decolonialization, most states agreed that the right to self-determination was to be limited to overseas colonies of Western colonial empires, in an unspoken rule that came to be known as "saltwater colonialism." See, for example, James Mayall, "Self-Determination and the Organization of African Unity" in I.M. Lewis, ed., *Nationalism and Self-Determination in the Horn of Africa*, (London: Ithaca Press, 1983). Unsurprisingly, many secessionists rejected the saltwater colonialism rule. Ironically, they were supported by at least one colonial power—Belgium— which, in a doctrinal argument that came to be known as the Belgian Thesis, argued that there existed no principled way in which to distinguish the anticolonialist struggle from the struggle for self-determination carried out by the indigenous peoples in the Americas. See Buchheit, *Secession*, pp. 74–75; and F. Van Langenhove, *The Question of Aborigines before the United Nations: The Belgian Thesis* (Brussels: Royal Colonial Institute of Belgium,

1954). Although Belgium was accused of engaging in a hypocritical effort to salvage its empire, its thesis highlighted the problem with the saltwater rule.

Many international legal scholars have since contested the strict limitation of secessionism to settings of saltwater colonialism. They have argued that the limitation is neither normatively nor legally grounded. See, for example, Alexis Heraclides, *The Self-Determination of Minorities in International Politics* (London: Cass, 1991), p. 38; Antonio Cassese, "The Self-Determination of Peoples," in Louis Henkin, ed., *The International Bill of Rights* (New York: Columbia University Press, 1981), pp. 91, 94–95, 112; John Collins, "Self-Determination in International Law: the Palestinians," *Case Western Reserve Journal of International Law*, vol. 12 (1980), pp. 137, 153; Ved Nanda, "Self-Determination under International Law: Validity of Claims to Secede," *Case Western Reserve Journal of International Law*, vol. 13 (1981), pp. 257, 266; Ernest Petric, "Self-Determination: Security, Integrity and Sovereign States" in Konrad Ginther and Hubert Isak, eds., *Self-Determination in Europe: Proceedings of an International Workshop Held at the Akademie Graz July 5–6, 1989* (Vienna: Bohlau, 1991), pp. 23, 32–33; and Eise Suzuki, "Self-Determination and World Public Order: Community Responses to Territorial Separation," *Virginia Journal of International Law*, vol. 16 (1976), pp. 779, 861.

4. See Arnold Toynbee, "Self-Determination," *Quarterly Review*, vol. 484 (1925), p. 319.

5. This double-standardism was most evident under the League of Nations minority protection regime that was applicable only to a select number of countries, all losers of World War I. See generally Inis Claude, *National Minorities: An International Problem* (Cambridge, MA: Harvard University Press, 1955); and Patrick Thornberry, *International Law and the Protection of Minorities* (Oxford: Clarendon Press, 1991), pp. 38–40. In the modern era, France is most guilty of double-standardism in this domain. While pushing for minority rights in the Balkans (and elsewhere) on international legal grounds, France has always placed a reserve on the minority rights provisions included in international human rights treaties. Yves Plasseraud, "Qu'est-ce qu'une minorité en France aujourd'hui?" in *Les minorités a l'age de l'État-nation* (Paris: Groupement pour les droits des minorités, 1985), pp. 271, 274. According to these reserves, these provisions have no applicability in France, because France does not have distinct minorities.

6. This idea may be traced to Cassese, "Self-Determination of Peoples," pp. 92, 95.

7. See G.A. Res. 1573, December 19, 1960.

8. See *Le Monde Diplomatique*, January 1995.

9. For the argument, see, for example, Ben Bagwell, "Yugoslavian Constitutional Questions: Self-Determination and Secession of Member Republics,"

Georgia Journal of International and Comparative Law, vol. 21 (1981), pp. 489, 516–22.

10. See, for example, Marc Gjidara, "Cadre Juridique et Regles Applicables aux Problemes Europeens de Minorité," *Annuaire Français de Droit International*, vol. 37 (1991), pp. 349, 367.

11. See, for example, Bagwell, "Yugoslavian Constitutional Questions," p. 508, n. 8, 10.

12. One can point to the internationally sanctioned mass expulsions that took place after both world wars. After World War I, Greece, Turkey, and Bulgaria signed multilateral treaties whereby they agreed to exchange minority populations. See, for example, *Convention between Greece and Bulgaria Respecting Reciprocal Emigration, Nov. 27, 1919*, League of Nations Treaty Series 1, 1919, p. 67. These treaties were registered with the League of Nations, and the Permanent Court of Justice decided several issues arising in the course of their implementation. See, for example, *Advisory Opinion No. 17, Interpretation of the Convention between Greece and Bulgaria Respecting Reciprocal Emigration*, Permanent Court of International Justice, ser. B, no. 17, July 31, 1990. This involvement of the League organizations in administering forced population exchanges only contributed to enhancing their international legitimacy.

In the wake of World War II, many East European countries also engaged in mass expulsions in an effort to homogenize their countries ethnically. These expulsions were not minor affairs. According to realistic estimates, 14 million to 15 million people were forced to relocate. See Alan Dowty, *Closed Borders: The Contemporary Assault on Freedom of Movement* (New Haven, CT: Yale University Press, 1987), p. 98. Most, but by no means all, of these people were ethnic Germans. Several East European countries agreed to exchange their minorities, and some of those agreements were carried out, at least partially. See Alfred M. de Zayas, "International Law and Mass Population Transfers," *Harvard International Law Journal*, vol. 207 (1975), pp. 225–26. Instead of condemning these forced population movements, the great powers condoned them. See Claude, *National Minorities*, p. 115.

Chapter 3

Collective Spinelessness: U.N. Actions in the Former Yugoslavia

THOMAS G. WEISS

L ONG BEFORE the presidents of Serbia, Croatia, and Bosnia initialed a peace settlement culminating three weeks of roller-coaster negotiations at Wright-Patterson Air Force Base, the United Nations was at the center of ongoing controversy in the former Yugoslavia. Throughout four years of fratricide, the world organization was embroiled among competing ethnic groups and confronted thorny questions about sovereignty, human rights, and the use of force to sustain international norms. This chapter details the painful dithering and ineffectiveness of U.N. actions from the beginning of the end of Yugoslavia on June 25, 1991, until the agreement on November 21, 1995, that partitioned Bosnia-Herzegovina into a Muslim-Croat federation and a Bosnian Serb entity while preserving the fiction of a central government of a multiethnic state with its seat in Sarajevo.

The record of the United Nations in the former Yugoslavia since early 1992—epitomized by the debacles in Bihac in late 1994 and throughout Bosnia in mid-1995, when Serbs repeatedly ran roughshod over international directives, took hundreds of U.N. soldiers hostage, and humiliated some of them as human shields—makes the organization's limitations clear. Time and again, U.N. actions in the Balkans were far too little and came far too late. This has been true since the first televised images of emaciated prisoners behind the barbed wire of concentration camps and reports of widespread Serbian and Croatian war crimes began to filter out of the region, conjuring up images of Europe's fascist past and provoking a general public outcry. And it was true of both of the "two United Nations"—the first, where governments meet and make decisions, and the second, comprising the various secretariats, officials, and soldiers who implement these decisions.[1]

In the absence of effective military engagement by the member states of the North Atlantic Treaty Organization (NATO) in support of Security Council resolutions, U.N. humanitarian efforts became a substitute for an overall strategy for bringing the war in the former Yugoslavia to an end. Despite lip service to the concept of collective security since the end of the Cold War, the international response can best be described as collective spinelessness. That peace appears plausible after face-to-face negotiations in Dayton and three and a half years of carnage, which followed closely upon NATO's willingness to use air power in late summer 1995, underlines rather than contradicts this argument. Significant Western military force was applied only after Croatia's rout of the Serbs in the Krajina and after blue helmets had retreated from the front lines.

Furthermore, the response of the "second United Nations" has been inadequate—even though at its peak in late summer, before the Dayton talks, U.N. forces in the former Yugoslavia were significant: approximately 50,000 soldiers and police officers from 36 countries (with almost 35,000 in Bosnia-Herzegovina after the addition of the rapid reaction force), as well as 3,000 civilian personnel, at an annual cost of some $2 billion.[2] In order to provide assistance for the million-plus refugees who fled across borders and another three million displaced persons who did not, the office of the United Nations High Commissioner for Refugees (UNHCR) was spending $500 million in the region annually, and various other governmental agencies, intergovernmental bodies, and nongovernmental organizations (NGOs) another $1 billion. These efforts added up to the most expensive, dangerous failure of any operation undertaken by the international community to date.

As the Cold War drew to a close, many believed that the role of the United Nations as a regional conflict manager would be limited to the Third World. Yet the organization is now a factor in security politics in the heart of Europe—in fact, at the end of 1995, European operations accounted for more than half of the U.N. soldiers and more than half of the world organization's military budget worldwide. The Republic of Yugoslavia was suspended in 1991 from membership in the Organization for (formerly, Conference on) Security and Cooperation in Europe (OSCE) for having started the war, but four years later there were shooting wars in eight of the 52 remaining member states. Even outside involvement in the former Soviet Union—which seemed improbable, if not inconceivable, a few short years ago—now appears likely in view of the ongoing crises there.[3]

In such circumstances, what lessons may be learned from the world's responses to the military, diplomatic, and humanitarian crises resulting from Yugoslavia's wars?

Military Force and Diplomacy in Support of Humane Values?

Since the beginning of Yugoslavia's wars, the international community has repeatedly weighed the costs and benefits of deploying military force in support of humanitarian objectives. However, the disparities between its rhetoric and its willingness to act have caused great confusion on the ground in Bosnia-Herzegovina and in what were the so-called U.N. protected areas (UNPAs) of the Serb-controlled Krajina within Croatia. When the international community switched its rhetorical response to the crisis in Bosnia from the pacific settlement of the dispute (based on chapter VI of the U.N. Charter) to physical enforcement (chapter VII), albeit with the purpose of protecting international military and humanitarian personnel rather than civilians, it did so without the will to commit the necessary military means to implement its mandates. U.N. credibility was thereby undermined, and U.N. soldiers condemned to "wander in the void" between peacekeeping and coercion.[4] Rhetoric and operational reality also diverged in the protected areas, where traditional peacekeeping activities assumed cooperation on the part of Serbs and Croats. The U.N. secretary-general subsequently has argued that "the organization has come to realize that a mix of peacekeeping and enforcement is not the answer to a lack of consent and cooperation by the parties to the conflict."[5]

Governments, NGOs, and the United Nations are now hesitating at a fork in the road. One route leads back toward the use of minimum force as a last resort and only in self-defense in support of narrow mandates. The other leads toward the application of superior military force in support of more ambitious international objectives, including the enforcement of humane values.[6]

Two main groups resist taking the latter fork toward "military humanitarianism."[7] The first consists of many developing countries, whose reticence or outright hostility toward U.N. intervention is based on four arguments: first, that state sovereignty does not permit outside intervention; second, that state sovereignty provides an element of protection against the bullying of major powers; third, that intervention is messy; and fourth, that the Security Council's definition of what constitutes a "threat" to international peace and security is far too broad.

Whatever one's views may be about the evolution of what the French government and its highly visible former minister of humanitarian affairs, Bernard Kouchner, have championed as the *devoir* or even *droit d'ingérence* (literally, the duty, or even the right, to interfere), or about the possible existence of a de jure right of intervention on humanitarian or human rights grounds, there does exist a de facto right of intervention when the Security Council decides that certain events constitute aggression or are a threat to international peace and security.[8] The restrictive claims of domestic jurisdiction of Third World naysayers have little relevance once the Security Council weighs in, since in ratifying the charter, member states agreed to acquiesce in the Council's own interpretation of its functions. Threats to international peace and security effectively constitute what Stanley Hoffmann has called an "all-purpose parachute."

It is inevitable that the major powers will flex their muscles in pursuit of their interests. What is not inevitable is that they will subject themselves to international oversight and law. For the foreseeable future, the Security Council's decision to intervene or not to intervene in a particular conflict will reflect not internationally agreed-upon objective criteria, but the domestic imperatives of the major powers. Its directives will reflect what the international political traffic will bear at a particular moment. Although efforts to refine the criteria for intervention are laudable, pleas against selective intervention amount to arguing that the United Nations should not intervene anywhere unless it can intervene everywhere in analogous circumstances. This is a case of the best being the enemy of the good.

However imperfect the U.N. system, the dangers of big-power abuse actually are reduced by relying on intervention under the Security Council's auspices. Beginning with the April 1991 decision creating havens for Kurds in northern Iraq, access to civilians has become a recognized basis for intervention, building logically on precedents established by the actions of developing countries themselves against white minority governments in Rhodesia and South Africa, where violations of human rights were considered not just an affront to civilization but also a threat to international peace and security. The logic has been extended subsequently in Haiti to intervene to restore a democratically elected government.

The other group of dissenters with respect to military humanitarianism is led mainly by civilians—not only analysts but some field staff as well—who believe that the terms "humanitarian intervention" and, worse yet, "humanitarian war" are oxymorons.[9] Their reluctance goes beyond eschewing violence on religious or philosophical grounds. They argue that humanitarian initiatives are by nature strictly consensual and necessitate independence and impartiality. Political authorities in armed conflicts must be persuaded to allow access to civilians, who are protected by the international law of armed conflict, of which the International Committee of the Red Cross (ICRC) is the custodian. Intervention, the dissenters argue, not only raises the levels of violence in the short run but also makes reconciliation more difficult in the longer run.

These humanitarians have found unlikely allies in those American military officers who have yet to recover from the failed interventions in Vietnam and, more recently, Somalia, as well as among critics who see U.S. dominance of multilateral military efforts as akin to an earlier hegemony that rarely, if ever, produced salutary results. A further objection to humanitarian intervention comes from those for whom the sine qua non of emergency relief is strengthening civilian institutions within countries experiencing war. In their view, outside military forces make the task of an affected country's own civilian authorities more problematic, with intervention leading to further instability and weakened democratic institutions.

Although humanitarian intervention may be uncomfortable for some, and is arguably counterproductive for the long-range task of democratization, with one in every 115 of the world's people forced into flight from war, sometimes it may be the only means of halting genocide, massive abuses of human rights, and mass starvation.[10] For this reason, others (this author included) are receptive to intervention by outside military forces to assist civilians trapped in the throes of war. When consent cannot be extracted from either local governments or insurgents, economic and military sanctions can be justified on operational *and* ethical grounds to create and sustain access to civilians. When the cause of starvation is war and there is sufficient political will, an effective humanitarian response may include military backup that goes far beyond the minimal use of force in self-defense permitted U.N. peacekeepers. Rather than suspending relief and withdrawing from an active war zone, the international community should be able to use force to guarantee access to civilians, protect aid workers, and disarm recalcitrant belligerents. Kofi Annan, once again the U.N. under-secretary-general for peacekeeping operations after a short period as special representative of the secretary-general in the former Yugoslavia, had earlier acknowledged, "The reality is there are situations when you cannot assist people unless you are prepared to take certain [military] measures."[11]

The international community's unwillingness to react militarily in the former Yugoslavia, until August 1995, however, provides a case study of what not to do in a humanitarian crisis. In the words of analyst Rosalyn Higgins, "We have chosen to respond to major unlawful violence not by stopping that violence, but by trying to provide relief to the suffering. But our choice of policy allows the suffering to continue."[12] This inaction has left many of the inhabitants of the region mistrustful of the United Nations and has lent a new and disgraceful connotation to the word "peacekeeping." Bound by the traditional rules of engagement (fire only in self-defense, and only after being fired upon), U.N. troops never fought a single battle with any of the factions in Bosnia that routinely disrupted relief convoys. The rules of engagement led to the appeasement of local forces rather than to the enforcement of U.N. mandates. Among the most unsafe locations in the Balkans, indeed in the world, were the so-called safe areas.

U.N. peacekeepers in Croatia were unable to implement their mandate because they received no cooperation from the Croats or Krajina Serbs. In Bosnia, the situation was even more problematic. The U.N. force there was present under chapter VII and was constantly challenged, but it lacked the capability to apply coercive force across a wide front. Under such conditions, observed Major Richard Barrons, chief of staff of British forces, at their headquarters in Split, "Day One success can turn into Day Two failure, unless you are prepared to conduct full-scale conventional war in support of humanitarian objectives." Even those U.N. soldiers who might be prepared to challenge Serbian troops would require "a completely different package of forces."[13]

Unable to create the conditions for its own success, the United Nations Protection Force (UNPROFOR) was not militarily credible. Shortly before resigning in January 1994 from a soldier's nightmare as U.N. commander in Bosnia-Herzegovina, Lieutenant General Francis Briquemont lamented the disparity between rhetoric and reality: "There is a fantastic gap between the resolutions of the Security Council, the will to execute those resolutions, and the means available to commanders in the field."[14]

The provisions for economic and military sanctions in the U.N. Charter were designed to back up international decisions to counteract aggression and to halt atrocities in such situations as the one in Bosnia. What actually happened was somewhat different.

In February 1994 NATO outrage over violations of the 12-mile artillery "exclusion zone" around Sarajevo boiled over, and the subsequent downing of four Serbian military aircraft temporarily reversed two years of empty saber rattling. But just as NATO, the United Nations, and the Clinton administration began to hope that these modest military actions would end the siege of Sarajevo and facilitate a diplomatic solution, the Serbs began new ethnic cleansing activities in Prejidor and Banja Luka and attacked the so-called safe area for Muslim refugees in Gorazde. Two American F-16s carried out another NATO "first" in April, bombing Serbian ground positions outside Gorazde. Although the stated purpose of these strikes was to protect the handful of U.N. observers and relief workers in Gorazde, the real target was, at long last, the Serbs.

The attacks enraged the Bosnian Serbs, who responded by killing a British soldier, shooting down a British Harrier aircraft, detaining 200 U.N. personnel, and taking over Gorazde. The Serbs had called NATO's bluff, not for the first nor the last time. And, as before, the Western alliance proved unwilling to confront the Serbian aggression for fear of all-out war between the 100,000-strong Serbian rebel forces and the significantly outnumbered U.N. forces. The Serbs subsequently withdrew many of their troops and weapons to beyond a 20-mile radius of Gorazde. Then, in a continuation of their usual cat-and-mouse game, they fortified their positions just outside the exclusion zone and increased the number of "policemen" within it. In April NATO had empowered the U.N. commander in Bosnia to set up exclusion zones like the one around Sarajevo around four other safe areas (Tuzla, Zepa, Srebrenica, and Bihac) in the event of attack or the infiltration of heavy artillery. However, when Admiral Leighton W. Smith, Jr., the U.S. commander of NATO's air cover for U.N. operations in Bosnia, subsequently proposed using force to menace the Serbs who were shelling Tuzla, UNPROFOR's force commander, General Bertrand de Lapresle, refused.

In July 1994 the "contact group"—which had been formed earlier that year and was made up of representatives of the United States, France, Germany, Britain, and Russia—offered the warring parties in Bosnia a take-it-or-leave-it partition of the country into two more or less equal parts. It was thought that a combination of carrots (easing economic sanctions against Belgrade) and sticks (the threat of NATO military action and the lifting of the arms embargo against the Bosnian Muslims) would prompt the Serbs—of Bosnia, Croatia, and Serbia—to accept *only* 49 percent of Bosnian territory instead of the more than 70 percent that they controlled. (This was after the first Vance-Owen plan had been judged a year earlier as morally and politically unacceptable in the West, although it had proposed even less territory as a prize for the aggressor Serbs.) The Bosnian government accepted the plan unconditionally, but the Bosnian Serbs attached so many conditions to their acceptance that their response amounted to a rejection. In a referendum the following month, 96 percent of the Bosnian Serbs who voted flatly rejected the plan.

Again, verbal rebukes rather than action emanated from the contact group, and there was a tepid call for more sanctions. Despite two symbolic attacks in August and September—against an antitank gun and an abandoned tank—it soon became clear once again that the international community was unprepared to employ significant air power against the Serbs or to arm the Muslims. In a curious mixture of wishful thinking and self-deception, the contact group instead took up a Russian proposal to ease sanctions against Belgrade. The Serbian government agreed to permit the deployment along the Yugoslav-Bosnian border of 135 civilian observers under the supervision of retired Swedish general Bo Pellnas to monitor its compliance with its announced decision to stop supplying the Bosnian Serbs with war matériel. In exchange, the contact group decided in late September to reward Serbian president Slobodan Milosevic with a temporary (100-day) easing of certain sanctions related to commercial travel and participation in international sporting and cultural events. At the same time, the contact group, in its wisdom, refused the promised lifting of the arms embargo that would have allowed the Bosnian Muslims to arm themselves more adequately.

November witnessed a new twist in the violence. After an unexpected string of victories in the Bihac pocket by the Bosnian army, nationalist Serbs counterattacked with artillery, tanks, and, finally, aerial bombing. This was especially embarrassing for the United Nations in that the attacks were staged from the Udbina airfield inside the Serbian-controlled Krajina, an area of Croatia supposedly patrolled by U.N. troops. The folly of the international efforts up to that point was encapsulated by the scene of cluster bombs and napalm dropping into a so-called safe area from planes based in a UNPA, and the attacks by Serbian soldiers supplied with weapons and fuel from Serbia in violation of Belgrade's agreement with the contact group.

The Security Council authorized NATO to attack Serbian ground targets as well as Serbian aircraft over Bosnian airspace. The sixth NATO attack—by 39 U.S., British, French, and Dutch aircraft—damaged the Udbina runway and the airfield's antiaircraft defenses but left aircraft untouched. Shortly thereafter, some 50 NATO aircraft attacked three Serbian missile sites—two in Bosnia and one in the Krajina—after attacks on two British planes on routine patrol.

Optimists heralded these gestures as a possible sign of a new commitment by the West to use force, but the air strikes amounted to little more than bluster. The United Nations, afraid that continued action would provoke retaliation against its troops and international aid workers, asked that the bombing be stopped. U.N. inspectors on the Bosnian border raised no objections as fuel and, no doubt, weapons shipments from Serbia passed through Serb-held parts of Bosnia en route to the Krajina. The remains of a pilot whose jet fighter crashed near Bihac were identified as those of a member of the Yugoslav (Serbian) air force. Moreover, the abrupt appearance of surface-to-air missiles in both the Krajina and Serbian-occupied Bosnia—also linked to Belgrade—now posed a threat to NATO aircraft, and permitted Serbs to advance with impunity and to recoup lost territory.[15]

When several hundred of their soldiers were detained by the Serbs in central Bosnia in December, U.N. forces demonstrated that they were unable to protect themselves, let alone Muslim civilians. The French and British governments refused to utter the word "hostage" because to have done so would have necessitated action. The United Nations and foreign governments tried to downplay the fact that the detained troops were Serbian pawns. Lieutenant General Sir Michael Rose, the commander of U.N. forces in Bosnia, euphemistically called them "life insurance" against bombing raids. The fate of UNPROFOR and of some four million people dependent on the United Nations for their daily survival hung in the balance as governments scampered to save face. Secretary-General Boutros Boutros-Ghali discussed openly a U.N. withdrawal, and 2,000 U.S. Marines were deployed in the Adriatic Sea in case they were needed. President Clinton announced that the United States would commit up to 25,000 soldiers to a force two or three times that size to evacuate what at the time were 24,000 U.N. troops in Bosnia.

The Clinton administration soon joined the French and British in appeasing the Serbs. Flights of NATO warplanes over Bosnia were halted in the hope that the Serbs would free the U.N. hostages and accept reformulated peace terms. In mid-December 1994 former U.S. President Jimmy Carter arrived in Bosnia to mediate—that is, to solidify Serbian gains in exchange for a renewable four-month cease-fire and a cessation-of-hostilities agreement that might permit UNPROFOR to interpose itself eventually between the hostile parties. The agreement held as winter set in, and the belligerents began yet another series of negotiations. As the cease-fire (by some accounts, the thirtieth to have been negotiated in the preceding three years) went into effect on New Year's Day, Bosnian President Alija Izetbegovic spoke to his compatriots over the radio: "We will negotiate where we can and make war where we have to. If the enemy does not show readiness for reasonable political solutions within the next four months, the cease-fire will not be extended."[16]

Later that month Croatian President Franjo Tudjman announced that he would not allow UNPROFOR to remain in the Krajina when its mandate expired at the end of March. Although he had made similar threats before, this time he appeared to mean what he said. He had come to the conclusion that the Serbs would never give up the quarter of Croatia that they occupied so long as U.N. soldiers shielded them. The West resisted, understanding that withdrawal of these troops could open up the possibility of a renewed Serbo-Croatian war.

In mid-March 1995 Tudjman admitted that his demand that UNPROFOR leave Croatia was, for the moment at least, the latest in a series of bluffs. He had wished to emphasize the dangers inherent in a permanently divided Croatia. As a result, however, it was agreed that the number of U.N. troops (about 14,000) in Croatia's protected areas was to be reduced substantially (to 8,750). Those remaining were to be redeployed to monitor the international borders with Serbia instead of only the cease-fire lines in the Krajina, and its name was to be altered: the U.N. Confidence Restoration Operation (UNCRO). The objective was to show that the Serb-occupied Krajina was still part of Croatia; to impede arms shipments from Serbia to Serb rebels; and to permit the U.N. soldiers to continue holding the lid on the Bosnian cauldron. As we shall see, the U.N.'s actual downsizing and withdrawal would await a Croatian military offensive a few months later.

Following a continual unraveling of the cease-fire in early spring, the United Nations finally called in NATO bombers for two successive days in late May 1995. Prodded by the Clinton administration, Rose's successor as commander of U.N. forces in Bosnia, Lieutenant General Rupert Smith, agreed from the U.N. side to target the Serbian arms depot in Pale. In what could be described as "Bihac revisited," the Serbs responded as they had earlier after milder air strikes. They held over 300 U.N. soldiers hostage—chaining several to potential targets as human shields—recovered heavy arms from the U.N.-controlled collection sites, and fired the deadliest shell of the war into the safe area of Tuzla.

On the basis of an accurate extrapolation of past reactions, including backing down in the face of comparable Serbian tactics in Bihac, the Serbs were unconvinced that NATO would press its assault. They were correct. U.N. blue helmets eventually were released; but their release appeared a quid pro quo for an agreement by the United Nations to abide strictly by the principles of traditional peacekeeping—a clear translation for no more NATO air strikes, the demand made by Bosnian Serb General Ratko Mladic and President Radovan Karadzic.

On paper, nonetheless, the military reaction appeared more muscular. In June NATO defense ministers, joined on the occasion by those from Sweden and Finland, established two separate rapid reaction forces. The Security Council approved the addition of 12,500 heavily armed soldiers for Bosnia—an increase of over 50 percent—from the British 24th Airmobile Brigade in central Bosnia and the joint English, French, and Dutch one in Croatia. For the first time in August 1995— two months being "rapid" for a U.N.-related rapid deployment force— the United Nations had artillery, light tanks, and battlefield-support helicopters. NATO also argued that there would be no "dual key," meaning that the force would no longer be subject to a veto by the cautious civilian head of the U.N. operation, Yasushi Akashi, then special representative of the secretary-general. In addition to other problems, the approval of the new force provided an ideal occasion for the Republicans in Congress to continue the larger battle to scale back U.S. contributions to the United Nations and to embarrass the president.

Although humanitarian motives figured prominently in justifications for the U.N. mission, concern about the safety of peacekeepers always had been the primary reason for the reluctance to respond vigorously—no matter how outrageous the Serbian provocation. For some time Bosnians had commented with derision that the word "self" should have been inserted before "protection" in UNPROFOR's title. As if to prove the point, before leaving his command in Bosnia, General Rose had coined the expression "Mogadishu line" to indicate that strict impartiality by U.N. soldiers was a necessity to avoid their becoming participants in the war. Consolidating positions, rather than remaining scattered in locations around Bosnia, and beefing up military capacities for self-protection made perfectly clear that U.N. soldiers were more concerned with protecting themselves than with any humanitarian mission, which necessarily would have involved crossing the line and taking sides on behalf of victims.

In July the Serbs moved to recover safe areas in eastern Bosnia. The symbolism was perfect. As Dutch peacekeepers retreated and widespread massacres of Muslims took place, the first safe area to be eliminated was Srebrenica, where the vacuous policy of safe areas actually had originated in March–April 1993. There French Lieutenant General Philippe Morillon, then the commander of U.N. troops in Bosnia, made a brave personal stand, which prevented the town from being overrun by rampaging Bosnian Serbs and resulted in the Security Council's designating Srebrenica and five other locales as "safe areas." The next to fall was Zepa, where Ukrainian peacekeepers were unable to resist Serbian advances. Gorazde was the next obvious target because the Serbs sought, as they had since 1992, an uninterrupted and purged swath of territory in eastern Bosnia bordering on Serbia itself.

The Bosnian Serbs' greed pushed NATO to announce after the fall of Srebrenica and Zepa their decision to use air power to deter further attacks. The latest in a series of lines drawn in continually shifting sands was around Gorazde. However, the most important result was that it catalyzed Croatia. The Tudjman government immediately mobilized soldiers to recover the Krajina and eventually other areas as well in western Bosnia. In spite of the arms embargo, Croatia's long coastline and cooperation by Hungary had permitted the government to procure heavy weapons for its 100,000-man army and 180,000 reserves, who also had been receiving technical assistance and training from a number of sources, including a Virginia-based company formed by retired American officers and called Military Professional Resources, Inc.

In only a few days, the Croatian army overran Knin, the capital of the self-styled breakaway republic, and recovered most of the Krajina that had been occupied for four years. The West talked, but Croatia acted. NATO's bluster had at least served to tie down the Bosnian Serbs— whose leaders, Karadzic and Mladic, had just been indicted by the War Crimes Tribunal and were busy infighting over civilian and military prerogatives—so they could not come to the aid of their Croatian counterparts, who were quickly routed. At the same time, Slobodan Milosevic had decided to steer clear in the hopes of getting sanctions lifted from Serbia itself. In an ironic twist, the largest refugee flow of the war—indeed the largest in Europe since the Soviet crushing of the Hungarian uprising in 1956—resulted from a successful Croatian military campaign. This time the estimated 125,000 to 150,000 refugees and 50,000 soldiers were all of Serbian origin. They fled into Serbia itself and toward Serbian-dominated Bosnia, especially Banja Luka.

In late August 1995 Serbian shells killed 38 people in the same Sarajevo market where twice as many deaths had catalyzed the first NATO air strikes in February 1994. The Western response this time was swifter and firmer than in the past. The effort to make Sarajevo safe involved both artillery from the rapid reaction force and NATO warplanes. The explanation for the largest military action since the founding of the Western alliance in 1949 was twofold: Serbs were on the defensive and leadership in disarray after the Croatian trouncing in the Krajina; and U.N. soldiers had withdrawn completely from the exposed areas in eastern Bosnia, thereby removing the contradiction that blue helmets were potentially endangered by Western air power.

The number of Serbian refugees continued to grow when Croatian forces (both from the Croatian Government Army and from Bosnia) and the Bosnian Government Army occupied land in western and central Bosnia that had been cleansed earlier by the Serbs. Aided by the NATO bombing that worsened long-standing supply problems, the rout of the Serbs continued. Bosnia and Croatia sought to strengthen their negotiating hands as they themselves took over the territory that had been slated to be returned to them as part of the negotiated 51–49 division. Western pressure to have the offensive come to a halt was motivated by a desire to facilitate face-to-face negotiations and to keep Serbia itself from intervening.

From the beginning of the war, the West's vacillation over the use of military force led to comparisons between the United Nations and its toothless predecessor. Jamasheed K.A. Manker, about to retire in late 1994 after two years as Pakistan's chief representative to the Security Council, stated: "This is not the League of Nations. That would be an exaggeration." But he also noted the similarities between the international community's performance in the 1930s and its response to the current clash "between a weak multiethnic democracy and a militarily strong fascist regime prepared to use force ruthlessly."[17] Milosevic clearly understood that the West had a high tolerance for the worst atrocities in Europe since the Nazi era and would only reluctantly force him or his proxies to abandon the ethnically pure areas created as a basis for a Greater Serbia. Fred Cuny, a veteran of many humanitarian tragedies who lost his life on a humanitarian mission in Chechnya in 1995, earlier had commented to this author bitterly about the international community's impotence and misplaced neutrality from his perspective in Sarajevo: "If the U.N. had been around in 1939, we would all be speaking German."

Military Choices

The United States seems to be pursuing a zero-casualty foreign policy. Ironically, the only country to project military power worldwide is timid while lesser powers with considerably less capacity are far more willing to sustain the deaths and casualties that are often concomitants of the present generation of U.N. peacekeeping. In Washington there is considerable political resistance to resort to military means alongside a growing need to employ military might to quell ethnic violence, create humanitarian space, and protect fundamental human rights. In such a world, the conflict in the former Yugoslavia illuminates the stark choices that confront policymakers considering the use of force in support of humanitarian objectives.[18]

When and Where?

Even when Western publics, legislatures, and governments wish to avoid external commitments, media coverage of egregious human rights abuses, widespread violence, and starvation sometimes elicits halfway measures: the "CNN factor" often can provoke action, but it also encourages wishful thinking and an underestimation of the costs of action. The media coverage of conflicts injects additional uncertainty into the policymaking process, and its effect is magnified considerably by the essentially formless agenda of the post–Cold War era.[19] Governments frequently react to crises in a random fashion without a well-articulated rationale and subsequently are buffeted by successive shifts in public opinion.

In Bosnia the media spotlight may well have pushed policymakers to substitute humanitarian gestures for an overall strategy to end the war.[20] The Brookings Institution's John Steinbruner notes that in such periods of ideological flux, governments are "particularly prone to crisis induced reactions chosen for their symbolic value and ease of execution rather than their decisive effect."[21] Such visceral reactions lead either to "quick fixes" or to ad hoc policies based on the hope that warring parties will somehow come to their senses. The analysis of the conflict in the former Yugoslavia provides compelling evidence that neither reaction is the basis for a workable policy and that both are potentially counterproductive.

The history of European and American efforts to address the breakup of the former Yugoslavia is rife with examples of wishful thinking and piecemeal action. The 14,000 U.N. blue helmets initially authorized in early 1992 to act as a buffer between the Croats and the Serbs in the newly independent Croatia never achieved the two most critical objectives of their mandate: they neither collected heavy arms from the Serbs in the Krajina nor facilitated the return of the Croatian refugees who had been "cleansed" from this area. The Serbs' use of the Krajina as a staging area for attacks against the Bihac pocket in November 1994 was the most dramatic illustration of the utter failure of U.N. forces. It should have come as no surprise that the Croatian army took matters into its own hands in August 1995.

This initial deployment of U.N. troops in Croatia had been accompanied by a token presence in Sarajevo. But symbols have been of limited value in staving off atrocities in Bosnia-Herzegovina. Some 1,000 soldiers were sent to Bosnia initially, followed by a steadily growing number of additional troops, mainly from NATO countries; no-fly zones were imposed but not enforced; other forms of saber rattling, including low-altitude sorties over Serbian positions and warnings about possible retaliatory air strikes, were tried; the Security Council passed what *The Economist* called "the confetti of paper resolutions"; and a seemingly endless number of cease-fires were negotiated. As Lawrence Freedman observed, the Security Council had "experimented with almost every available form of coercion short of war."[22]

But the West's token half measures under U.N. auspices did nothing to halt Serbian irredentism in either Croatia or Bosnia, nor did they prevent the initial expansion of Croatian claims to Bosnia territory. The arms embargo instituted in September 1991 primarily benefited the Serbs, who controlled the bulk of the military hardware of the former Yugoslav People's Army (YPA). Given traditional U.N. operating procedures and constraints—not to mention U.N. forces' small numbers and inadequate equipment—U.N. soldiers were powerless to deter the Serbs. But their presence impeded more assertive intervention by the international community because these troops, along with aid workers, were vulnerable targets and potential hostages until August 1995, when they regrouped and consolidated themselves in central Bosnia.

It is ironic that as the withdrawal of UNPROFOR was discussed more openly following the debacle in Bihac, little attention was devoted to the effects of such a pullout on humanitarian activities. The protection of relief workers had been the rationale for committing troops to Bosnia in the first place, and the fear of reprisals against troops and aid personnel had deterred the application of greater military force against the Serbs all along. Moreover, as war engulfed Bosnia, civilian efforts were restricted, and beginning in late 1993 U.N. troops had replaced aid agencies as the major humanitarian actor in Sarajevo and in many parts of Bosnia. The exit of U.N. troops would therefore have created a vacuum.

After the assault on Bihac had made a virtual dead letter of the idea of safe areas, the overall ineffectiveness of UNPROFOR and the temporary abandonment of air support for relief missions led to a Serbian ban on armored-vehicle escorts for food convoys in eastern Bosnia, even if this move backfired. Still, it is inaccurate to argue that nothing had been accomplished. Assistance to refugees relieved suffering; air drops of food salved consciences—and saved lives. All the while, however, human rights abuses continued virtually unabated, and the endless round of negotiations conferred legitimacy on the perpetrators of war crimes.

Whither Command and Control?

The second problem confronting policymakers with respect to the use of military force in support of humanitarian objectives is in deciding whether to place military command and control in the hands of the U.N. secretary-general. This is no longer a question in Washington, but it is still being asked in the capitals of some troop-contributing countries. In the former Yugoslavia, as elsewhere, U.N. military operations have been hampered by a low level of professionalism. The capacity to plan, support, and command peacekeeping operations, let alone peace-enforcement missions, is scarcely greater now that it was during the Cold War. As Michael Mandelbaum notes, "The U.N. itself can no more conduct military operations on a large scale on its own than a trade association of hospitals can conduct heart surgery."[23]

After holding steady at about 10,000 in the early post–Cold War period, the number of U.N. troops began to increase rapidly, rising to between 70,000 and 80,000 in the mid-1990s. The annual U.N. "military" (peacekeeping) budget approached $4 billion in 1995. These statistics only hint at the magnitude of overstretch. With accumulated arrears hovering around $3.5 billion in 1995, the world organization's financial juggling act had become a considerable feat—three times its annual budget or the annual tab for peacekeeping. Fortunately, the NATO force was not in the world organization's budget because, as the secretary-general lamented, "the difficult financial situation . . . is increasingly proving to be the most serious obstacle to the effective management of the organization."[24] Dismantling the U.N. military presence in Bosnia and Croatia by the end of January 1996 would alleviate this problem but cause another in that the peacekeeping budget had permitted the United Nations greater flexibility in meeting cash flow problems.

Deficiencies in U.N. command and control in general stem from three sources. First, multiple languages, different procedures, and incompatible equipment make communications difficult, and this problem is exacerbated by the absence of common training. Second, operations suffer as a result of multiple chains of command within theaters and between the military and civilian sides of the U.N. Secretariat. Third, the normal tendency for contingents to seek guidance from their own capitals intensifies operational complexity and danger.

The U.N. operations in the former Yugoslavia were hampered, in addition, by an unusually dispersed military structure for what in fact constituted three distinct operations.[25] The Security Council formally split UNPROFOR into three units on March 31, 1995. The headquarters for the Bosnia-Herzegovina command was at Kiseljak, near Sarajevo, which retained the UNPROFOR label. The majority of its 35,000 troops were from France, Britain, and seven other Western countries, with NATO providing air support and air drops. Until Croatia regained most of the Krajina, the four sectors of the UNPAs had reported separately to Zagreb, which always had served as the headquarters for the entire U.N. operation and as of April 1995 was labeled the United Nations Peace Forces Headquarters, or UNPF-HQ. The Macedonia command's headquarters is in Skopje. This dispersed structure for control over U.N. troops in the former Yugoslavia exacerbated the usual tendency for the different national contingents to emphasize their own narrow modi operandi, as opposed to a general U.N. one, which ultimately detracted further from military cohesion and effectiveness.

There has been some conceptual progress with respect to multilateral military undertakings—as evidenced by Secretary-General Boutros-Ghali's *An Agenda for Peace*, the products of the veritable cottage industry on peacekeeping, and the revised thinking in many staff colleges and defense ministries.[26] Yet there have been few operational improvements within the United Nations, and certainly not enough to make the militaries of major or even most middle powers feel at ease about placing the United Nations in charge of combat missions.[27]

In the mid-1990s the United Nations was bogged down in multifaceted operations in a myriad of civil wars—a circumstance hardly imagined by the framers of the U.N. Charter and certainly not an area in which success has been commonplace in the past. There arose increasing political, economic, and military pressures on Washington and other Western capitals to avoid engagement.[28] The May 1994 Presidential Decision Directive (PDD) 25, limiting U.S. participation in multinational operations, reflected this reticence on Washington's part and represented yet another 180-degree policy reversal by President Clinton, away from the "assertive multilateralism" trumpeted at the outset of his administration. The transformation of American attitudes toward the United Nations and the meandering of the administration's foreign policy was dramatic. Only three years separate the bullish optimism that accompanied guaranteeing the survival of the Kurds in northern Iraq and the utter cynicism in ignoring Rwanda's tragedy. Over the same period and beyond, Washington's approach to the former Yugoslavia was characterized by Iraq-like rhetorical firmness and Rwanda-like operational timidity.

Yet American leadership is still the sine qua non of meaningful U.N. initiatives, especially those involving combat forces. As Thomas Friedman of the *New York Times* points out, "There is no multilateralism without unilateralism."[29] But the Clinton administration gradually had abandoned the pro-U.N. stance of candidate Clinton. Symptomatic of this shift was the contentious debate in Washington that began in mid-1993 about the wisdom of placing U.S. combat troops under U.N. command, as recommended for some purposes in a draft presidential decision directive, portions of which were leaked to the media. These tensions surfaced again in September 1993 in the minority report of the U.S. Commission on Improving the Effectiveness of the United Nations, which was issued in the same month as President Clinton delivered his maiden speech before the General Assembly and a few weeks before heavy American casualties were sustained in Mogadishu.[30] The Defense Department's "Bottom-Up Review" questioned the feasibility of multilateral military efforts in general and the wisdom of sending American troops as part of a U.N. effort to restore elected government in Port-au-Prince in particular.

After a year of fierce interagency feuding, ill-fated military operations in Somalia and Haiti, and dithering over the former Yugoslavia, President Clinton signed PDD 25. This directive reveals the extent to which Washington had abandoned the mantle of leadership. It spells out strict guidelines for determining whether U.S. troops can be sent abroad, based on such considerations as American interests, the availability of troops and funds, the necessity for U.S. participation, congressional approval, a set date for the withdrawal of U.S. forces, and command and control arrangements. The directive made it clear, moreover, that Washington would not approve any new U.N. operation, whether U.S. soldiers were involved or not, unless other restrictive criteria were satisfied. A crisis must represent a threat to international peace and security (such threats include lack of access to starving civilians), involve gross abuses of human rights, or have resulted from the violent overthrow of a democratically elected government. American approval also will depend on clearly stated objectives, the availability of troops and funding, and, most important, the consent of the parties to the conflict as well as a realistic exit strategy.

These criteria will rarely, if ever, be met. And as the subsequent mobilization for the deployment by NATO demonstrated, only strong presidential leadership could overcome the significant stumbling block for U.N. operations, which in fact had been placed by the administration. Experiences in Somalia most influenced the content of the directive. While the residue was felt in the former Yugoslavia, the first real test of the new policy came in Rwanda. As one senior State Department official put it during an off-the-record discussion, "It was almost as if the Hutus had read it [PDD 25]." Three months later—with perhaps as much as ten percent of Rwanda's population dead and at least half of those who remained alive displaced by grisly violence—Washington finally decided to send U.S. troops to neighboring Zaire as part of a belated humanitarian response.

It was in the midst of the chaos in East Africa that Secretary-General Boutros-Ghali originally had suggested that the Security Council should seriously consider withdrawing U.N. forces from Bosnia in the event that the Bosnian Serbs agreed to the so-called peace proposal from the contact group. In a Clintonesque reversal, Boutros-Ghali began to argue that only the major powers would be able to enforce the peace. After the change in military balance in August, NATO's bombing in September, and the continued rout of the Serbs by both Croatian and Bosnian forces, the secretary-general recommended to the Security Council that the U.N. role be replaced by a "multinational" one modeled on earlier efforts in the Gulf War and Haiti.

As could have been predicted, American contingents in the new international force will remain under U.S. and NATO command and control. The exact role for the troops from 14 non-NATO members remains to be worked out in the field, but a face-saving formula seems to have been found for Russian troops. U.S. Defense Secretary William J. Perry and Russian Defense Minister Pavel S. Grachev agreed that a Russian brigade of two or three infantry battalions (that is, about 1,500 combat soldiers) would take part in the NATO force by being part of an American division. The commander of the Russian force, Colonel General Leonti P. Shevstov, will take orders from Major General William Nash of the First Armored Division, who takes order from General George A. Joulwan. This arrangement was reached in the corridors at Dayton and superseded an earlier agreement for a noncombat role for Russian troops. Both approaches indicated that the Russians were willing to use the fiction that orders would emanate from Joulwan not in his role as supreme NATO commander but rather as the top soldier of American forces in Europe.

The Republican-dominated Congress used its constitutional power to declare war and control spending to question the president's ability to commit U.S. troops to the peacekeeping effort in the Balkans. But short of a constitutional crisis, which could develop should things turn sour on the ground, American and other forces new to the region will continue to serve along with the troops from NATO and other countries already in UNPROFOR and UNCRO in an integrated NATO structure. As elsewhere in the world, the Pentagon will cede command and control to the U.N. secretary-general only for safer and smaller operations such as the one in Macedonia, and then only when no bullets are flying. This is neither surprising nor regrettable.

Regional versus Universal Institutions

The third choice facing policymakers is whether to make use of regional organizations as alternatives to the United Nations. Some believe regional institutions are the more attractive alternative because they supposedly have greater incentives and qualifications to act than does a global institution. Since the member states of these institutions suffer the most from the destabilizing consequences of war in their locales, it is argued, they have a greater stake in the management and resolution of regional conflicts. Regional actors are also more likely than outsiders to understand the dynamics of a particular conflict and the influence of local cultures on it, and are thus in a better position to mediate. Finally, issues relating to local conflicts are more likely to be given full and urgent consideration in regional forums than in global forums, where there are broader agendas, competing priorities, and other distractions.

These advantages exist more in theory than in practice, however.[31] Most regional institutions have virtually no military experience or resources. They normally also include among their numbers powers seeking regional hegemony whose presence makes non–self-interested intervention problematic. Regional groupings of small countries—as, for example, the Contadora Group or the Association of Southeast Asian Nations (ASEAN)—are less threatening and sometimes can be helpful on the diplomatic front. In military terms, however, the interests of geopolitically important neighbors normally disqualify them from objective mediation and enforcement. Syria's occupation of Lebanon under the auspices of the Arab League or Nigeria's of Liberia under the auspices of the Economic Community of West African States (ECOWAS) illustrate the more general reality. Similarly, Russia's overtures, beginning in 1993, to obtain the blessing of the United Nations and U.N. financing to arbitrate disputes in the former Soviet Union appear to have been little more than traditional Russian hegemony dressed up in the guise of Commonwealth of Independent States (CIS) peacekeeping.[32]

Between late June and late July 1994, the Security Council approved Moscow's scheme to deploy Russian troops in Georgia to end the three-year-old civil war there; France's intervention in Rwanda to help stanch three months of bloodletting by a government that it had armed, trained, and supported economically; and the U.S. plan to spearhead a military force to reverse the military coup in Haiti. These decisions demonstrated a growing acquiescence on the part of the Security Council in major-power intervention in regional disputes. The Clinton administration's "benign realpolitik" straightforwardly recognizes this reality, which amounts to a revival of spheres of influence, albeit with U.N. oversight.[33] *Foreign Policy* editor Charles William Maynes, who coined this phrase, later dubbed the concept "benign spheres of accountability," but whatever the policy is called, it is not so much regional institutions that count but regional powers. In granting the requests of Russia, France, and the United States to take matters into their own hands, the Security Council seems to be experimenting with a new form of the great-power politics that the United Nations was founded to end.

The conflict in the former Yugoslavia provided what social scientists might deem the "best case" for relying on regional institutions, yet even Europe's well-endowed regional organizations failed the test. The European Community (now Union) and the Conference on (now Organization for) Security and Cooperation in Europe were unable to develop a common policy for recognizing independence with guarantees for minorities; NATO and the Western European Union (WEU) dithered continually over taking action.

A robust military response by NATO before autumn 1995 to counter either Serbia's initial cross-border aggression or the various civil wars would hardly have been an "out-of-area" operation. In fact, this phrase has fallen into disuse as a result of the efforts of NATO's late secretary-general, Manfred Wörner, who helped to convert NATO into a mechanism that could respond to U.N. requests for help in the former Yugoslavia. The lack of resolve that characterized European and American diplomacy until the second half of 1995 was complicated by the existence of two decision-making centers. Thus, Brussels slowed and sometimes impeded meaningful reactions from the Security Council in New York.

Moreover, even after the Security Council decided to use chapter VII language, some Western governments continued their foot-dragging within NATO. This was particularly true of Britain and France. Although they provided the core of forces in Bosnia, and especially of the rapid reaction force, they obstructed and objected to decisions within NATO that would have given military meaning to the palaver emanating from New York. This hypocritical behavior put London and Paris on a collision course with Washington until blue helmets abandoned outlying safe areas and the Croatian offensive put the Serbs in disarray. As one analyst noted: "The conflicting agendas of the three Permanent Members of the Security Council, who are also major actors in NATO, emphasize that without consensus neither organization can work effectively, let alone in tandem."[34]

The result of Western disunity was the continued resistance to lifting the arms embargo—and the European threat of the withdrawal of their ground troops in the event that it was lifted unilaterally, as repeatedly proposed by the U.S. Congress—and the postponement of meaningful military engagement. The February 1994 ultimatum with respect to the Serbs' heavy weapons around Sarajevo, the subsequent downing of four Bosnian Serb aircraft, and the bombing raids against Serbian positions around Gorazde momentarily restored NATO's tattered credibility. However, the West's unwillingness to respond after the Serbs' rejection of the contact group's August ultimatum, and the timidity of the responses both to renewed Serbian onslaughts against Bihac in November and December as well as to their overrunning two safe areas and taking 300 blue helmets hostage in May and June 1995, and others again in July, exposed the disarray within NATO and the United Nations. The disconnect between the diplomatic decisions taken by governments in New York and the operational ones taken in Brussels was a constant.

"It is unfair to blame NATO for the war in Bosnia," Manfred Wörner used to say with some frequency. But it is certainly not unfair to ask why the Western alliance was unable to stop the war sooner rather than later. Europe's regional institutions compare favorably with the United Nations, which is not a compliment. Disparities in viewpoint between the United States and Europe meant that neither the military nor the diplomatic means were sufficient to make a difference until Croatia took matters into its own hands and changed the balance of military forces on the ground. With the Serbs on the defensive, the West's primary collective defense organization was embrazened sufficiently to act.

Another Military Choice?

What emerges from the history of the world's military floundering in Yugoslavia's wars is the international community's desperate need for a new guiding concept: the prevention of both interstate and intrastate war. As he was leaving office in 1993, the U.N. under-secretary-general for administration, Dick Thornburgh, characterized the continuing overextension of U.N. military activities as a "financial bungee jump."[35] Apart from saving money, however, preventing violence is preferable to picking up the pieces of war or humanitarian intervention. If the consequences of civil war are becoming more dire, and if such wars are developing faster than the international community's ability to respond to them, would it not be more reasonable to act earlier and head them off?

Preventive diplomacy is the latest conceptual fashion, "an idea in search of a strategy."[36] Such preventive actions as the symbolic deployment of a detachment of U.N. soldiers to Macedonia and the expanded use of fact-finding missions, human rights monitors, and early-warning systems are beginning to be implemented. And although ultimately an emphasis will have to be on economic and social development as a necessary if insufficient buffer against war, effective prevention today and tomorrow necessarily also will entail the deployment of troops. If they are to be an effective deterrent, however, such troops must be provided with contingency plans and reserve firepower for immediate retaliation against aggressors. This would amount to extending advance authorization for chapter VII action in the event a preventive force was challenged. Although such backup firepower would be no easy matter to assemble—and acknowledging that the combined forces of the Yugoslav People's Army, or YPA, and the Bosnian Serbs would have been hard to intimidate—it is absolutely essential. Otherwise, the currency of U.N. preventive action will be devalued to such an extent that it should not be attempted in the first instance.

The rub is that prevention is cost-effective in the long run but cost-intensive in the short run. In the former Yugoslavia the "long run" lasted over three years, whereas in Rwanda it was reduced to a matter of weeks. The argument that an earlier use of force would have been more economical in the former Yugoslavia runs up against the theoretical inability of governments to look very far into the future and of their consequent tendency to magnify the disadvantages of immediate expenditures and to discount those of future expenditures. In Rwanda, the costs of at least 500,000 dead, four million displaced persons, and a ruined economy were soon borne by the same governments that had refused to respond militarily only a few weeks earlier. The United States and the European Union ended up providing at least $1.5 billion in emergency aid in 1994 alone. If cost savings are important enough and the West is unable to ignore massive human tragedies, perhaps prevention will become more plausible and prevalent.

Humanitarian Choices

The human toll from Yugoslavia's wars has been overwhelming—something like a quarter of a million dead and four million displaced. Moreover, the future likely holds more displacement and international operational problems associated with humanitarian help as the peace settlement is designed to bring refugees and displaced persons back to their prewar homes to claim property that has been destroyed or occupied by voluntary or involuntary migrants from other parts of the former Yugoslavia. It will take some time to straighten out the chain of illegal property transfers that accompanied ethnic cleansing. As so much housing and infrastructure have been destroyed, it is unclear to what extent returnees and the resulting displaced (that is, the illegal occupants who themselves often were chased from their own property) can be accommodated. Preliminary estimates from the UNHCR suggest that repatriation, if all goes well, will involve over the next two years some 2.7 million people in three phases.[37] The first will concentrate on 1.3 million displaced persons within Bosnia living in temporary quarters. The second will involve both refugees and displaced persons from Croatia (463,000) and Serbia (330,000), most of whom will wish to return to Bosnia. And the final phase will involve some 700,000 refugees settled in other European countries, about half located in Germany.

It might be assumed that it would be easier in the humanitarian than in the military arena for the United Nations to reconcile first principles with political and operational realities, and hence to mount coherent and effective programs of action. Yet, in the former Yugoslavia, the international community has begged ethical and operational questions in three important ways, with distinctly negative consequences for the shape and impact of U.N. operations.

Human Rights Trade-offs

The United Nations—member states and also, less justifiably, the political, humanitarian, and military leadership of international secretariats—has been too timid in confronting the perpetrators of human rights abuses and war crimes. Secretary-General Boutros-Ghali has set the tone by reaffirming in his writings a fairly conventional interpretation of sovereignty when this principle clashes with other international norms. Upon his return from a visit to Somalia in October 1993, the secretary-general announced: "The United Nations cannot impose peace; the role of the United Nations is to maintain the peace."[38] Thus, in spite of mandates overriding sovereignty in Iraq, Somalia, Haiti, and the former Yugoslavia, the head of the United Nations was already backtracking from the earlier bullishness spelled out in his 1992 *An Agenda for Peace*; that the United Nations was no longer in the peace-enforcement business became official policy in the 1995 *Supplement to an Agenda for Peace*.[39]

If there are now square brackets around chapter VII as there were during the Cold War—that is, if warring parties must consent to U.N. humanitarian as well as military efforts—then this policy shift should reduce considerably the world organization's overstretch. But the United Nations henceforth would have a minor role at best in confronting the moral and operational challenges that are clearly the dominant challenges of our turbulent times.[40]

Operational implications arise from sustaining the shibboleth of Charter article 2(7), with its emphasis on nonintervention in "matters which are essentially within the domestic jurisdiction of any state." Some U.N. practices themselves have been antihumanitarian, including the decisions to prevent civilians from leaving Sarajevo and other besieged areas in Bosnia and from entering or leaving protected areas. Moreover, the conscious restriction of activities has precluded U.N. staff from confronting political authorities about human rights abuses as a routine part of their missions.

The need to reinforce the neutrality of the United Nations provides the most sanguine explanation for such behavior. The world organization's leadership wished to sidestep confrontations with states, move ahead with negotiations, and be seen as an impartial partner once ceasefires were in effect. However, the promotion of human rights is a victim of such misplaced evenhandedness. In the former Yugoslavia, U.N. personnel acted as if the most, and sometimes only, essential undertaking was the delivery of relief goods. They downplayed such tasks as protecting fundamental rights, gathering information about war crimes, and assertively and routinely investigating alleged abuses.

Dealing mainly with the products of war rather than with its causes, the United Nations has ignored opportunities for at least documenting and publicly denouncing some of the causes. The main exception has been the UNHCR, whose staff has fairly consistently, and sometimes openly, exposed abuse. The treatment of human rights as a nonessential luxury rather than as a central element in U.N. operations has led Human Rights Watch to point to the "lost agenda" that has "led to a squandering of the U.N.'s unique capacity on the global stage to articulate fundamental human rights values and to legitimize their enforcement."[41]

Moreover, potentially significant innovations in meeting the human rights challenges in the former Yugoslavia have received so little financial and political support from governments as to be the subject of ridicule.[42] Among these innovations were a first-ever emergency session by the U.N. Commission on Human Rights after the discovery of concentration camps in western Bosnia; the appointment of a commission of experts to report on breaches of the Geneva Conventions; the deployment of field monitors by the U.N. Human Rights Center and the assignment of human rights responsibilities to the UNHCR protection officers; and, most significant, the convening of an ad hoc international war crimes tribunal. In relationship to the last of these, one observer has summarized: "Lacking the political will to act decisively to curtail abuses of prisoners and civilians, they endorsed or went along with the creation of the tribunal," a lamentable charade that constituted a "black eye."[43] The lack of resources and leadership undermines the utility of these initiatives, with repercussions not only for today's victims in the former Yugoslavia but also for the victims of tomorrow's armed conflicts. Their value—not simply as moral statements but also as effective deterrents—should not be minimized.

Many senior officials, both in the field and in Geneva, have said that the UNHCR should never again become involved in providing emergency relief in an active civil war, a task that they believe is better left to the ICRC. According to this logic, the UNHCR's preoccupation with the nuts and bolts of delivering massive emergency aid in the former Yugoslavia detracted from its ability to fulfill its central protection role. The protection of refugees and internally displaced persons is most problematic when a state not only is a host country for refugees from other states but also produces refugees and internally displaced persons of its own. Such has been the case in all three major theaters of conflict in the former Yugoslavia, where protection problems should have received the undivided attention of the UNHCR.

A crucial shortcoming of the U.N. system is a lack of specialization—the failure to ascertain who does what best. More effective international responses to humanitarian crises require a clear division of labor among humanitarians. Unfortunately, although everyone is for coordination, no one wishes to be coordinated. It would be wrong to denigrate the courage and dedication of individuals—or the efforts of the UNHCR and other humanitarian agencies—in the former Yugoslavia. At the same time, it cannot be ignored that while emergency delivery has been marred by duplication and competition, human rights have been ignored.

In December 1991, in response to the numerous operational problems that had been encountered in the Persian Gulf crisis, the General Assembly authorized the secretary-general to appoint a humanitarian coordinator and create the Department of Humanitarian Affairs (DHA).[44] However, DHA has made no appreciable difference in the former Yugoslavia, in terms of enhancing either overall leadership or the coverage and performance of the various U.N. and other humanitarian agencies present—not surprising when the coordinator has no real budgetary authority and does not outrank the heads of the agencies that he is supposed to coordinate.

Tough Calculations

The United Nations also must confront the need to allocate limited resources in a more cost-effective manner. Humanitarian assistance in the former Yugoslavia, especially in Bosnia-Herzegovina, often has been a double-edged sword—meaning that the "age of innocence" for humanitarians is now over.[45] Assistance to refugees no doubt decreased their suffering, but it also fostered ethnic cleansing by facilitating the movement of unwanted populations—one of the central war aims of the Serbs. It has been reported that in some instances up to two thirds of the shipments of food and medicine intended for civilians were diverted to soldiers. While such reports are virtually impossible to verify, there is no doubt that too many concessions have been made to belligerents. A more principled approach with fewer "deals" might have led to less extortion.

In February 1993 the U.N. high commissioner for refugees, Sadako Ogata, called a temporary halt to the UNHCR's activities in Bosnia in protest against the failure of the warring parties to honor their agreements and guarantee access to civilians, only to be overruled by the secretary-general. Organizations that are entrusted with mounting humanitarian efforts in a war zone should have the authority to suspend their efforts when political and military authorities make a mockery of international norms—or to withdraw completely under certain extreme circumstances. The latter is anathema to many in the United Nations and in other humanitarian organizations, but such a visceral rejection should be reexamined. The ICRC considers it to be an acceptable and honorable practice in extreme circumstances, as, for example, when its delegate, Frederic Maurice, was assassinated in Sarajevo in May 1992.

There is also a growing disparity between available resources and the skyrocketing demand for military intervention and humanitarian action. In the view of many humanitarians and development specialists, "compassion fatigue" and "donor distraction" are too often facile and unacceptable excuses for avoiding responsibility.[46] But domestic recessionary and budgetary problems in the West are eroding the public's willingness to help out in the world's increasing number of crises. In the words of retired U.S. Marine Corps General Bernard Trainor: "One would like to use the doctrine of limited tears. We can't cry for everyone, so we should have some sort of measure that helps us decide where and when to get involved."[47]

Since the United Nations is a global organization with a universal mandate as well as a worldwide operational network, there is no crisis that is *not* on the U.N. agenda. However, as High Commissioner Ogata—who, on occasion, has referred to herself as the "desk officer" for the former Yugoslavia—realizes: "The time has come for a major dialogue on the hard choices that will have to be made in the face of finite humanitarian resources and almost infinite humanitarian demands."[48] If the United Nations is to remain a force for maintaining world order, policymakers and citizens can no longer avoid painful choices. Like the surgeon on the battlefield, the international community must increasingly confront the stark and morally repugnant task of triage and decide who needs no help, who cannot be helped, and who can and must be helped.

In this regard, humanitarian practitioners estimate that 10 to 20 times more could be accomplished with the same limited resources by attacking what the United Nations Children's Fund (UNICEF) has called poverty's "silent" emergencies, rather than the "loud" emergencies caused by warfare.[49] Each day, for example, 35,000 to 40,000 children worldwide perish from poverty and preventable diseases. What claim should they have on the resources that now finance soldiers and humanitarians in war zones?

A New Institutional Capacity

As in Iraq and Haiti, the efforts of U.N. humanitarian organizations in the former Yugoslavia have taken on political connotations by association with military and economic sanctions.[50] The ineffectiveness of U.N. forces deployed in the former Yugoslavia and of economic sanctions imposed on the Federal Republic of Yugoslavia (Serbia and Montenegro) have created hardships that, ironically, the UNHCR, UNICEF, and the World Food Programme (WFP) have been called upon to alleviate.

The United Nations is supposed to be both "tough cop" and "good cop," at one moment applying pressure and in the next cushioning the plight of the vulnerable. Aid workers point out that sanctions cause the most suffering among the most vulnerable members of society. The sanctions against Serbia led several U.N. agencies, along with many NGOs, to lobby actively for lifting sanctions once they began to exert significant pressure on Belgrade. These groups were groping for what the former president of the U.S. United Nations Association, Edward Luck, has wryly labeled "painless sanctions with bite."[51] Along with the experience in South Africa, Milosevic's failure to assist the rebel Serbs in both Croatia and Bosnia in August and September 1995 and his subsequent twisting of their arms in Dayton in exchange for a gradual lifting of sanctions seems to provide evidence that economic sanctions can be an important factor influencing a regime's calculations.

As Shashi Tharoor, the leading U.N. official in New York centrally involved with the former Yugoslavia, quipped: "It is extremely difficult to make war and peace with the same people on the same territory at the same time."[52] Dealing with this institutional schizophrenia requires overcoming the inherent contradictions between the politico-military and humanitarian spheres within the United Nations. It is true, for example, that the review process for economic sanctions often mocks humanitarian values and the provisions of the Geneva Conventions. The Sanctions Committee of the Security Council has on numerous occasions held up or barred the delivery of such items as seeds, tools, fertilizer, and medicine. In 1992 and 1993, delays of two months in granting permission even for shipments of basic foodstuffs and medicine to the former Yugoslavia were common. Consequently, U.N. organizations were identified with the anti-Serbian stance of the Security Council and with the political agendas of the Western countries supporting sanctions.

In order to assess beforehand the likely impact of U.N. coercive action on vulnerable groups, the Security Council and the secretary-general should consult U.N. humanitarian organizations as a matter of course prior to deciding to impose sanctions. In deciding to take such action, the Security Council also should commit the U.N. system to dealing with the consequences. Therefore, in addition to taking into consideration the financial implications of enforcement by the United Nations, member governments should consider the costs of emergency aid and the medium-term reconstruction needs that may flow from punitive economic and military sanctions once the stated objectives of such sanctions have been realized.

Such modifications could help mitigate the tensions between the "good" (humanitarian) and the "bad" (politico-military) United Nations, but a dramatic new mode of operation also is required for delivering emergency aid to active war zones under chapter VII or military sanctions.[53] This would involve the creation of a cadre of volunteers able to function in the midst of armed conflict.[54] These volunteers would not be part of the ordinary U.N. staff system because they would have to be appropriately insured and compensated for the danger that they would face. An international agreement to treat attacks against such humanitarian personnel as an international crime would build on precedents set in dealing with terrorists and airplane hijackers, whose effective prosecution is no longer subject to the vagaries of national legislation or the extraditional whims of host countries. Resources and capable relief specialists could be siphoned from existing humanitarian agencies with distinguished records in armed conflicts—such as UNICEF, the UNHCR, and the WFP. Under such an arrangement, U.N. humanitarian agencies would not be present as long as chapter VII was in effect. They would have to withdraw whenever a peacekeeping mission turned into an enforcement mission.

Like the military forces deployed in a humanitarian intervention, this new civilian delivery unit would form part of a unified command that would report directly to the Security Council, not to the secretary-general. The troops authorized by the Security Council to deal with a particular crisis and the staff from the new humanitarian unit would together comprise a cadre of soldiers and civilians in possession of both humanitarian expertise and combat readiness—a "HUMPROFOR," or Humanitarian Protection Force. There would have to be ground rules for mounting and suspending deliveries of humanitarian aid. Troop contributors would have to agree that their forces would be bound by the Geneva Conventions and Additional Protocols and held accountable for their actions.

Assistance would go to refugees and internally displaced persons without regard for their juridical status. It might be a good idea for the new humanitarian unit to be dominated by retired military personnel, who would be less likely to reject out of hand the necessity of subordinating themselves to and working side by side with military protection forces within a hierarchical structure. Members of such a unit should in any case be experienced in working with military personnel and able to bridge the military-civilian cultural divide that often leads to ineffectiveness. The advantage of such an arrangement is that responsibility will be clearly defined. In the present, decentralized U.N. structure, everyone, and hence no one, is responsible, and buck passing is the norm.

Removing this unit from the control of the secretary-general and attaching it directly to the Security Council would insulate the office of the U.N. chief executive from decisions for the use of force, thus preserving its impartiality and its ability to take on other tasks, including the critically important one of administering "collapsed" or "failed" states.[55] Recent calls for the recolonization of countries that "are just not fit to govern themselves"[56] are implausible, not least of all because former imperial powers are not interested. The United Nations will therefore no doubt be called upon to pick up the pieces after certain humanitarian interventions and perhaps to assume temporary trusteeship in some cases.

The difficulties of nation-building should not be underestimated. And although local populations themselves ultimately must take responsibility for the reconstitution of viable civil societies, they will require buffers and breathing space following periods of prolonged violence. This is where U.N. peacekeepers and modified trusteeship or conservancy will be valuable—*after* the warring parties are exhausted or humanitarian intervention has helped to stabilize a violent situation. The genuine vision and independence required for nation-building would be best served by distancing and insulating the U.N. secretary-general and the U.N. humanitarian network from the use of force. There is a precedent for this in the appointment of Rolf Ekeus as executive chairman of the Special Commission on Disarmament and Arms Control in Iraq. Ekeus was appointed by and reports to the Security Council. As part of the chapter VII enforcement mechanism governing the terms of the cease-fire in the Gulf War, he is clearly the Security Council's emissary. Thus Secretary-General Boutros-Ghali has been able to maintain his distance, thereby remaining a potential interlocutor for the pariah regime in Iraq or its successor.

Learning from the Former Yugoslavia

When confronted with the crisis caused by Yugoslavia's dissolution, the West used the United Nations to pursue a course of shameless diplomatic compromise mixed with inadequate military responses and well-intentioned but counterproductive humanitarianism. Combined with halfhearted sanctions and a well-orchestrated negotiating charade on the part of Belgrade and the nationalist Serbs, U.N. action thus constituted a powerful diversion and served as a substitute for more creative Western diplomatic pressure, more vigorous military action, or arming the Bosnian Muslims to defend themselves.

Fecklessness in Bihac at the end of 1994 and across Bosnia in mid-1995 after the Serbian takeover of safe areas, abuse of civilians, and use of U.N. soldiers as human shields was a microcosm of U.N. actions in the former Yugoslavia—which Boutros-Ghali called "mission impossible."[57] With the Serbs taking over territory as they liked and making a mockery of international norms and of Security Council resolutions, U.N. forces were helpless even to free their own comrades held hostage. U.N. troops inhibited one thing, an effective multilateral military response.

Until the renewed and brutal shelling of Sarajevo in August 1995 goaded the West to act, the sum of the international community's ad hoc and inappropriate operational decisions in the former Yugoslavia had added up to an intervention—but one that worked in favor of Bosnian and Croatian Serbs and their patrons in Belgrade. The idea of limited and impartial intervention is, as Richard Betts has pointed out, a delusion, and "the West's attempt at limited but impartial involvement abetted slow-motion savagery."[58]

The moral of the international community's actions in the former Yugoslavia is that halfhearted or symbolic action is worse than no action at all. This is not to minimize the serious difficulties of intervening in ethnonational conflicts generally or of working around the perennial obstacles to U.N. action. Nor is it to deny the value of traditional peacekeepers in contexts where consent is present, which is no doubt what the United Nations will concentrate on once again in the near future. In the former Yugoslavia, however, earlier and more robust military intervention should have taken place, or the warring parties should have been left to settle their disputes among themselves. Instead, appeasement produced the worst possible outcome: large expenditures, unspeakable suffering, and diminished NATO and U.N. credibility.

The West was so anxious to stop the fighting in the Balkans that the options brokered by the contact group were devoid of principle. Although partition is now all that is possible, it should at least be presented honestly. What could be a more massive case of self-deception than the West's efforts to persuade itself that Milosevic has been compelled to accept its conception of international norms and fairness? We have accepted his.

The agreement initialed in Dayton and signed in Paris suggests that there are prospects for tense coexistence, if not peace, because an erstwhile multiethnic fabric now has ethnically homogeneous swaths. A restored Croatia (minus for the time being the oil fields in eastern Slavonia but with control over contiguous territory in western Bosnia), an enlarged Serbia (although not as big as the proponents of "Greater Serbia" had hoped), and a rump Bosnia dominated by Muslims now correspond to ethnic and military realities.

Some 20,000 American soldiers are now enforcing a settlement that they should have earlier fought to prevent. Their presence is essential not simply to give peace a chance and shore up NATO's credibility but also to sustain American interests. Ironically, Congress and the public are asking not "Why did it take so long?" but instead "Why are we involved?" After a cursory consideration of U.S. and Western interests, debate has shifted to specifying "exit strategies" and avoiding "mission creep." The portion of Bosnia reserved for Muslims is, in fact, an economically nonviable camp whose population will depend indefinitely on Western aid and military protection.

The post–Cold War glow of multilateralism had already dimmed in Washington with PDD 25. An operational debacle in the Balkans risks sealing the fate of the United Nations, leaving it a marginal actor in the task of maintaining international peace and security. Such an eventuality appears particularly plausible with the Republican-dominated Congress displaying a visceral skepticism, even hostility, toward multilateralism.

At this juncture, it is more important than ever that the administration clearly communicate its goals to the American public with respect to the Balkans. Perhaps a realistic goal would be to try to keep the lids on the other ethnic and political cauldrons in the former Yugoslavia. If they boil over and there is no immediate and robust response—to outbreaks of ethnic violence in Kosovo or Macedonia, for example—it will be obvious just how naked the NATO emperor is. The best argument for NATO's expansion may, in fact, be to counter those forces that have exploded in the Balkans and to test the resolve of would-be members, which has become more central to the administration's position.[59]

A wider war in the Balkans remains a distinct possibility, and a classic constitutional crisis looms between the congressional power to declare war and control spending and the presidential prerogative to deploy troops in pursuit of foreign policy interests.[60] Now U.S. soldiers constitute one third of the largest operation in NATO's history. They are not guaranteeing the Dayton agreement single-handedly, although the sole superpower is widely caricatured as Superman swinging into action. Nonetheless, NATO's success requires presidential leadership and congressional support. Growing isolationism accompanied by the administration's dithering had placed war criminals at ease in the former Yugoslavia, until autumn's Croatian offensive and Serbian disarray goaded Washington and NATO to act. Assistant Secretary of State Richard Holbrooke took the lead in reversing what he earlier had aptly labeled "the greatest collective failure of the West since the 1930s."[61]

Holbrooke would find it difficult to take issue with David Forsythe, a leading academic analyst of human rights, who has noted: "Some had hoped for an elementary, partial consensus on U.S. action to help guarantee at least the right to life in the form of no mass starvation and no mass murder. Events in the 1990s in both Bosnia and Rwanda indicate much remains to be done to achieve even this minimal objective."[62] Moreover, as Richard Haass of the Council on Foreign Relations reminds us, "effective multilateralism is not an alternative to U.S. leadership; it will be a consequence. The question is whether the world's only superpower will choose to behave like one."[63]

Some 58,000 deaths in Southeast Asia contributed to the Vietnam syndrome, the axiom that American troops should only rarely be placed in harm's way. Less than two decades later, the threshold was lowered dramatically—18 dead marines in Mogadishu brought a rapid retreat and ushered in the Somalia syndrome. Today the ritual incantation of "not a single body bag" deters a thoughtful review of the national interest. There is, it seems, none worth fighting for in the Balkans, or by extension perhaps anywhere else.

There is a dangerous irony in the new international military order. Parliamentarians, the public, and pundits within the only country capable of projecting military power worldwide are timid about using such power, particularly to reinforce multilateral decisions. At the same time, major Western powers such as France and Britain as well as middle powers such as Canada and the Netherlands lack the capacity but expect their troops to participate in risky international efforts. In fact, Canadian and Dutch shortcomings in Mogadishu and Srebrenica did not produce an American-style backlash within their domestic politics, but rather a demand that their armed forces do their difficult jobs better. Fifty-four French soldiers have died and 600 more have suffered casualties in the line of duty in Bosnia. Soldiering is inherently risky, but responsible membership in the family of nations requires that risks be accepted.

In the fall of 1995 Dutch Minister of Defense Joris Voorhoeve articulated the rationale for the continued presence of Dutch troops abroad: "The pursuit of a well-ordered international society in which human rights are respected and social justice is prevalent is an important national interest."[64] Does the United States have less to lose than the Netherlands from a world in which international law is violated with impunity? Do we not gain from a world in which our own fundamental values are upheld jointly by the larger community of states? Without a menacing Soviet Union, what is the justification for annual military expenditures of $260 billion, particularly in support of a zero-casualty foreign policy? Stability in Europe, the prosecution of war criminals, and the elimination of ethnic cleansing as a policy option for would-be thugs are all in the U.S. national interest.

After NATO responded vigorously against the Bosnian Serbs at the end of August 1995, Bosnian President Alija Izetbegovic stated, "the world has finally done what it should have done a long, long time ago."[65] If the conduct of the world and Yugoslavia's wars reveals anything, it is that collective security remains a distant aspiration. Collective spinelessness is too often still the order of the day.

Notes

This chapter draws on "U.N. Responses in the Former Yugoslavia: Moral and Operational Choices," Ethics and International Affairs, 8 (1994), pp. 1–22.

1. See Thomas G. Weiss, David P. Forsythe, and Roger A. Coate, *The United Nations and Changing World Politics* (Boulder, CO: Westview, 1994).

2. Only a few hours before the expiration of the mandate of what had been known as the United Nations Protection Force (UNPROFOR) on April 1, 1995, the Security Council decided to split the operation into three separate contingents: "UNPROFOR" would henceforth apply only to the operation in Bosnia; the peacekeeping tasks in the Krajina would be handled by the U.N. Confidence Restoration Operation in Croatia; and the efforts in Macedonia would be handled by the U.N. Preventive Deployment Force. Zagreb formerly served as the headquarters for UNPROFOR but became the United Nations Peace Forces Headquarters. In this chapter, "UNPROFOR" normally refers to the U.N. operations in Bosnia, Croatia, and Macedonia, as was actually the case for most of the period under review. In October 1995, on the eve of the Dayton negotiations, the approximate numbers were as follows: 1,100 in Macedonia; 22,000 in Bosnia along with 12,500 in the rapid reaction force; and 13,000 (supposed to be 8,750 and scheduled to be reduced to 2,500 by late fall) in Croatia. On November 30 the Security Council extended the mandate for the Macedonia force for another six months, but for Croatia and for Bosnia for only 45 and 60 days, respectively. Thus, the controversial U.N. operation would begin to wind down immediately, coinciding with the arrival of the advance party from NATO and preceding the final signature of the peace treaty in Paris.

3. See Jonathan Dean, *Ending Europe's Wars: The Continuing Search for Peace and Security* (New York: Twentieth Century Fund, 1994); Jarat Chopra and Thomas G. Weiss, "Prospects for Containing Conflict in the Former Second World," *Security Studies*, vol. 4 (Spring 1995), pp. 552–83; Thorvald

Stoltenberg, "Introducing Peacekeeping to Europe," *International Peace-keeping*, vol. 2, no. 2 (Summer 1995), pp. 215–23; and Shashi Tharoor, "United Nations Peacekeeping in Europe," *Survival*, vol. 37, no. 2 (Summer 1995), pp. 121–34.

4. John Gerard Ruggie, "Wandering in the Void," *Foreign Affairs*, vol. 72, no. 5 (November/December 1993), pp. 26–31. See also David Rieff, "The Illusions of Peacekeeping," *World Policy Journal*, vol. 11, no. 5 (Fall 1994), pp. 1–18.

5. Boutros Boutros-Ghali, *Report of the Secretary-General on the Work of the Organization, August 1995*, document A/50/1, para. 60.

6. See Adam Roberts, "The Crisis in Peacekeeping," *Survival*, vol. 36 (Autumn 1994), pp. 93–120.

7. This term was first used by Thomas G. Weiss and Kurt M. Campbell, "Military Humanitarianism," *Survival*, vol. 33 (September/October 1991), pp. 451–65.

8. See Bernard Kouchner and Mario Bettati, *Le devoir d'ingérence* (Paris: Denoël, 1987); Bernard Kouchner, *Le malheur des autres* (Paris: Odile Jacob, 1991); Mario Bettati, *Le droit d'ingérence* (Paris: Odile Jacob, 1996).

9. Adam Roberts, "Humanitarian War: Military Intervention and Human Rights," *International Affairs*, vol. 69 (1993), pp. 429–49.

10. See U.N. High Commissioner for Refugees, *The State of the World's Refugees 1995: In Search of Solutions* (New York: Oxford University Press, 1995).

11. As quoted in Stanley Meisler, "U.N. Relief Hopes Turn to Despair," *Washington Post*, October 25, 1993, p. A4.

12. Rosalyn Higgins, "The New United Nations and Former Yugoslavia," *International Affairs*, vol. 69 (July 1993), p. 469.

13. As quoted in Larry Minear et al., *Humanitarian Action in the Former Yugoslavia: The U.N.'s Role, 1991–1993*, Occasional Paper, no. 18 (Providence, RI: Watson Institute, 1994), p. 86.

14. "U.N. Bosnia Commander Wants More Troops, Fewer Resolutions," *New York Times*, December 31, 1993, p. A3.

15. Roger Cohen, "Despite Vow, Serbia Is Said to Supply Serbs Fighting in Bosnia," *New York Times*, December 12, 1994, p. A11.

16. Stephen Kinzer, "Cease-fire in Bosnia Starts, and Sides Meet on Details," *New York Times*, January 2, 1995, p. A3.

17. As quoted in Barbara Crossette, "At the U.N., Thoughts about Bosnia but No Action," *New York Times*, December 9, 1994, p. A12.

18. The following discussion on military lessons builds on Thomas G. Weiss, "Intervention: Whither the United Nations?" *Washington Quarterly*, vol. 17 (Winter 1994), pp. 109–28.

19. See James F. Hoge, Jr., "Media Pervasiveness," *Foreign Affairs*, vol. 73 (July/August 1994), pp. 136–44; Jonathan Benthall, *Disasters, Relief and the*

Media (London: Tauris, 1993); and Robert I. Rotberg and Thomas G. Weiss, eds., *From Massacres to Genocide: The Media, Public Policy, and Humanitarian Crises* (Washington, DC: Brookings Institution, 1996).

20. Nik Gowing, *Real-time Television Coverage of Armed Conflicts and Diplomatic Crises:* Press, Politics, Public Policy Working Paper, no. 94–1 (Cambridge, MA: Harvard University, 1994), p. 30. See also Johanna Neuman, *Lights, Camera, War* (New York: St. Martin's, 1996).

21. John Steinbruner, "Memorandum: Civil Violence as an International Security Problem," reproduced in Francis M. Deng, *Protecting the Dispossessed: A Challenge for the International Community* (Washington, DC: Brookings Institution, 1993), annex C, p. 155.

22. "In Bosnia's Fog," *The Economist*, April 23, 1994, p. 16; and Lawrence Freedman, "Why the West Failed," *Foreign Policy*, no. 97 (Winter 1994–95), p. 59.

23. Michael Mandelbaum, "The Reluctance to Intervene," *Foreign Policy*, no. 95 (Summer 1994), p. 11.

24. Boutros-Ghali, *Report of the Secretary-General*, para. 22.

25. For a succinct depiction of the military problems of UNPROFOR, see Åge Eknes, "The U.N.'s Predicament in the Former Yugoslavia," in Thomas G. Weiss, ed., *The United Nations and Civil Wars* (Boulder, CO: Lynne Rienner, 1995), pp. 109–26. See also Dick A. Leurdijk, *The United Nations and NATO in Former Yugoslavia* (The Hague: Netherlands Atlantic Commission, 1994).

26. Boutros Boutros-Ghali, *An Agenda for Peace* (New York: United Nations, 1992). The best examples of the growing analytical literature are William J. Durch, ed., *The Evolution of Peacekeeping: Case Studies and Comparative Analysis* (New York: St. Martin's, 1993); Paul Diehl, *International Peacekeeping* (Baltimore: Johns Hopkins, 1993); Mats R. Berdal, *Whither U.N. Peacekeeping?* Adelphi Paper, no. 281 (London: International Institute for Strategic Studies, 1993); John Mackinlay, "Improving Multifunctional Forces," *Survival*, vol. 36 (Autumn 1994), pp. 149–73; A. B. Fetherstone, *Towards a Theory of United Nations Peacekeeping* (New York: St. Martin's, 1994); and Steven R. Ratner, *The New U.N. Peacekeeping* (New York: St. Martin's, 1995).

27. For a review of these concerns, see Frank M. Snyder, *Command and Control: The Literature and Commentaries* (Washington, DC: National Defense University, 1993); *U.N. Peacekeeping: Lessons Learned in Recent Missions* (Washington, DC: General Accounting Office, 1993); and *Humanitarian Intervention: Effectiveness of U.N. Operations in Bosnia* (Washington, DC: General Accounting Office, 1994).

28. See Thomas G. Weiss, "The United Nations and Civil Wars," *Washington Quarterly*, vol. 17 (Autumn 1994), pp. 139–59.

29. Thomas L. Friedman, "Round and Round," *New York Times*, April 2, 1995 p. A15.

30. U.S. Commission on Improving the Effectiveness of the United Nations, *Defining Purpose: The U.N. and the Health of Nations* (Washington, DC: Government Printing Office 1993).

31. See S. Neil MacFarlane and Thomas G. Weiss, "Regional Organizations and Regional Security," *Security Studies*, vol. 2, no. 1 (Fall/Winter 1992–93), pp. 6–37; and ———, "The United Nations, Regional Organizations, and Human Security," *Third World Quarterly*, vol. 15 (April 1994), pp. 277–95.

32. See "Moscow Counts on Itself to Stem Conflicts in CIS," *Peacekeeping Monitor*, vol. 1, no. 1 (May–June 1994), pp. 4–5, 12–13; and Andrei Raevsky and I. N. Vorobev, *Russian Approaches to Peacekeeping Operations*, Research Paper no. 28 (Geneva: U.N. Institute for Disarmament Research, 1994).

33. Charles William Maynes, "A Workable Clinton Doctrine," *Foreign Policy*, no. 93 (Winter 1993–94), pp. 3–20.

34. Gordon Wilson, "Arm in Arm after the Cold War? The Uneasy NATO-U.N. Relationship," *International Peacekeeping*, vol. 2, no. 1 (Spring 1995), p. 74.

35. See Dick Thornburgh, *Reform and Restructuring at the United Nations: A Progress Report* (Hanover, NH: Rockefeller Center, 1993). See also other cautionary notes by Charles William Maynes, "Containing Ethnic Conflict," *Foreign Policy*, no. 90 (Winter 1993), pp. 3–21; and Stephen John Stedman, "The New Interventionists," *Foreign Affairs*, vol. 72, no. 1 (Winter 1992/93), pp. 1–16.

36. Michael S. Lund, *Preventive Diplomacy and American Foreign Policy* (Washington, DC: U.S. Institute of Peace Press, 1994), p. 27. For a critical view about the political and operational infeasibility of prevention, see Stephen John Stedman, "Alchemy for a New World Order," *Foreign Affairs*, vol. 74, no. 3 (May/June 1995), pp. 14–20.

37. Christopher S. Wren, "Resettling Refugees: U.N. Facing New Burden," *New York Times*, November 24, 1995, p. A15.

38. As quoted in Julia Preston, "U.N. Officials Scale Back Peacekeeping Ambitions," *Washington Post*, October 28, 1993 p. A40.

39. Both documents have been reprinted in Boutros Boutros-Ghali, *An Agenda for Peace 1995* (New York: United Nations Press, 1995).

40. See Michael E. Brown, ed., *Ethnic Conflict and International Security* (Princeton, NJ: Princeton University Press, 1993); and Ted Robert Gurr and Barbara Horff, *Ethnic Conflict in World Politics* (Boulder, CO: Westview, 1994).

41. See Human Rights Watch, *The Lost Agenda: Human Rights and U.N. Field Operations* (New York: Human Rights Watch, 1993); and ———, *Human Rights Watch World Report 1995* (New York: Human Rights Watch, 1994), p. xiv. See also Alice H. Henkin, ed., *Honoring Human Rights and Keeping the Peace* (Washington, DC: Aspen Institute, 1995); and Paul LaRose-Edwards, *Human Rights Principles and Practice in United Nations Field Operations* (Ottawa: Department of Foreign Affairs, September 1995).

42. See Roberta Cohen, "Strengthening International Protection for Internally Displaced Persons," in Louis Henkin and John Lawrence Hargrove, eds., *Human Rights: An Agenda for the Next Century* (Washington, DC: American Society of International Law, 1994), pp. 17–49.

43. David P. Forsythe, "Politics and the International Tribunal for the Former Yugoslavia," *Criminal Law Forum*, vol. 5, nos. 2–3 (1994), p. 403; and ———, "The U.N. and Human Rights at Fifty: An Incremental but Incomplete Revolution," *Global Governance*, vol. 1, no. 3 (September–December 1995), p. 314.

44. See Larry Minear and Thomas G. Weiss, "Groping and Coping in the Gulf Crisis: Discerning the Shape of a New Humanitarian Order," *World Policy Journal*, vol. 9 (Fall/Winter 1992–93), pp. 755–88.

45. Thomas G. Weiss, "Military-Civilian Humanitarianism: The 'Age of Innocence' Is Over," *International Peacekeeping*, vol. 2 (Summer 1995), pp. 157–74.

46. See Judith Randel and Tony German, eds., *The Reality of Aid 94* (London: Actionaid, May 1994); and Ian Smillie and Henry Helmich, eds., *Nongovernmental Organisations and Governments: Stakeholders for Development* (Paris: Organisation for Economic Co-operation and Development, 1993).

47. Bernard Trainor, "Going In," *Boston Globe*, September 18, 1994, p. 74.

48. "Emergency Relief and the Continuum to Rehabilitation and Development," Statement to the Economic and Social Council on Coordination of Humanitarian Assistance, Geneva, July 1, 1993, p. 4.

49. This argument was made most effectively by the late James P. Grant, *The State of the World's Children, 1993* (New York: Oxford University Press, 1993). See also Boutros-Ghali, *An Agenda for Development 1995.*

50. This is a major theme developed in Larry Minear and Thomas G. Weiss, *Mercy under Fire: War and the Global Humanitarian Community* (Boulder, CO: Westview, 1995); and ———, *Humanitarian Politics* (New York: Foreign Policy Association, 1995).

51. See David Cortright and George A. Lopez, eds., *Economic Sanctions: Panacea for Peacebuilding in a Post–Cold War World?* (Boulder, CO: Westview, 1995).

52. "The Changing Face of Peace-Keeping and Peace-Enforcement," Speech of September 9, 1995, at the Annual Conference of the International Institute of Strategic Studies, p. 10.

53. The argument for this new institutional activity was first made in Thomas G. Weiss, "Overcoming the Somalia Syndrome—Operation Restore Hope?" *Global Governance*, vol. 1 (May/August 1995), pp. 171–87.

54. For a discussion of the inadequacy of the U.N. civilian delivery system in war zones by two practitioners, see Frederick C. Cuny, "Humanitarian Assistance in the Post–Cold War Era," and James Ingram, "The Future Architecture for International Humanitarian Assistance," in Thomas G.

Weiss and Larry Minear, eds., *Humanitarianism across Borders: Sustaining Civilians in Times of War* (Boulder, CO: Lynne Rienner, 1993), pp. 151–93.

55. Gerald B. Helman and Steven R. Ratner, "Saving Failed States," *Foreign Policy*, no. 89 (Winter 1992–93), pp. 3–20.

56. See Paul Johnson, "Colonialism's Back—and Not a Moment Too Soon," *New York Times Magazine*, April 18, 1993, p. 22.

57. Press release SG/SM/5804, November 1, 1995, p. 3.

58. Richard K. Betts, "The Delusion of Impartial Intervention," *Foreign Affairs*, vol. 73, no. 6 (November/December 1994), p. 24.

59. See Strobe Talbott, "Why NATO Should Grow," *New York Review of Books*, vol. 42, August 10, 1995, pp. 27–30.

60. See David Rieff, "The Lessons of Bosnia: Morality and Power," *World Policy Journal*, vol. 12 (Spring 1995), pp. 76–88; and ———, *Slaughterhouse: Bosnia and the Failure of the West* (New York: Simon and Schuster, 1995). See also Susan L. Woodward, *Balkan Tragedy: Chaos and Dissolution after the Cold War* (Washington, DC: Brookings Institution, 1995).

61. As quoted by Tim Weiner, "Clinton's Balkan Envoy Finds Himself Shut Out," *New York Times*, August 12, 1995, p. A5.

62. David P. Forsythe, "Human Rights and US Foreign Policy: Two Levels, Two Worlds," *Political Studies*, vol. 43 (Special Issue 1995), pp. 129–30.

63. Richard N. Haass, "Military Force: A User's Guide," *Foreign Policy*, no. 96 (Fall 1994), p. 37.

64. Joris J.C. Voorhoeve, Speech at the Institute of Social Studies in The Hague, October 10, 1995.

65. Quoted by R.W. Apple, Jr., "Goal of Bombers: The Bargaining Table," *New York Times*, August 31, 1995, p. A1.

Chapter 4

Yugoslavia: Implications for Europe and for European Institutions

STANLEY HOFFMANN

T HIS CHAPTER describes, first, what European institutions and powers did to cope with the disintegration of Yugoslavia; second, it discusses some of the key issues involved; third, it examines the implications of and reasons for the European fiasco. It covers events up to the Western reaction—in the form of the bombing campaign of the North Atlantic Treaty Organization (NATO)—to the murderous shelling of Sarajevo on August 28, 1995. Once the bombing started, leadership of the external effort, military and diplomatic, shifted decisively to the United States. While European actors continued to perform on the stage, they read from a largely American script (lifted from earlier European drafts).

European Actions

Far more detailed accounts of European actions in the Yugoslav crisis can be found elsewhere.[1] Here, only the main points will be mentioned.

Early Offers of Agreement and Aid

Before the Slovenian and Croatian declarations of independence on June 25, 1991, Western statesmen (the American secretary of state as well as the British foreign minister and French officials) proclaimed their support for the territorial integrity of Yugoslavia, in accordance with the Helsinki Principles included in the 1975 Final Act of the Conference on Security and Cooperation in Europe (CSCE). In May 1991 the

president of the European Community (EC) Commission, Jacques Delors, and the prime minister of Luxembourg had gone to Belgrade offering an association agreement and aid ($4 billion) if a peaceful solu-
tion of Yugoslavia's internal conflicts could be found, and "asserting
that the Community would refuse to recognize breakaway republics or
offer them benefits."[2] The mission failed.

CSCE and EC Involvement

After June 25, both the CSCE and the EC got involved quickly. The
CSCE summoned the Consultative Committee of the Conflict Prevention Center, which was created in July, and its equally recent Committee of Senior Officials, whose mission is to deal with serious emergencies; the latter, which met in Prague on July 3–4, condemned any use of
force, offered to send a good offices mission if "Yugoslavia" was
willing, and called for a cease-fire.

The EC jumped into action, with Luxembourg's foreign minister
claiming: "this is the hour of Europe."[3] It moved on several fronts. First,
the Yugoslav federal government asked the Community to take part in
its negotiations with Slovenia and Croatia; on July 8, at Brioni, a common declaration was drafted, in which Slovenia and Croatia accepted a
three-month moratorium on independence, and all parties accepted a
cease-fire, negotiations on Yugoslavia's future, and EC observers to
monitor compliance. Second, after the war in Slovenia ended but the
conflict in Croatia got worse, the EC foreign ministers discussed (in-
conclusively) the French idea of sending a force of interposition, agreed
on the principle of the inviolability of the internal borders of Yugoslavia
(on July 29), increased the number of cease-fire monitors in Croatia to
300, decided (on August 27) to summon a conference on Yugoslavia's
future because of the failure of the parties to do so, set up an Arbitration
Commission of five members (two appointed by the Federal Presidency
of Yugoslavia, three by the EC), and threatened sanctions if no cease-fire
was achieved by September 1. Such a cease-fire was obtained after a
"laborious compromise" among the 12 EC members.[4] The EC sent its
observers even though several of the conditions listed in the cease-fire
agreement of September 1, concerning the demobilization of Croat and
irregular forces and the withdrawal of the Yugoslav army, were not
met. As a result, the cease-fire did not hold. Yugoslavia, Austria, France,
and several other countries then asked the U.N. Security Council to deal
with the issue; the Council adopted unanimously a draft resolution
introduced by four European countries (Austria, Belgium, France, and
the United Kingdom) plus the Soviet Union and, under chapter VII of
the U.N. Charter, on September 25, 1991, called for a complete arms
embargo. On the basis of that resolution, the U.N. secretary-general

appointed Cyrus Vance as his envoy, and it was Vance who finally succeeded in obtaining a lasting cease-fire on February 11, 1992. Thereafter the Council established and sent to the parts of Croatia occupied by the Serbs the peacekeeping United Nations Protection Force (UNPROFOR).

Having, so to speak, dumped the military aspects of the conflict in the lap of the United Nations, the EC concentrated on the peace conference, summoned by its envoy, Lord Peter Carrington. The principles that he tried to get the parties to accept, and that the EC endorsed, linked the future recognition of the secessionist republics to the acceptance of a settlement that would entail a loose association among the republics, adequate arrangements for the protection of minorities, and the acceptance of the principle of the inviolability of borders. Even though the most elaborate version of Lord Carrington's plan, presented on October 18, 1992, contained provisions for a "special statute" for regions dominated by an ethnic minority as well as for a Human Rights Court, Serbia rejected the draft. This led the EC to denounce its trade and cooperation agreement with Yugoslavia and to suspend the peace conference on November 8.

When Vance and the secretary-general of the United Nations decided to summon a new international conference on the future of Yugoslavia in August 1992, Lord Carrington resigned. This intractable issue thus became a joint U.N.-EC responsibility, but the new conference led nowhere. As an American participant later remarked, it "resulted in a package of useful agreements among the parties," but "in the days and weeks that followed, the Serbs willfully ignored every accord reached and commitment made."[5]

On December 16, 1991, five days after the Maastricht Treaty on European Union was signed, the 12 nations gave up the idea of linking recognition of the new republics to an overall agreement and decided to recognize, collectively, on January 15, 1992, all the republics that sought recognition and met a long list of conditions drawn from Lord Carrington's plan, including respect for the inviolability of borders and guarantees for the rights of ethnic groups and minorities. On the issue of borders, the Arbitration Commission had already been asked to give an opinion, at Yugoslavia's request. On January 11, 1992, it extended the U.N. Charter's protection of international borders to internal borders, because the Yugoslav Republic was breaking up. On the issue of minorities, Yugoslavia asked the commission whether Serb minorities in Croatia and Bosnia-Herzegovina were entitled to the right of self-determination; the commission restricted it to "minorities and entities established as territorially defined administrative units of a federal nature."[6] On December 18, after several months of domestic debate and diplomatic exhortation favoring such a move, Germany recognized Slovenia and Croatia, before the commission could report on whether those republics had met the conditions set on December 16. The commission subsequently declared that Slovenia and Macedonia had met these conditions. However, Greece blocked Macedonia's recognition by the EC, and the EC recognized Croatia on January 15 even though Croatia had failed to amend its constitution so as to incorporate the Carrington plan's notion of a "special status" for minorities, which figured in the EC list of conditions of December 16 and in the commission's judgment on Croatia's demand for recognition.

The Fate of Bosnia-Herzegovina

Subsequently, the key issue became the fate of Bosnia-Herzegovina. On October 1, 1991, EC delegates had succeeded in getting the federal foreign minister and the prime minister of Bosnia-Herzegovina to accept the stationing of European observers in Bosnia-Herzegovina. After the EC decisions of December 16, Bosnia-Herzegovina asked for recognition; the Arbitration Commission based itself "on the human right of minorities and ethnic groups to equal participation in government" and declared on January 11, 1992, that in the absence of a referendum on independence, "the popular will for an independent state had not been 'clearly established.'"[7] Such a referendum was held on March 1, 1992; 63 percent of the electorate voted for independence (but the Serbs boycotted the vote); the EC recognized Bosnia-Herzegovina on April 6.

Worried by the attitude of Serbs and Croats in Bosnia-Herzegovina, Lord Carrington had asked, in January 1992, a Portuguese diplomat, José Cutileiro—Portugal having now the presidency of the European Community—to run a conference on the future of Bosnia-Herzegovina. On March 18 the representatives of the Serbs and of the Croats and the Muslim prime minister agreed that Bosnia-Herzegovina would be a state composed of three "constitutive units," each one entitled to a veto; but a week later the Serbs proclaimed the "Serb Republic of Bosnia-Herzegovina," which was to be an integral part of the new Yugoslavia. In April and May, war spread all over Bosnia-Herzegovina. The U.N. Security Council imposed a trade embargo on the new Federal Republic of Yugoslavia (Serbia plus Montenegro) on May 27 and, on June 7, endorsed Secretary-General Boutros Boutros-Ghali's proposal to extend UNPROFOR's mandate so as to have it keep the Sarajevo airport open for humanitarian assistance. The contingents began to arrive only after French President François Mitterrand's surprise visit to Sarajevo on June 29, and Europeans have since provided the majority of the U.N. forces in Bosnia-Herzegovina. But the EC as such did not play a major part: the negotiations led by Cutileiro failed, and the EC observers were withdrawn after one was murdered on May 3. As for the CSCE (now the Organization for Security and Cooperation in Europe, or OSCE), which, in the summer of 1992, with Yugoslavia's consent, sent human rights monitors to Kosovo and Vojvodina, it had earlier urged Serbia, on April 15, to cease supporting the violation of Bosnia-Herzegovina's integrity and later followed a recommendation of its Committee of Senior Officials to suspend Yugoslavia's participation.

From the summer of 1992 until the NATO bombing campaign three years later, attention centered on the efforts of the U.N. envoys (Vance, later Thorvald Stoltenberg) and of the EC representative (Lord David Owen) to find a political solution for Bosnia-Herzegovina; the U.N. Security Council, which extended sanctions several times and established a "no-fly" area and "security zones" in Bosnia-Herzegovina; the United States; and NATO, as a kind of sword protecting the shield (UNPROFOR) from Serbian attacks in Bosnia. Britain and France effectively vetoed the Clinton administration's proposal to lift the embargo on arms to the Bosnian government and to resort to air strikes against Serbian forces in Bosnia-Herzegovina, after Serbs in that country rejected the Vance-Owen plan in the spring of 1993. Only in the fall of 1993 did the EC take a new initiative, aimed at persuading the Serbs and the Croats of Bosnia-Herzegovina to make territorial concessions to the Muslims in order to get the Owen-Stoltenberg partition plan (which the latter had rejected in September) accepted, in exchange for a gradual lifting of sanctions. This, again, failed.

The Ambiguous Roles of Britain and France

In 1994 the EC (by then transformed into the European Union, or EU) practically vanished as an actor, except for its endorsement of one more plan in the summer: the plan conceded 49 percent of Bosnian territory to the Bosnian Serbs and gave the rest to the Croat-Muslim federation that had emerged under American pressure. But this plan—a later version of which was enshrined in the Dayton accords—resulted mainly from the efforts of the "contact group" consisting of the United States, Britain, France, Germany, and Russia. The key European actors have been Britain and France; both consistently stressed the need to reach a peaceful settlement of the Bosnian war and showed considerable reluctance to use military force either to stop Serbian attacks on Muslim areas or to pressure the Bosnian Serbs into accepting a settlement. They supported NATO air raids after the market massacre in Sarajevo in February 1994. But until August–September 1995 these raids were never more than pinpricks. Britain and France continued to resist American suggestions for getting the Security Council to lift the arms embargo on Bosnia—a suggestion first made by George Bush, shortly before he left office. At various moments, British and French officials suggested that in the absence of a settlement, or should violence escalate, they would pull their men out of UNPROFOR.

In the spring and early summer of 1995, it became even clearer that the presence of UNPROFOR, far from deterring the Bosnian Serbs from attacking the "safe areas" the Security Council had designated in May 1993, allowed them to intimidate the states whose soldiers served in the U.N. force, and to deter them from any military riposte in order not to compromise the military personnel's safety. A few bombs dropped, without adequate consideration of consequences, around the Bosnian Serb headquarters in Pale in May 1995, resulted in hundreds of U.N. soldiers' being taken as hostages. Two "safe areas" fell to the Serbs without any international reaction other than verbal indignation. In London, on July 21, 1995, an international conference once more threatened the Serbs with air strikes should new assaults on safe areas occur. Those strikes—for the first time carried out with persuasive force—began some six weeks later. Ten weeks later still came the agreement reached at Dayton.

European Issues

The Europeans faced four main issues: preventive action, a choice of principles, the problem of recognition, and the problem of coercion.

Preventive Action

The breakup of Yugoslavia been easy to predict. In September 1989 the Slovenian parliament voted for a "Declaration of Sovereignty," and in December 1990, in a referendum, 95 percent of the Slovenes voted for independence should an agreement on a new, looser Yugoslav Federation not be concluded within six months. In December 1990 a new Croatian constitution contained a similar provision. In Bosnia-Herzegovina, in November 1990, the election winners were the parties representing each of the three ethnic groups. In Croatia, the new constitution of December 1990 defined Croatia as the "national state of the Croatian people," and President Franjo Tudjman later took a number of anti-Serb measures; in reply, the Serbs in the Krajina and Slavonia, in a referendum, expressed their determination to remain in Yugoslavia.[8]

There was very little preventive diplomacy. Except for the belated Delors mission, neither the EC nor the CSCE tried to find a peaceful solution for the reconstruction of Yugoslavia. This was partly, as one author has written, because any move that entailed accepting the idea of a possible breakup of Yugoslavia might become a self-fulfilling prophecy—at a time when the United States, the Soviet Union, Britain, and France were supporting Yugoslavia's territorial integrity.[9] But this is not a convincing explanation: since the parties were evidently incapable of agreeing on a new common structure, outside good offices would have provided the best chance for saving Yugoslavia. The real explanations are elsewhere.

The CSCE, after its solemn conference in November 1990 in Paris, was still in the process of establishing its new institutions, and no one tried to activate the new conflict prevention machinery until *after* the Slovenian and Croat declarations of independence. As for the EC, it suffered from two handicaps. First, foreign policy cooperation and coordination among the 12 members was not yet a *Community* function, carried out under the Treaty of Rome and the Single Act of 1987 that had amended the treaty. This meant that except for external trade policy, the supranational Commission, which is not the legislator of the EC (the Council of Ministers is the legislative arm) but is both the initiator and the enforcer of policy, could not play its customary planning and prodding role. Foreign policy was entirely an intergovernmental exercise among the foreign ministers of the member nations. Called "European Political Cooperation," it had started in the 1970s and had rarely gone beyond common declarations of approval or disapproval. Second, in the first half of 1991, attention among EC members was focused on the negotiations of the Maastricht Treaty—the details of the planned monetary union and the reshaping of the EC's institutions to allow them to cope with the new functions that would be entrusted to the EC, including defense and diplomacy. The plate was too full for preventive foresight. Third, when, in 1990, the United States suggested that NATO discuss the coming crisis in Yugoslavia, France rejected the idea because of its opposition to American notions about the continuing predominance of NATO in post–Cold War European security issues. Indeed, in 1991, when EC efforts at peacemaking failed, the French turned to the United Nations, not NATO, and it was not until 1994 that a more flexible French government and an American administration less dogmatic than Bush's about NATO's supremacy and American domination of it could agree on a NATO mission in Yugoslavia.

After the wars in Slovenia and Croatia started, the 12 EC members had fewer excuses for passivity regarding the next chapter in the book of disasters—Bosnia-Herzegovina. Its government called for European observers in July 1991, but the foreign ministers of the EC nations replied that they had to concentrate on "the Serbo-Croat problem which is the heart of the Yugoslav crisis."[10] Only in September did the Dutch president (the Netherlands held the Community presidency for the last half of 1991) begin to worry and act so as to enable the EC to send observers. But other EC actions, to be discussed, contributed to the crisis in Bosnia-Herzegovina.

A Choice of Principles

From the beginning, the Europeans' effort to mitigate the crisis had to face a conflict of principles. The federal presidency of Yugoslavia wanted to maintain the territorial integrity of the federation, while the secessionist forces that dominated several of its member states invoked the right of self-determination. At first, the CSCE and the EC tried to avoid a clear-cut choice. The CSCE concentrated on condemning the use of force, while, in accord with the Helsinki principles of respect for sovereignty and nonintervention, seeking the consent of the federal Yugoslav government to the sending of a good offices mission. The EC also emphasized the need for a halt to the use of force and tilted somewhat in the direction of the federal government, both in the composition of the Arbitration Commission and in the language of the cease-fire agreement of September 1.[11]

Once it became clear that the secession of Slovenia and Croatia was irreversible and that condemning it would only encourage the Serbs' resort to force, a new choice confronted the Europeans. The Slovenes and the Croats asserted that the right of self-determination belonged to their states as geographic entities; the Serbs argued that it belonged not to artificial multiethnic units but to "peoples" (referring thus to the language of the U.N. Charter and the Helsinki Declaration), and specifically to the Serbian people, who refused to accept Croatian rule in Croatia and Muslim rule in Bosnia-Herzegovina. The use of force by the Serbian army "was essential to protect the Serbian people from extermination."[12]

Thus confronted with the fatal indeterminacy of the principle of self-determination, the EC opted for the approach that was deemed the least conducive to endless trouble and fragmentation in disintegrating empires: the ministers and the Arbitration Commission endorsed, in effect, the Slovenian and Croatian position, by proclaiming the inviolability of internal borders. As an observer who is generally very critical of the EC nevertheless put it, "a shift towards endorsing the principle of self-determination [for peoples] would have opened up a Pandora's box throughout Yugoslavia and incidentally implied that the EC was condoning the use of force."[13] This explains why it did not appear to the EC member nations that they were inconsistent in, on the one hand, acknowledging the disintegration of the multiethnic state of Yugoslavia and endorsing, on the other hand, the possibility of independence for the multiethnic state of Bosnia-Herzegovina.

To the Serbs' argument that this formalistic limitation of the right of self-determination to establish "administrative units of a federal nature" was unfair, because it submitted Serb minorities to the will of hostile ethnic majorities, the EC replied, in effect, by granting to the Serbs extensive rights as minorities and ethnic groups, including, said the Arbitration Commission, "the right to choose their nationality." The Commission in this case, however, "defined the right to self-determination not as a people's right to independence but as a human right of minorities and groups," who "were not entitled" to territorial secession.[14] This was unacceptable to the Serbs, as was shown by the fate of Lord Carrington's plan, which had gone extremely far toward accommodating President Slobodan Milosevic, by recommending an association of states with a status of its own under international law and a "special statute" for regions dominated by an ethnic minority. The Serbs clearly put the right of self-determination, conceived as a people's collective right to secession, above the principle of the sanctity of borders—except (some exception!) insofar as Serbia itself was concerned: Kosovo was clearly not entitled to the people's right of self-determination. The EC's position, to quote Lord Owen, was that "self-determination is a qualified right . . . there are other international criteria as well: sovereignty, territorial integrity and human rights, to name only three."[15]

The Problem of Recognition

Recognition is certainly one of the messiest aspects of the EC's action. From July 1991 on, the 12 member nations were split—Germany and Italy (as well as Austria, a candidate for EC membership) argued for prompt recognition of Croatia and Slovenia, which were seen as exercising their right to self-determination; the United States, the U.N. secretary-general, and his envoy, Cyrus Vance, supported the position of the Dutch foreign minister, the French, the British, and Lord Carrington against immediate recognition: such a move "would not incite these republics to moderation; and also, who would defend their independence, after it had been recognized?"[16] Germany seems to have believed that recognition would deter the Serbs from further military action; those who opposed early recognition thought it would make the situation worse.

The French foreign minister later argued that the Europeans' decision, "under German pressure," to recognize Croatia and Slovenia had been a mistake, and that it would have been wiser to preserve a confederal framework for Yugoslavia.[17] Certainly Belgrade viewed the EC's decision of December 16 as hostile, and it would have been better if recognition could have accompanied or followed an agreement on such a framework; this is exactly what Lord Carrington had wanted. But by December 16 it had become clear that Milosevic did not accept that plan's point of departure—the dissolution of the old Yugoslavia and the need to rebuild it on the basis of the new republics—nor was he willing to accept that the idea of a special statute for minorities be applied within Serbia or, indeed, to Bosnia-Herzegovina, which he saw not as a Muslim nation with Serb and Croat minorities (as had been Bosnia-Herzegovina's official definition in the last years of the old Yugoslavia) but as a reunion of three equal communities. The problem for the EC was whether to postpone recognition until the Slovenes, Croats,

Macedonians, and so on accepted the principle of Yugoslav continuity, demanded by Serbia—a most unlikely event—or until Milosevic had a change of mind so that a new framework could be agreed upon. But would denying recognition to the new republics have encouraged Milosevic to be more flexible?[18] In fact, throughout November and December 1991, the Serbs devastated Vukovar and bombed Dubrovnik. We will never know whether a delay in recognition would have facilitated a compromise on a settlement—especially while war or the prospect of war hardened every party's attitude. But it seems most unlikely.

In evaluating the effects of the EC's moves, we need to separate the different cases. In that of Slovenia, recognition came when the country was at peace, the government exerted full control over the state's territory, and the republic had met all of the EC's conditions for recognition. The latter did not incite any new violence.

In the case of Croatia, two issues arose. One was the failure of the government to meet the very strict EC request for a constitutional commitment to the notion of a special status of autonomy for the Serb minority. Having demanded such a commitment, the EC should have insisted on its being met before granting recognition. The other issue is the fact that the Croatian government was clearly not in full control of its territory, since the Serbs had established their own rule in roughly one third of Croatia. But to apply, in this instance, the traditional criteria for recognition would have condoned the Serbs' use of force and given them a precious reward for having occupied the Krajina and detached it from the rest of Croatia. It is a fact that the recognition of Croatia encouraged President Tudjman to be more intransigent during the negotiations on the Vance plan that led to a cease-fire and to the deployment of UNPROFOR in February 1992. But it is also a fact that this agreement was reached partly because of Croatian exhaustion, partly because the three U.N. "protected areas" in which UNPROFOR was stationed remained outside the jurisdiction of Croatian laws and institutions. Recognition did not affect the situation on the ground.

Far more serious appears the brief against the recognition of Bosnia-Herzegovina. The risk of its disintegration was so high that President Alija Izetbegovic had, in vain, asked Vance for a preventive deployment of U.N. peacekeepers.[19] When the EC decided, on December 16, 1991, no longer to link recognition of the new republics to a global political settlement and stated it would recognize those republics that asked for recognition (and met EC conditions), a fatal *engrenage* was set in motion. For Bosnia-Herzegovina (whose parliament had voted a statement of "sovereignty" in October) not to ask for recognition as an independent state would have meant remaining tied to and dependent on a "Yugoslavia" dominated by Serbia. And for the EC not to recognize Bosnia-

Herzegovina after the republic had met all of the Community's conditions would again have appeared to encourage Serbian hostility and would have been in contradiction with the "declaration of principles" the leaders of the three ethnic groups of Bosnia-Herzegovina had signed on March 18, 1992, under Cutileiro's pressure; this declaration stated that Bosnia-Herzegovina would be a single state. But the failure of the parties to agree on the meaning of the declaration and the EC's recognition were followed by a war that is still going on.

The EC was in a catch-22 situation: if it had postponed the recognition of Bosnia-Herzegovina because of the failure of the Izetbegovic government to control the Serb and Croatian parts of the country, it would have rewarded, and in no way prevented, a Serbian resort to force—unless, in this case at least, recognition was once again linked to an agreement on Bosnia-Herzegovina's future. But this would have given the Serbs a strong incentive to delay any agreement that did not meet their demand for, in effect, a partition along ethnic lines—a demand the Muslims would have resisted even if Bosnia-Herzegovina had *not* been recognized. The critics of the premature "recognition" of Bosnia-Herzegovina need to prove that there would have been no war in Bosnia-Herzegovina if recognition had been denied or postponed. The gap between the Serbs' position and the Muslims' insistence on a multiethnic state was such that it is hard to see how war could have been avoided.

The Problem of Coercion

The EC (as well as the CSCE) came out strongly against the use of force in Yugoslavia; the EC endorsed the inviolability of internal borders and rejected the Serb interpretation of the principle of self-determination. It sought a political settlement, first for the whole country, later and more specifically for Bosnia-Herzegovina. But it became clear quickly that the Serbs were using force, both in Croatia and (later) in Bosnia-Herzegovina, in order to enforce their interpretation. (Croatia's role in Bosnia-Herzegovina was more ambiguous, since the local Croats supported independence from Serbia, but with the help of Croatia's army carved out their own area and resorted to their own "ethnic cleansing.") The EC, which had seen the Yugoslav crisis as an opportunity, now faced an unwelcome challenge. It could decide and declare that the behavior of the parties made any further good offices futile and that it would wash its hands of the whole mess; but this would have been seen as a cowardly retreat. Or else it could decide that what was at stake was nothing less than the future of the post–Cold War European order. Just as those who had, in early 1991, argued against any encouragement to secession within Yugoslavia had in mind the precedent this would have created for the tottering Soviet Union, those who, in the summer of 1991 and later, argued against condoning ethnic cleansing and Serbian behavior had in mind the chaos that could result all over eastern Europe and the former Soviet Union if the Serbs' thesis about the self-determination of "peoples" and Serbia's use of force became the model. But to prevent this from happening meant a willingness to threaten and, if necessary, to fight the Serbs. It meant, in effect, being willing to declare that they were aggressors and to put in motion collective security or collective self-defense on the side of the Muslims in Bosnia, just as had been done against Iraq a few months earlier.

In the case of Croatia, the French, in July–August 1991, argued for a "force of interposition," aimed at making a cease-fire stick—at a time when each new one was collapsing at once. But this scheme to send Western European Union (WEU) forces to Yugoslavia would have required an invitation by the parties, which did not come, and unanimity among the 12 member nations, which was not present. The United Kingdom opposed the idea uncompromisingly (hence the French decision to turn to the Security Council). The EC did not go beyond a vague threat of "international action" against uncooperative parties and the imposition of economic sanctions on—at first—Yugoslavia (November 8, 1991) and later only Serbia and Montenegro (December 2). As indicated before, a lasting cease-fire was established finally in February 1992, and it is hard to argue that EC sanctions contributed to the Serbs' acceptance of a deal that left them, in effect, in control of much of Croatia and left Croatia's future in suspense.

The issue of coercion became much more crucial in the case of Bosnia-Herzegovina. But as of the summer of 1992 it became a U.N. issue, and none of the permanent members of the Security Council was willing either to allow openly outside arms to reach the Muslims in Bosnia or to threaten force against Serbia, except to protect humanitarian efforts from attack and except for President Clinton's suggestions, which France and the United Kingdom turned down. Britain and France insisted on presenting international action on the ground as purely humanitarian (supplemented by sanctions and by the efforts at a Vance-Owen settlement, later a Stoltenberg-Owen settlement, and still later by the "contact group" settlement). The presence of U.N. forces in Bosnia-Herzegovina, protecting relief operations, became an argument against letting the soldiers be endangered by a resort to military action, and the nonparticipation of Americans in the U.N. force became an additional reason for resisting American arguments for the use of force. Vance and Owen insisted that a resort to threats of force would compromise their efforts, which failed anyhow.

Thus, the pursuit of diplomacy and of humanitarian intervention became obstacles to military coercion—even though throughout history (and as Lord Owen belatedly acknowledged), "if there is no international will to take arms, it reduces . . . diplomatic room for maneuver"; even though it has been argued that humanitarian action puts one almost inevitably on a slippery slope toward military action—and even though it can be argued that U.N. humanitarian efforts have kept alive men, women, and children only so that they would remain the hapless targets of Serbian atrocities.[20] Even when a little bit of force was used, in 1994 around Goradze, to punish the Serbs for having seized a tank that was under UNPROFOR's guard, and in the spring of 1995 around Pale and Srebrenica, the action was minimal, in intensity and in scope. (It was meant to protect the U.N. personnel, not the Muslims, and no effort was made to get the siege of Sarajevo lifted.) When, at the end of 1994, Bosnian Serbs and Serbs from the Krajina largely overran the "safe zone" of Bihac, British and French opposition to any effective use of force seemed on the verge of provoking a major crisis in NATO; however, rather than opposing its chief allies, the United States chose to align with them, and the United Nations and NATO even agreed to reduce their surveillance flights. After the disastrous air raid near Pale in May 1995, when hundreds of UNPROFOR soldiers were seized by the Bosnian Serbs, the United Nations and NATO ceased to enforce the heavy weapons exclusion around Sarajevo.

As in some other cases, the effects of economic sanctions have been both slow (in the meantime, the Serbs have occupied the greatest part of Bosnia-Herzegovina) and harder on the poor and the civilians than on the rulers and the armed forces. Moreover, both the Europeans and the Russians have kept dangling a promise of reducing or lifting sanctions as a way of coaxing the Serbs into a more cooperative diplomacy. Basically, no EC nation was willing to use force—and without such a willingness or the willingness to lift the arms embargo on Bosnia, there was no way to prevent Serbian victory on the ground. The Europeans' opposition to any collective lifting of the arms embargo and to America's halfhearted inclination toward a unilateral lifting both harmed the Bosnian government's attempt to defend itself and failed to reach its stated objective—avoiding more war and helping to bring peace.

The Impact of Failure

What does the European fiasco mean for Europe and its institutions? There have been five major impacts.

First, the Yugoslav crisis has confirmed the obvious, in the case of the OSCE (the former CSCE): it is too unwieldy an organization to be either an effective diplomatic agent or a force for collective security. It was handicapped initially by the principle of unanimity, which made moves opposed by the federal government of Yugoslavia impossible. Later it developed the notion of "consensus minus one," which certainly facilitates OSCE interventions in internal conflicts; and as we have seen, it suspended Yugoslavia's membership. It also "strengthened the tools available for human rights enforcement" and for conflict prevention and crisis management; the emergency mechanism can be, and was, activated at the request of only 12 members.[21] Nevertheless, even "consensus minus one" is a slow and clumsy process in an organization of more than 50 members (several of which in the future could face ethnic conflicts comparable to Yugoslavia's and were not eager for external involvement in a domestic crisis). The OSCE is likely to be more useful as a body stating principles (and deploring their violation), as a fact-finding agency, and perhaps as a preventive alarm bell than as a major actor among international and regional organizations. The relatively modest role the OSCE has played in the Yugoslav crisis is not likely to induce states in conflict or parties locked in ethnic or religious disputes within a troubled state to turn to it for help. The major powers among its members, both European and non-European, have not shown enough enthusiasm for boosting its role to provide such an incentive to anyone.

Second, the problem of the EC was and still is to some extent an institutional one. Even after the Maastricht Treaty went into effect, the EC as an actor in foreign policy and defense remained handicapped by the rule of unanimity. It is true that the extension of the new union's functions to diplomacy and security makes it possible for the Commission to insert itself into these areas insofar as they are linked to the areas in which the Commission represents the Community abroad, such as foreign trade. However, this is a very narrow opening, and, at this stage certainly, many governments (France and Britain especially) are most unwilling to let the Commission exploit it, and the Commission is badly equipped to do so. It played an important role in shaping the foreign economic policies of the EC, but that was partly because of its considerable expertise in that domain. It has none in diplomacy and defense. Even if the Council unanimously decides to proceed in some areas of foreign and defense policy, with a qualified majority rule, as the Maastricht Treaty allows, no effectiveness can be guaranteed. Even though, since the Single European Act of 1985, foreign economic policy is a realm in which qualified majority rule now prevails in the Council, serious tensions have arisen both among members and between "minority" members and the Commission, as the 1993 drama over French adherence to the General Agreement on Tariffs and Trade (GATT) showed. Inclusion of diplomacy and security in the jurisdiction of the Union may make foreign policy consultations among the members even more intense than in the past, but it is not clear that under the Maastricht Treaty the members must allow the Commission to play an autonomous role. As in the past, the alternatives remain deadlock (hence impotence) vs. compromise. The Yugoslav crisis has shown that compromises may be clumsy and ineffectual, as in the case of the common agreement of December 16, 1991, on collective recognition, which was an apparent compromise between the German push for prompt recognition and the Carrington approach. Immediately after its adoption, it was undercut by Germany's unilateral recognition of Slovenia and Croatia. The future effectiveness of the European Union in security and foreign policy matters is tied to a reform of its institutions in a more federal direction—a very "iffy" subject especially in these domains, where traditions of independence die hard or tend to revive.

Another factor, besides the rule of unanimity, turned out to be nefarious and could strike again: linkage. Often in the history of the EC/EU progress has resulted from package deals; mutual concessions across different areas resolved conflicts and broke deadlocks. In the Yugoslav case, linkage occurred—informally—over the issue of recognition. What made the compromise of December 1991 possible was a complex deal: Germany would agree not to break ranks but to wait for collective recognition, in exchange for a British and French agreement to separate the issue of recognition from that of a global settlement; and Britain and France agreed to do this in exchange for German concessions in the Maastricht negotiations (over Monetary Union, to accommodate the distrustful United Kingdom; over institutional reform, to please the reluctant French). The injection of these completely extraneous issues into the handling of the Yugoslav crisis was not a mark of wisdom.

The deal on collective recognition resulted also from another concern, which seems to have affected French diplomacy particularly (but not exclusively), in December 1991: the main consideration was not the future of Yugoslavia, or even the effectiveness of the EC in this first major postwar crisis in Europe; it was the preservation of the appearance of unity among the 12 members. A repetition of the disarray that had been so conspicuous during the Gulf crisis had to be avoided, and the only way of succeeding, given Germany's strong stand, was an agreement on collective recognition that provided a European costume for a policy made in Bonn. Later, when the war in Bosnia broke out and Germany became aware of the contradiction between its strong anti-Serbian stance and the constitutional restrictions on German military action outside the old NATO area, the same desire for surface unanimity led German diplomacy to follow, however reluctantly, those who were now the most determined (against a strong resort to force): the British and French.

Third, the French would have liked to be able to use this crisis as a lever to activate the WEU, but the latter remains a shadowy institution, despite its "operationalization" in July 1992 and its role in enforcing the arms embargo.[22] The one asset the WEU had was that, unlike NATO, it is not bound to eschew out-of-area actions (or to undertake them only when all its members agree to heed a call from the United Nations). But it could not overcome three handicaps. One—again—was the principle of unanimity, and as we have seen, the 12 member nations split over the issue of a force of "interposition." A second handicap was the lack of logistical autonomy, of an integrated command, and of readily available forces (other than the Franco-German corps, which was regarded as not usable because of Germany's constitutional restrictions on military action abroad). A third handicap explains the second: the preference of several of the WEU's members (especially the United Kingdom and the Netherlands) for NATO and their unwillingness to act without the United States. (Indeed, in 1993, in discussions about the eventual deployment of peacekeepers in Bosnia-Herzegovina after a cease-fire agreement there, even the French conceded that NATO could provide the secular arm the Security Council would request and sanctioned such a NATO role, in 1994, even before any agreement.) WEU is not likely to be an effective instrument of collective security in Europe as long as there is no coherent common foreign policy of the European Union, and the quasi-theological question of the WEU's relationship to NATO is not resolved. The recent agreement that allows future autonomous actions by the European members of NATO both removes some of the grounds for that theological quarrel and makes the WEU less, and NATO more, significant. (For the time being, NATO plays a residual "reassurance" role with respect to the countries of central and eastern Europe, although its military functions are as problematic as those of the WEU.)

Fourth, it may be true, as Thomas Weiss argues in chapter 3, that regional organizations are not a viable alternative to the United Nations (although his excellent critique of the United Nations suggests that the world organization is not a very effective alternative to regional organizations). The key problem is the need for better *coordination between the global and the regional agencies.* During the Croatian crisis, Slobodan Milosevic, the Serbian leader, played the United Nations against the EC, which he distrusted because of German and Italian hostility, whereas he thought that Yugoslavia would benefit from the sympathy of both the former nonaligned nations and the Soviet Union in the United Nations.[23] The EC envoy of the Dutch president found Vance more willing to lean toward Serbia than the EC negotiators and Lord Carrington had been. For France and the United Kingdom, U.N. involvement became both an alleged necessity, given the absence of a common foreign policy and defense system in pre-Maastricht Europe (what Delors described as the situation of "an adolescent—the Community—facing the crisis of adulthood"), and an all-too-easy way of preserving the EC's cohesion despite the splits among its members by essentially moving all the coercive aspects of the tragedy to the United Nations and sharing with it the rather unrewarding diplomatic function.[24] Boutros-Ghali at times showed his exasperation with the Security Council's preoccupation with a conflict that, to him, was only one among many, and that had been added to all the other U.N. operations mainly at the request of the Europeans.

The issue of coordination is difficult. On the one hand, "what many considered the regional organizations' comparative advantage—proximity to and interest in resolving the conflict—proved to be a serious limitation," because of the conflicting ties several of the members had with different parties in the Yugoslav breakup.[25] On the other hand, not only are members of the Security Council likely to be just as contradictorily involved, but the United Nations is not equipped to handle every crisis adequately. Suggestions have been made, but general guidelines may have to be bent to the specific features of each case.[26] In this one, the experiences of both the United Nations and the European organizations have been unedifying. Basically, there is no substitute for the common resolve of a concert of key powers operating as the leaders in the Security Council and the regional organizations. When there is such a concert, as in the Gulf War, things work. When there is not—as in Yugoslavia—they do not. What we witnessed was an unseemly mess: a string of Security Council resolutions that gave to U.N. peacekeepers, in areas where there was no peace (Bosnia) or only a shaky one (Croatia), missions without the means to carry them out; a U.N. presence in Bosnia that could use force only in self-defense (and often did not do so, out of concern for its own protection), but not in order to protect the Bosnians' "safe areas," and had to depend on NATO air power for that purpose; a chain of command so complex—going from the secretary-general of the United Nations to his delegate in the field, from the latter to the commander of UNPROFOR, and from him to NATO—as almost to ensure snags and clashes; for much of the time a military commander (General Rose) whose behavior seemed closer to the British position than to the spirit of many of the Security Council's resolutions; a U.N. secretary-general of the U.N. complaining of "micromanagement" by the members of the Security Council; a U.S. government complaining about U.N. inefficiency and timidity but obstinately unwilling to take the only decision that might have given it some leverage: contributing ground forces to UNPROFOR.

Fifth, and ultimately, the most striking and disturbing aspect of the drama was this: sensing the hesitations of and divisions among the major powers faced with the problem of Serbian moves in Croatia and in Bosnia-Herzegovina, the Serbian civilian and military leadership decided to reach its objectives by force and through murderous "ethnic cleansing" unless the European and U.N. "mediators" acquiesced in the Serbian program of dismemberment of multiethnic states in the name of the Serbian people's right to self-determination. And the major powers allowed this to happen. They did so for a number of reasons, different in each case. Here I mention only those of the Europeans.

Germany was the state that took, at the outset, the most anti-Serb stand. Domestic politics played a role: most of the Yugoslav workers in Germany were Croats, the Croats' lobby was influential with the Bavarian Christian Social Union (CSU), and the press supported the Slovenes and the Croats. However, there is no doubt that for Germany's leaders, if not always its vociferous media, the principle of self-determination was by itself a powerful motive, and sympathy for the Serbian version of it—"ethnic self-determination"—was precluded by Serbian inconsistency and behavior (perhaps also by the similarity between this Serbian version and the Nazi one). But the strong German stand proved doubly counterproductive, and this fact should also be a lesson to the new Germany. On the one hand, it only fed Serbian paranoia about Germany's sinister role in the breakup of Yugoslavia, ancient hostility to the Serbian people, sympathy for Croat "fascists," dreams of revenge against the victors of World War II, and desire for hegemony in the Balkans. On the other hand, it increased tensions within the EC, between France and Britain on the one hand and between Germany and the two of them on the other.

Moreover, Bonn's position was undercut by the constitutional restrictions on Germany's military action abroad: the most severe critic of Serbia could not take part in military operations against it. (The only exceptions until everything changed in August 1995, and even they required a big internal battle, have been the participation of German cargo aircraft in the nightly drops of supplies to beleaguered Bosnian towns and of German AWACS planes in the surveillance of the "no-fly" zone in Bosnia-Herzegovina.) It is true that Germany has accepted by far the greatest number of refugees from the former Yugoslavia—a quarter million in 1992—but this, in turn, provoked a backlash and a constitutional revision against the previous asylum policy. Germany's ambivalence is well illustrated by the writings of the gifted political analyst Josef Joffe, who forcefully criticized Serbian behavior (all the way back to Sarajevo 1914!) but who also argued that only a most unlikely and risky massive military intervention could have saved the Muslims of Bosnia-Herzegovina, given the terrain, the scope of "tribal warfare," and the likelihood of its recurrence.[27]

If Germany's problem was righteous indignation without the means to enforce it, *Britain*'s position was devoid of ambivalence. Whether the old and curious sympathy that had linked the United Kingdom and Tito under Churchill was still at work, or whether Britain's leaders had concluded that forcible outside intervention in so savage and multi-sided a conflict could lead only to endless frustration, escalating casualties, and exitless entrapment—as in Northern Ireland, but on a far greater scale—they decided not to listen to Lady Thatcher's (as usual) shrill advice and to let force settle the issues, with only a minimum of humanitarian intervention to bring some food and medication to the victims (and great reluctance to tighten and expand sanctions). American suggestions to "lift and strike" were invariably met with the argument that such measures would force the British to get out of UNPROFOR. The British agreement in the summer of 1995 to the setting up of a rapid reaction force appears to have been intended as a way of helping UNPROFOR withdraw eventually rather than as a means to protect the Muslims.

This was a defensible policy *if* one is willing to close one's eyes to the precedent thus established in a world full of ethnic powder kegs, *if* one considers that the Yugoslav crisis is a self-contained drama with no serious risk of overflowing (for instance, through an explosion in Kosovo), *if* one believes that no amount or threat of punishment could have deterred Serb aggression (especially in Bosnia), and *if* one is absolutely convinced that, even at first, only a massive use of air power and ground forces had any chance of stopping Serbia. However, if one is disturbed both about the precedent and about the potential for a broader Balkan crisis, and if one believes that, as a good Leninist, Milosevic kept pushing because he met only mush but might have moderated his demands and his acts if he had met steel far short of a colossal military action by European or U.N. powers, Britain's policy appears deplorable (and sadly reminiscent of the 1930s, although, of course, Milosevic is not as mighty as Hitler). It condones an often atrocious use of force to change borders recognized by the international community and huge violations of human rights aimed at destroying the very possibility of a multiethnic state. It quietly proclaims that such occurrences, in an important part of Europe, do not gravely matter.

It is to Mitterrand's *France* that Joffe's verdict on the European peacemaking effort applies particularly: "good will without the will to power."[28] "Good will" may not have been universal; many French diplomats and military men have "historic" sympathies for Serbia and its army, or show themselves receptive to Serbian arguments about the "danger" of a "Muslim state" in Europe. But these were not the factors that shaped official policy. French priorities, set by President Mitterrand, were the end of war—through a combination of economic sanctions and diplomacy—and humanitarian assistance. When the first of these objectives appeared beyond the reach of the divided EC, the French turned to the United Nations. They played an important role in the sharpening of sanctions in the spring of 1993 and in the establishment of security zones. For many months, one of Mitterrand's ministers, Bernard Kouchner, the apostle of the *droit d'ingérence*, pleaded for a tougher approach to humanitarian intervention, and much of the French intelligentsia mobilized itself in favor of the Muslims in Bosnia. But when it came to the use of force for any goal other than protecting the humanitarian efforts from direct attack, Mitterrand remained aloof; his daring visit to Sarajevo in the summer of 1992 was, characteristically, both a demonstration of concern and a substitute for more forceful action. He remained, in this respect, close to the British position (and the "cohabitation" government that took over in March 1993 did not try to modify this stand). As in the 1930s, France, in effect, followed Britain into spinelessness.

Did Mitterrand feel, in 1991–92, that given the United Kingdom's position and Germany's paradoxical paralysis, France could not in any case move without the United States? But when the United States, under Clinton, finally recommended lifting the arms embargo on Bosnia and resorting to air strikes against Serbia, the French said no, arguing that the first of these measures would only prolong the war and that the second would jeopardize the humanitarian effort and the lives of those who protected it. They repeatedly warned about taking their contingents back if the war were not settled or if it escalated through measures taken by the United Nations or Western powers. The contradiction between Mitterrand's enthusiasm for the principles of collective security in 1990–91, during the Gulf crisis, and his failure to invoke them in 1991–93, over Yugoslavia, is striking and hard to explain, except in terms of the domestic priorities (especially the issue of unemployment), of the shabby state of France's conventional forces, and of the concentration, in 1991–92, on Maastricht and its ratification. Preserving the chances for a European Union and thus avoiding obviously divisive issues was understandable, but the price was a demonstration of European impotence and futility—a boon for all those who argue that in the absence of American leadership, Europe, now habituated to dependence, cannot act.

French policy changed considerably after the election of Jacques Chirac to the presidency in May 1995. His position remained somewhat acrobatic, insofar as his (and his government's) endorsement of a diplomatic solution led him to insist that he did *not* support any one side in the conflict. But he came out repeatedly in favor of a far more militant, or military, approach by NATO and by the rapid reaction force London and Paris have been establishing. His attitude has been described as "*on tire ou on se tire*"—we fire or else we flee.[29] (As a result, the threat of a withdrawal of UNPROFOR in case of demonstrated impotence was added to the threat of withdrawal should the arms embargo on Bosnia be lifted and a bigger war ensue.)

The reasons for this change were, in part, Chirac's own character, which is highly activist, in part a sense of shame at the humiliation of French soldiers in UNPROFOR by the Bosnian Serbs—the honor of French soldiers is as important to him as the lives of American soldiers are to Clinton—in part indignation at the new atrocities committed by the Bosnian Serbs in Srebrenica in July 1995 and in Sarajevo in August. On July 14, 1995, Chirac compared the international handling of the conflict to Chamberlain's and Daladier's handling of the Sudeten crisis of 1938. This new stance led to serious cracks in the previous *entente cordiale* between London and Paris. However, France does not have the military means to act alone, and as was shown at the international conference in London in July 1995, its proposals for ground action (which would have required extensive American logistical support and therefore were opposed by Washington) were shelved in favor of the strategy traditionally preferred by the Americans: bombardment from the air.

Reckoning the Costs

I can only conclude that the British and French preference for "sustained negotiations" without deterrence or uses of force—and without even the lifting of an unfair arms embargo that mainly helped the aggressor—was both a political and a moral mistake.[30] Are the Europeans willing to threaten or to resort to force only when their oil supplies or the physical safety of their own people are in danger? The treatment of the breakup of Yugoslavia by the west Europeans was a tragic and blatant example of their ambivalence about those central and eastern European countries that had remained outside the Community and the European Free Trade Area and under communist rule—even though, in Yugoslavia's case, it was a dissident communism, and hundreds of thousands of its citizens had found work in western Europe. Rhetorically, west European intellectuals and politicians always viewed these countries as part of Europe—temporarily alienated brothers, whose future lay in a reunion with their more fortunate kin in the West. This explains not only the moments of enthusiasm for the liberation of the former Soviet satellites in 1989 but also the rush of the EC, eager to show its capacity to act on the world stage, into the Yugoslav labyrinth in the summer of 1991. On the other hand, this enthusiasm has waned whenever the risks and costs have begun to be visible: witness the niggardliness of the EC's economic association agreement with the eastern countries, the EC's and EU's hesitation to offer full membership to them, and the contortions over Yugoslavia described here. European responsibility for Yugoslavia, proclaimed in the summer and fall of 1991, was partly shed and dumped on the United Nations (and the United States), partly resented insofar as involvement on the ground in Croatia and Bosnia became increasingly seen as a trap (and an excuse for not doing more). Given America's reluctance, both under Bush (at the time of the Serb attack on Dubrovnik in 1991 and throughout 1992) and under Clinton, to take the lead in this case as it had in the Gulf crisis in 1991, given the inability of the United Nations to be effective when its key members are both divided and reluctant to act, the Yugoslav tragedy became a kind of orphan of world politics—a blot on Western consciences, but just a blip on the diplomatic screen.

Indeed, there is a lesson that goes beyond the Europeans' responsibility and applies to the United States, Russia, and the United Nations as well. Yugoslavia's crisis has been handled in a way that reminds one of the Italo-Ethiopian conflict and of the way in which it was handled by Britain, France, and the League of Nations. In both cases, the international "community" had to deal with two issues: the settlement of the crisis (which in the Yugoslav case must include both the fate of Bosnia and the borders and composition of Croatia) and the issue of force—of the means used by one of the parties to impose its solution. In the case of Yugoslavia, the means used by Serbia were doubly unacceptable: because of their brutality—they amount to a massive violation of human rights as well as to a violent attempt at preventing acts of secession recognized by the international "community"—and because they prejudged the outcome of international efforts at a settlement.

In both cases, the major powers and the international organization in charge tried to cope with both issues at once, and each of these attempts interfered with the other. Punishing Serbia (even only mildly) did not make it more accommodating in the discussions on consecutive "plans." But the continuing negotiations aimed at resolving the crisis served as an alibi for "moderation" in the imposition of sanctions, as a pretext for suggesting that they could become a bargaining chip, and as a reason for not "enlarging the conflict" by resorting to force or by lifting the arms embargo on Serbia. It was a mistake to negotiate with Serbia as if all the parties to the dispute had the same moral standing; this left the negotiations at the mercy of the most intransigent—Serbia—while justifying the reluctance of the outside powers to create the incentives that might have obliged Serbia to negotiate fairly and to accept a morally just deal—economic pressure has not been sufficient to do so and military pressure has, on the whole and until very late, been missing. As a result, each new "plan" became a capitulation to the realities that the Serbs had imposed on the ground, except for the plan of the "contact group," which would have imposed a partial Serb retreat but still ratified ethnic cleansing and recognized a huge chunk of the Bosnian Serbs' land grab. In any case, the Bosnian Serbs' intransigence has paid off. As in the process that ended in Munich in September 1938, the major powers gradually increased their concessions to Bosnian Serb demands, in the name of "realism."

A case should have been made for giving priority to stopping Serbian violations first and negotiating the best possible solution afterward. What was done instead was a dreadful mix: negotiations were altogether toothless (when the use of force was finally threatened by the United Nations and NATO, it was unrelated to any negotiating process) and in constant retreat. The reluctance to use the model of collective security resulted in the failure to send UNPROFOR preventively to Bosnia, the long delay in enforcing the ban on Serbian air flights, the delay in protecting the "safe havens" (and the minimalist interpretation given it as well as, in several cases, the failure to attempt that protection), the maintenance of the arms embargo on Bosnia despite the charter's recognition of the individual and collective right of self-defense. The Western powers have walked only a few inches toward resorting to this model. The most striking move, the creation of an international tribunal on war crimes, may turn out to be the least effective, as Abram and Antonia Chayes suggest in chapter 8. While the West hesitated, the Russians reentered the picture, reinforcing the Europeans' fatal attraction to crippled diplomacy and making any further progress toward collective security even less likely. As for UNPROFOR, sent to Bosnia for a primarily humanitarian mission, its civilian and military leaders have, of course, been reluctant throughout to engage in forceful moves against Serbian or Bosnian Serb attacks—out of the conviction that this could only jeopardize its primary task. But it thus became the hostage of the Serbs, even in the performance of that task.

It is true that, as Pierre Hassner has suggested, the United Nations (and the European Union) need to establish a clear set of guidelines on self-determination and secession, indicating the conditions in which the latter will be accepted internationally; but, as he also states, there is also a need to treat explicitly as acts of aggression attempts at crushing by force secessions that meet such conditions.[31] The precedent set by the treatment of the Yugoslav crisis—the massive brutalization of international relations and the destruction through ethnic cleansing of a multinational state—is as shocking as it is disastrous.

Notes

1. See especially James B. Steinberg, "International Involvement in the Yugoslavia Conflict," in Lori Fisler Damrosch, ed., *Enforcing Restraint* (New York: Council on Foreign Relations Press, 1993), pp. 27–76.

2. Ibid., p. 34.

3. See John Zametica, *The Yugoslav Conflict*, Adelphi Paper, no. 270 (London: International Institute for Strategic Studies, 1992), p. 59.

4. Wynaendts, *L'engrenage*, Paris, Denoël (1993), p. 34.

5. David Gompert, "How to Defeat Serbia," *Foreign Affairs*, vol. 73, no. 4 (July–August 1994), p. 38.

6. Weller, "International Response to the Dissolution of the Socialist Federal Republic of Yugoslavia," *American Journal of International Law*, vol. 36, no. 3 (July 1992), p. 591.

7. Ibid., pp. 592–93.

8. See also Dusko Doder, "Yugoslavia: New War, Old Hatreds," *Foreign Policy*, no. 91 (Summer 1993), p. 18.

9. Zametica, *Yugoslav Conflict*, pp. 76–77.

10. Wynaendts, *L'engrenage*, p. 63.

11. Weller, "International Response to the Dissolution of the Socialist Federal Republic of Yugoslavia," pp. 576–77.

12. Ibid., p. 574.

13. Zametica, *Yugoslav Conflict*, p. 62.

14. Weller, "International Response to the Dissolution of the Socialist Federal Republic of Yugoslavia," p. 592.

15. David Owen, "The Future of the Balkans," *Foreign Affairs* vol. 72, no. 2 (Spring 1993), p. 8.

16. Wynaendts, *L'engrenage*, p. 100.

17. "Entretien avec Alain Juppé," *Politique Internationale*, no. 61 (Fall 1993), p. 16.

18. Aleksa Djilas, in his "Profile," *Foreign Affairs* vol. 72, no. 3 (Summer 1993), pp. 81–96, argues that Milosevic counted on war to unify the Serbs around him.

19. Wynaendts, *L'engrenage*, p. 141.

20. Owen, "The Future of the Balkans," p. 5. For arguments against intervention, see Adam Roberts "Humanitarian War: Military Intervention and Human Rights," *International Affairs*, vol. 69, no. 3 (1993) pp. 429–49; and Ernst Haas, "Beware of the Slippery Slope," in Carl Keyser, ed., *Emerging Norms of Justified Intervention* (Cambridge: American Academy of Arts and Sciences, 1993), pp. 63–87.

21. Steinberg, "International Involvement in the Yugoslavia Conflict," p. 57.

22. Ibid., p. 58.

23. Wynaendts, *L'engrenage*, p. 136.

24. Quoted in Zametica, *Yugoslav Conflict*, p. 66.

25. Steinberg, "International Involvement in the Yugoslavia Conflict," p. 57.

26. See the prudent suggestions of Tom Farer, "A Paradigm of Legitimate Intervention," in Damrosch, *Enforcing Restraint*, ch. 8.

27. Josef Joffe,"The New Europe: Yesterday's Ghosts," *Foreign Affairs: America and the World 1992-93*, vol. 72, no. 1, pp. 29–43.

28. Ibid., p. 31.

29. *Le Monde*, July 27, 1995, p. 1.

30. Zametica, *Yugoslav Conflict*, p. 63.

31. See Hassner's "Les impuissances de la communauté internationale," in Véronique Nahoum-Grappe, ed., *Vukovar, Sarajevo* . . . (Paris: Esprit, 1993), pp. 83–118. See also Jacques Julliard, *Ce fascisme qui vient* (Paris: Ed. du Seuil, 1994), esp. pp. 161–62.

Chapter 5

The United States and Yugoslavia's Wars

DAVID C. GOMPERT

ONTRARY TO A widely held view, the Bush administration was
well aware of the potential of a violent dissolution of Yugoslavia.
It simply knew of no way to prevent this from occurring. National Security Adviser Brent Scowcroft and Deputy Secretary of State
Lawrence Eagleburger, among others, had served in Yugoslavia and
understood its volcanic nature. The top floors of the State Department
and the West Wing of the White House saw clearly a year before the
fighting began that Yugoslavia was being led toward the abyss by a few
demagogic politicians. There was no American "intelligence failure," no
inattention due to preoccupation with the collapse of communism or
Iraq's invasion of Kuwait. Rather, despite considerable deliberation and
diplomatic activity, no good option emerged to arrest the accelerating,
awful logic of breakup and war.

From Warning to War

From the mid-1980s onward, Serbs were usurping power in Belgrade,
upsetting the delicate balances of Tito's Yugoslav federation; Slovenes
were determined to be independent from the usurpers; Croats were
bound to follow the Slovenes; Serbs, in turn, would kill and die before
accepting the fate of becoming a minority in an independent Croatia;
and the Bosnian powder keg was set to explode if the fuse was lit in
Croatia. The basic choices were clear to the Bush administration early
on: either Serbian leaders would have to be induced to embrace constitutional democracy and eschew domination of Yugoslavia, or else the

Slovenes would have to be persuaded to abandon their hopes and stay in an undemocratic Yugoslavia dominated by the Serbs.

Tall orders, both. Only a credible threat of force by the West would have been likely to halt Serbian power-grabbing, while nothing short of outright Western opposition would have tempered the Slovenes' wish to get free of the Serbs. Neither policy was politically feasible for the Bush administration, at home or with its European allies. More fundamental still, those American officials who knew the Balkans best believed that no external power, not even the sole superpower, could prevent Yugoslavs from killing each other and destroying their country, much less impose a fair and lasting peaceful solution.

If Washington was pessimistic by late 1990, it was not paralyzed. The United States declared its sympathy for the teetering Yugoslav federal government of Ante Markovic, who was committed to democracy, a civil society, and a market economy. But the prime minister wanted debt relief and a public signal of unreserved American political backing—commitments that seemed unwarranted in view of his government's apparent terminal condition.

The belief that the Markovic government was beyond help only partly explains why the Bush administration could not justify putting the dying Yugoslav federal authority on life-support systems. The capacity to take on such a daunting challenge was lacking. At the time, the United States was confronted with no less than a world political revolution (of which the disintegration of Yugoslavia was a manifestation) whose future course and consequences were far from clear. Communism and Soviet control were being vanquished from eastern Europe. The Soviet Union itself was hurtling toward turmoil and transfiguration. A new European power, unified Germany, was being created. West Europeans were crafting plans to transform their community into an economic and political colossus. In the volatile Middle East, a former Soviet client invaded Kuwait and threatened Saudi Arabia.

Neither Carrots nor Sticks

This swirling revolution, while full of opportunity, also placed heavy burdens on the United States in terms of defense commitments, foreign aid and debt relief, crises to be managed, and actual and possible force deployments. The difficulty in building and holding congressional and public support to meet these growing demands merely underlined the administration's perception that it was strapped. The entire annual U.S. assistance program for Europe's new democracies was but a few hundred million dollars—a minute fraction (in real terms) of what the United States had injected into Europe after World War II. An American economic commitment to Yugoslavia would have had to come out of this paltry east European account. Because Washington did not view even a violent breakup of Yugoslavia as likely to lead to a Europe-wide war or to threaten the democratic revolutions elsewhere in eastern Europe, a major program to shore up Belgrade's last federal government was no more seriously contemplated than was preemptive military action.[1]

Washington did step up its diplomacy in Yugoslavia. The Bush administration knew that the person chiefly responsible for turning up tensions, Serbian strongman Slobodan Milosevic, was also the only figure with the power to avert a violent outcome. It repeatedly directed U.S. Ambassador Warren Zimmermann to demand that Milosevic cease his oppression of the Albanian majority in Kosovo province as well as his illegal seizure of Yugoslav federal assets and authority. While the latter more directly fueled Slovenian secessionism, Washington stressed the former in response to flagrant Serbian abuse of human rights in Kosovo and heavy pressure from several members of Congress with vocal Albanian-American constituents. Milosevic was right if he perceived that the United States was more offended by his policies toward Kosovo than toward Slovenia. In any case, since the Bush administration was not prepared to take military action, it chose not to issue any explicit warnings, even though nothing less would have changed Serbian policy.[2] Milosevic could see by 1990 that he was safe to ignore American pressure, since no concrete threats, much less actions, accompanied Washington's stern demarches.

At the same time, the United States urged the Slovenes and Croats to consider new arrangements short of dissolution. While the identity of the archvillain—Milosevic—was never in doubt, the Bush administration had scant sympathy for Slovene and Croat separatists. The former seemed willing to trigger a Yugoslav war so long as they could escape both Yugoslavia and the war. The Croatian regime of Franjo Tudjman, which was hardly democratic, adopted policies regarding minorities that stoked the fears of Serbs living in Croatia of a revival of the infamous Ustashe fascist organization that had butchered their fathers and uncles during World War II. So American policymakers saw cynicism behind the declared "right" of Slovene and Croat nationalists to be free, democratic, and part of the (Roman Catholic) West, even though they knew that Milosevic was the main force propelling Yugoslavia toward a violent end.

The Bush administration's lack of enthusiasm for Slovene and Croat separatism has been wrongly ascribed to an attachment to an artificial single state, forsaking freedom in the interest of stability.[3] In fact, U.S. policy prior to the outbreak of hostilities was not motivated by a preference for a unified Yugoslavia but by a judgment, which proved all too correct, that a peaceful dissolution was infeasible. American interest in the integrity of Yugoslavia per se ended with the collapse of the Soviet threat to Europe. Indeed, the strategic importance of Yugoslavia was waning at the very moment the federation was coming unglued. If the end of Tito's communism made Yugoslavia's breakup certain, the end of Soviet communism made such a development seem less threatening to international peace and U.S. vital interests. Had peaceful dissolution been deemed a realistic possibility, the Bush administration would have favored it or at least accepted it, as it did the orderly breakup of Czechoslovakia on January 1, 1993.

By the end of 1990, the overriding concern among American officials was averting a Balkan war. They feared the worst: the disintegration of Yugoslavia was bound to be violent because Serbs would sooner fight than be abducted by an independent Croatia; the fighting would then engulf much of Yugoslavia, because the urge of each republic to secede would grow as others seceded; and the human toll would be terrible, because Yugoslavia was bristling with weapons and seething with old hatreds and fears. (The grisly particulars—detention camps, ethnic cleansing, mass rapes, shelling of civilian populations—were not predicted, though perhaps they could have been.) The ingredients needed for a peaceful dissolution were not at hand. Those who criticize the Bush administration for contributing to the outbreak of hostilities by favoring a unified state have yet to explain how favoring disunity would have prevented the conflict.

Washington's Principles

While increasingly gloomy, Washington advanced a set of principles that, if embraced by all parties, might have yielded a peaceful resolution: Yugoslavia should become democratic throughout; Yugoslavs should decide its future democratically; borders, external and internal alike, should be altered only by mutual consent, not unilaterally or by force; Yugoslavia should not be held together by force; members of minority groups throughout Yugoslavia should have the same rights as all other individuals.[4] That every one of these principles was thoroughly trashed within a year underscores the scale of the U.S. failure, but it does not invalidate the norms on which they were based. It is worth noting that essentially these same principles were observed in the breakup of Czechoslovakia, where not a shot was fired.

Of course, Czechs and Slovaks split by mutual consent, whereas Slovenes and Croats did not seek, and certainly could not have gotten, Serbian consent for their independence. Nonetheless, until 1991 the United States clung to the position that it could accept any outcome arrived at consensually by the republics of Yugoslavia. Then, knowing that disintegration meant a savage war, the Bush administration came to favor transforming Yugoslavia into a confederation of quasi-sovereign states, the details of which were to be left to the Yugoslavs. A specific proposal for such an arrangement was made in early 1991 by the leaders of Macedonia and Bosnia-Herzegovina, who saw great peril for their people in complete dissolution. Washington hoped that such a loose structure might satisfy the aspirations of most Slovenes (and thus Croats) and that the Serbs would see that it was the only way to hold Yugoslavia together. Many moderate Slovenes and Croats also favored such an outcome and welcomed the American stance, knowing as they did that secession would lead to bloodshed.

The administration's strategy, which culminated in Secretary of State James Baker's June 1991 visit to Yugoslavia, sought to persuade the Slovenes to postpone unilateral separation, while warning Milosevic and the leadership of the Serb-dominated Yugoslav People's Army (YPA) not to use force to hold Yugoslavia together.[5] But not even Baker the poker player could disguise the fact that the warning to the Serbs was not backed by the threat of force. Nor could the persuasive Baker give pause to the Slovenian separatists.

The Slovenes proved to be indifferent to the fatal consequences for others of their unilateral secession. Unfortunately, signals from western Europe did not consistently reinforce Washington's plea for restraint and negotiations. "Unofficial" Austrian and German encouragement spoke louder than American caution to Slovene nationalists, who hoped to see their Alpine nation soon tucked safely into a close economic and political relationship with Germany, en route to membership in the European Community (EC). So the Slovenes seceded—and pulled the Croats with them . Even hesitant Croats understood the dangers of remaining in a Yugoslavia ruled by Serbs once Slovenia bolted. When Slovenia seized control of its borders, the YPA declared itself obligated to act in defense of federal assets and of the union itself. The war began modestly—if any war can be modest—in Slovenia, whose separation Belgrade did not seriously contest because no Serbs lived there. Hostilities then spread quickly to and throughout those regions of Croatia inhabited by Serbs. Within weeks of Slovenia's decision to secede, Serbs and Croats were fighting as viciously as they had a half century earlier.

The Baker mission failed, but—contrary to the opinion of many analysts—the secretary had not given the Serbs a "green light" to use force to preserve Yugoslav unity.[6] Indeed, he had told Milosevic that the American people, if forced to choose, would come down on the side of freedom over unity. But since the United States was prepared neither to intervene militarily to protect the seceding republics nor to make empty threats, it is unclear just what U.S. policy at that point could have prevented or stopped the war. Indeed, had the United States championed Slovenian and Croatian secession instead of urging restraint, the results would hardly have been better.

Deferring to the Allies

Until blood began to flow, Europeans seemed to discount the mounting dangers, deluding themselves that Europe's peoples had progressed beyond outright war, even in the Balkans. The outbreak of fighting in Slovenia and Croatia in mid-1991 was therefore as shocking to west Europeans as it was predictable to American policymakers. (Later, disillusioned, some west Europeans rationalized that the Balkans were not part of the new Europe.) Caught unprepared for the war, Europe's leading governments proved purposeless, divided, and vulnerable to shifts in public emotion—just when the United States turned to them to take charge of managing the crisis.

America's decision to rely on its European partners to take the lead in Yugoslavia proved to be a grave mistake that compounded the West's failure. Before the fighting began, Washington had urged the EC to accept leadership responsibility out of the reasonable belief that the allies had more economic and political leverage in Yugoslavia than the United States did. American attempts in late fall 1990 to get the Europeans to face the peril were brushed aside: an American proposal to consult within the North Atlantic Treaty Organization (NATO) was declined, with the French accusing the United States of "overdramatizing" the problem. Not until spring 1991 was the EC seized with the risks of Serbian policies and Slovenian secession. The $4 billion aid carrot the EC then produced might have avoided war, had it not been dangled in front of the Yugoslavs at least a year too late.

At the highest levels and at every turn, the United States encouraged the allies to engage and offered its support. The Europeans favored EC leadership because Yugoslavia was viewed as an opportune foreign policy challenge at the very moment Helmut Kohl, François Mitterrand, and others wished to display the EC's ability to act effectively and cohesively.[7] Luxembourg's foreign minister, speaking for the EC's troika of emissaries, proclaimed it "the hour of Europe," a quote whose painful echo is a reminder of how badly the Europeans misjudged the dogs of this Balkan war.

Washington accommodated not only the Europeans' wish to lead but also their insistence that transatlantic cooperation take place within EC-U.S. channels, rather than in NATO's North Atlantic Council. While this meant awkward arm's-length coordination, in contrast to the possibility of fashioning a common European-American approach in NATO, the Bush administration chose not to object. Key European allies, already disappointed with Washington's cool reception to the idea of an EC-based common defense policy, would have considered unfriendly any attempt by the United States to frustrate their wish to treat Yugoslavia as a matter of EC common foreign policy. Difficult as it was for the United States to deal with the EC's ponderous, inflexible, and opaque policymaking, Washington went along. With the consent of the Bush administration, NATO was kept out of the crisis until 1993, when it became clear that the Bosnian conflict exceeded the capacities of all other international institutions.

Broadly speaking, the U.S. government's handling of the Yugoslav crisis from 1990 through 1992 contradicted and undermined its declaratory policy regarding the centrality and purpose of NATO in post–Cold War Europe. During that period, the Bush administration insisted that America's role in European security would be maintained despite the disappearance of the Soviet threat and that NATO was the keystone of European security and the proper venue for crisis management. The administration informed Congress that a residual American presence in Europe on the order of 150,000 troops was needed to preserve European stability and peace. The Rome summit at the end of 1991 endorsed NATO's new role as guardian of European stability and revised alliance military strategy to emphasize force projection over territorial defense. This new stance implied NATO responsibility to respond to precisely the sort of conflict by then raging in the Balkans.[8]

Despite this, the Bush administration did not press for the use of NATO to set and manage Western strategy, much less to intervene militarily in Yugoslavia, not simply because of the EC's desire to lead but also out of a concern that NATO involvement would shift responsibility to the United States and imply that the West was prepared to take military action to stop the bloodshed. The administration wanted the EC to succeed, but the clearer it became that it could not, the less eager Washington was to see the alliance, and thus itself, saddled with a "no-win" problem. (Speculation that Washington really wanted the EC to fail and thus display its impotence is without foundation.) Predictably, the attempt to hold the Yugoslavia crisis at arm's length did not spare the United States the effects of, or responsibility for, the failure that followed.

Military Options

The shelling of Dubrovnik and the destruction of Vukovar by the Serbs toward the end of 1991 prompted some U.S. officials to raise the issue of whether military intervention was warranted. The most readily available option was a show of force by the Sixth Fleet to save Dubrovnik. While it may have been possible to chase Serb gunners away from this romantic walled city on the Adriatic (to the joy of west European café intellectuals), it is less clear that such a limited action would have deterred Serbs from their more determined military operations elsewhere in Croatia. A more robust Western military option, by far, would have involved the accelerated assembling and deployment of the newly approved NATO "rapid reaction corps" to stop the fighting in Croatia. However, the Defense Department, its standing within the government enhanced by the victory in Kuwait, opposed any use of force by the United States. And the president was not about to overrule the Pentagon and launch the nation into another, possibly major war after just finishing one.

Having excluded the option most likely to stop the conflict—decisive military intervention—the U.S. government took the position, by default, that it was better to let the EC continue to take the lead than to adopt ineffective half measures or to seize the helm with no compass. As well, paralyzing interagency differences began to surface during the fighting in Croatia, differences that would dog U.S. policymaking and discourage initiative throughout Yugoslavia's wars. From late 1991 on, consensus proved elusive not only inside Washington but between the United States and its European allies and among the Europeans.

As hostilities worsened in Croatia, the United States resisted growing German and domestic pressures promptly to recognize the two breakaway republics. This hesitation stemmed from the conviction that premature recognition would scuttle the effort of U.N. Special Envoy Cyrus Vance to achieve a cease-fire and get a peacekeeping force deployed in Croatia—a conviction shared by Vance himself. George Bush declined to recognize Croatia despite intense pressure from the influential Croatian-American community, which as a result deserted him in the election of 1992. Washington was also reluctant to recognize Croatia and Slovenia before recognizing Bosnia-Herzegovina, lest it be implied that the latter was condemned by the West to live under the heel of Serbian nationalism in a rump Yugoslavia.

Both the U.S. government and the EC's Arbitration Commission, formed to search for a solution, held that recognition of Bosnia should await the outcome of a referendum there. Even though it was known that Bosnia's Serbs would resist separation from Serbia proper, the United States could not oppose a straight popular vote, which effectively denied the Serbs a veto. When two thirds of the Bosnians voted for independence (the Bosnian Serbs boycotted the referendum), the United States persuaded the EC to recognize Bosnia in return for U.S. recognition of Slovenia and Croatia. Washington was eager for the

Europeans to join in recognizing Bosnia, both to bolster its prospects for survival and to avoid leaving the United States with sole responsibility for a new state that might soon descend into civil war.

Western recognition of Bosnia did not precipitate the use of force there by the Bosnian Serbs any more than it deterred it. Very simply, Bosnian Muslims would not have stayed in a rump Yugoslavia dominated by Serbia, and Bosnian Serbs would not have stayed in a separate Bosnia dominated by Muslims. Thus, the logic of the war was complete without Western recognition. In any case, the United States had no legal basis for recognizing Croatia but not Bosnia-Herzegovina.

The West was divided and immobilized between the time of the EC's recognition of Slovenia and Croatia in December 1991 and the European-American agreement in March 1992 that Slovenia, Croatia, and Bosnia-Herzegovina should all be recognized. This transatlantic quarrel over recognition, which came during a critical pause between the Croatian and Bosnian wars, was the product of German irresponsibility. Bowing to right-wing Bavarian and Croat expatriate pressure, German leaders muscled their EC colleagues into recognizing Slovenia and Croatia against the better judgment of the United States, the United Nations, and for that matter most EC foreign ministries. In doing so, Bonn precipitated Bosnian secession, which triggered a war from which Germany, due to its history and its consequent constitutional restraints, could remain aloof while its partners faced risk and sacrifice.

Germans have consistently favored standing up to the Serbs, even though the responsibility for doing so would fall to others. Like the Slovenes with whom they sympathized, the Germans have been able—without admitted remorse—to escape the harmful consequences of policies in Yugoslavia that have served their special purposes. Germany, the champion of self-determination for Slovenia and Croatia, abetted a unilateral alteration of international borders along ethnic lines and made no effort to use its ample influence in the seceding republics to find an alternative to a step that was bound to lead to war. A proponent of strong European leadership in responding to the crisis, Germany had no intention itself of meeting the demands of such leadership. The most important and powerful country in Europe did little to prevent and has risked little to end Yugoslavia's wars.

Watching Bosnia Die

Consumed by their dispute over recognition, the Western powers failed utterly to prepare for a conflict in Bosnia they had every reason to anticipate. They failed even to demand the prompt departure of the YPA from the newly recognized country. Worse, the opportunity was lost to dispatch a peacekeeping force to Bosnia to discourage the outbreak of violence. Because the United Nations Protection Force (UNPROFOR) in Croatia was already shaping up as a major burden, there was no enthusiasm in the West or in the United Nations for a significant new commitment. The EC was inert and would remain so. Even on the eve of disaster, European governments did not seem to grasp the huge danger in Bosnia. At the same time, the Bush administration, which did understand the danger, was hardening its resolve to keep American troops out of Yugoslavia altogether. So the West simply watched as Bosnia slid into unspeakable violence.

The Bosnian Serbs and their YPA allies were ready to fight and quick to take the offensive. They embarked on a strategy of conquest and ethnic cleansing from which they did not stray. Their aim was as simple as it was monstrous: they wanted all Serbs, but only Serbs, on the land on which they meant to build Greater Serbia. This goal dictated that the Bosnian Serb army gain control and then "purify" 70 percent of the territory of Bosnia (although Serbs accounted for just 30 percent of the Bosnian population). By its essence, this strategy was bound—indeed, it was intended—to create massive human suffering. The atrocities perpetrated against civilians, the attacks on population centers, and the uprooting of two million Bosnians were all "necessary" to the successful execution of their strategy. Moreover, the abundant weapons stockpiles, indigenous military production facilities, and no-holds-barred tactics that were the legacy of Yugoslavia's experience in World War II and its preparations for resisting a Warsaw Pact invasion ensured that the Bosnian war would be highly destructive. These same factors also would make Western intervention difficult—too difficult, in the eyes of Western governments. Thus, in Europe (of all places!), weak and innocent people would be driven off, or killed off, to make room for a stronger group with a different god.

George Bush's decision not to allow American ground forces to play any role under any circumstances in Bosnia effectively precluded decisive Western military intervention. The president and his advisers knew that Western military intervention in Bosnia really meant American military intervention with token allied participation, owing to the allies' lack of serious intervention capabilities. After all, the Europeans had mustered a mere five percent of the coalition force that had just defeated Iraq. While such asymmetry could be excused—barely—in liberating Kuwait and protecting Persian Gulf oil, it could not be excused in a war in the middle of Europe.

The administration also feared that any involvement of U.S. ground forces, even to escort humanitarian relief convoys, would lead to a creeping, eventually massive U.S. engagement, since only the United States was both able to escalate and vulnerable to pressure to do so to ensure success. Intervention in Bosnia was viewed as more akin to the Vietnam experience (high casualties, lengthy stay, poor prospects) than to Desert Storm (few casualties, short stay, good prospects). Notwithstanding the public outcry over televised Bosnian horrors, the Bush administration was convinced that the American public, seeing no vital interests at stake, would not support the level of commitment and casualties that might be required for an intervention to succeed. The events of 1993 in Somalia suggest that this was an accurate political reading.

The selective use of force—for example, against the Serbian artillery being used against population centers, as requested in mid-1992 by Bosnian President Alija Izetbegovic—was rejected by the United States as likely to be ineffective militarily and the first step on the proverbial slippery slope to large-scale intervention. The Bush administration, no rookie when it came to using force, was not prepared to threaten force unless it was willing and able to execute not only the specific threat but whatever further steps might be needed to prevail. Panama and Kuwait were held up as evidence of the merits of acting only with "decisive force"; even administration hawks understood that Bosnia could prove to be a much harder proposition, both militarily and politically.

Nor was the administration inclined to gamble that the Serbs would lose their nerve when confronted with American might, as critics of the administration claimed they would. The likely Serb reactions to limited U.S. military action were pure guesswork, and the Bush national security team believed the consequences of guessing wrong were prohibitive. Unlike its successor, the Bush administration considered it essential that the United States never be forced to back down or be caught in a bluff. Thus, once committed, even in the absence of a vital interest and firm public support, the United States would have to use all necessary force to avoid failure.

Op-ed page advocacy of the selective use of force was treated by those with policy responsibility as uninformed and emotional. After all, columnists and analysts would not have to answer for the consequences of the acts of war they so cleverly devised and boldly urged. It is worth noting that not only the U.S. government but all the governments actually faced with the decision of whether to order the use of force in Bosnia—let alone the military commanders who would have to execute such orders—have been far less daring than those who have opined from the sidelines.

However sound the Bush administration's decision was not to become involved militarily in Bosnia, it belied the president's own assertion at the mid-1992 summit meeting of the Conference on Security and Cooperation in Europe (CSCE) that humanitarian relief would be delivered to Bosnian noncombatants, "no matter what it takes." These words, as well as subsequent American-inspired U.N. Security Council resolutions authorizing "all necessary force" to get relief supplies to those in need, were robbed of their credibility when Serbian interference with convoys went unchallenged. The Serbs quickly discovered that they could safely block U.N. relief deliveries. They learned as well that even explicit warnings from the United Nations could be ignored.

The London Conference of August 1992, attended by all key Yugoslav parties and external powers, was a lost opportunity, a turning point, and a sorry chapter in the West's mishandling of the conflict. At the conference, an accommodating Californian, Milan Panic, serving a brief stint as premier of the new "Yugoslavia," agreed to a package of concrete steps including a cease-fire, a military flight ban, support for relief operations, and restrictions on heavy weapons. If honored, these agreements would have curtailed the fighting, ended atrocities, reduced human suffering, and set the stage for political negotiations. In the days and weeks that followed, however, the Serbs willfully ignored every accord reached and commitment made. This drew no response from the West or the U.N. Security Council. The United States was disinclined to use force, even air power, to enforce the various London agreements, in part because of the perceived risk of being drawn into the conflict and in part because of the particular difficulty of policing restrictions on artillery from the air. The British reinforced American hesitation by insisting that they would participate in UNPROFOR convoy protection only if the United States did *not* introduce air power, lest it provoke the Serbs.

The Serbs Get the Message

Western inaction after London told the Serbs in unmistakable terms that there would be no intervention. The Serbs were emboldened further as it became clear that the British and French regarded their UNPROFOR contingents as virtual hostages and therefore sought to avoid provocation. Concerned about the dangerous precedent of bowing to threats against the U.N. blue helmets, the United States offered in late 1992 to use air power punitively against the Serbs if they harmed U.N. personnel. Britain declined the offer. London's repeated public display of concern for the safety of its UNPROFOR contingent invited the Serbs to threaten openly the U.N. forces as a means of derailing any Western attempts to interfere with their ethnic cleansing of the Bosnian Muslims. Had the West shown early on that harming UNPROFOR personnel was intolerable and would be punished, subsequent taking of blue-helmeted hostages by the Serbs might well have been deterred. Instead, it was invited.

The Europeans were also adamant about the need to maintain the arms embargo on the Bosnian Muslims. Until its final days, the Bush administration shared this reluctance to arm the Bosnian Muslims, despite the Serbs' failure to abide by the London accords. Its analysis showed that lifting the embargo would result in increased *Muslim* casualties, increased suffering of innocents, impaired humanitarian relief, and resulted in no change in the military fortunes of the parties. The fear of fueling the conflict to no good end outweighed the view that only the government in Sarajevo had the right to decide whether to accept the risks inherent in defending the Bosnian state and its people. When the Bush administration, responding to strong pressure from its Arab friends, reversed its position on the arms embargo before leaving office, London and Paris blocked any change in the policy. The presence of Europeans (and the absence of Americans) in UNPROFOR gave the allies a veto over U.S. action in this instance, just as it has given the Serbs a veto over Western action.

Even with most of the country under their control by late 1992, the Serbs pressed their attacks on Sarajevo and Muslim population centers in eastern, northern, and northwestern Bosnia in order to ensure land access to all Serbs in the former Yugoslavia and to complete the cleansing of what would be Greater Serbia. Not long after the London Conference, the Serbs could plainly see that the West was not going to intervene, not going to allow the Bosnian government to arm its forces, and not going to use all necessary force to deliver relief supplies.

In Washington, the Bush national security team that performed so well in other crises was divided and stumped. A proposal surfaced to make what was left of Bosnia a U.N. protectorate, where displaced Muslims could settle in safety behind a large peacekeeping force backed by U.S. air power. However, this idea was defeated by a combination of the Pentagon's aversion to military involvement and the State Department's distaste for what might appear to be an abandonment of the right of uprooted Muslims to return to their original homes in Serb-controlled areas.

The United States also considered pressing for an immediate "humanitarian truce" to get both displaced and entrapped Bosnian Muslims through the winter of 1992–93. This idea also was dropped out of concern that it might freeze the status quo and thus appear to accept the results of aggression and ethnic cleansing. The EC mediator, Lord Owen, reached the same conclusion on the grounds that the effort he had undertaken with Cyrus Vance to negotiate a comprehensive political solution would be undermined by a Western call for a simple truce. Owen was especially concerned that if the Serbs could obtain an unconditional cease-fire while holding 70 percent of Bosnia, they would have no incentive to accept a final settlement requiring territorial concessions on their part.

Thus, the United States, its allies, and U.N. authorities were willing neither to press for a truce nor to let the Bosnian government obtain the arms it needed for a fair fight. They wanted no part in condoning aggression, but they permitted it by embargoing arms for the Muslims. Of course, this gave the Serbs the strongest of all possible negotiating hands: they could hold out for a settlement codifying their conquests, knowing that if the conflict continued their military advantage would be preserved by the arms embargo and by the absence of Western intervention.

U.S. policy on Bosnia by late 1992 was driven not by a resolve to defeat aggression but by a desire to bring humanitarian relief to aggression's victims. The U.S. intelligence community and U.N. relief authorities estimated that over 100,000 Bosnians would perish in the winter of 1992–93 unless deliveries of food, fuel, and shelter materials were expanded. While in-country convoy escort duties were left to others, the United States played a major role in the "wholesale" end of the relief effort, which included staging operations through Zagreb and even through Belgrade. The Sarajevo airlift and the airdrops to remote Muslim enclaves would not have been possible without U.S. initiative, aircraft, and expertise. While the prewinter estimates of Bosnians "at risk" proved to be high, there is little doubt that the international relief effort saved tens of thousands of innocent lives. What it did not do, of course, was stop the ethnic cleansing and the atrocities that were generating refugees faster than the international community could feed and shelter them.

As the American presidential election approached, hawkish sentiments on Capitol Hill—whipped up by hauntingly familiar footage of detention camp inmates—was sidetracked into a farcical debate over a marginally useful Bosnian "no-fly" zone. The British at first argued that the Serbs' violations of the military flight ban they agreed to at the London Conference had little practical significance and should be tolerated, lest enforcement endanger U.N. blue helmets and humanitarian relief operations. Predictably, the Serbs were quick to exploit this anxiety, threatening dire consequences for U.N. personnel and operations if the flight ban (to which they had agreed) was enforced. Eventually, the United States convinced its allies to go along with enforcement of the ban, pointing out that the very credibility and effectiveness of the U.N. Security Council would be demolished if threats against U.N. personnel deterred the Council from implementing its own decisions.

South Balkan Dangers

In the last months of the Bush administration, American domestic politics did not have a major effect on U.S. policy in Bosnia. Domestic politics did, however, have a decidedly perverse effect on American policy toward Macedonia, the ethnically mixed, quasi-democratic, unstable southern republic that had seceded from Yugoslavia only when it was clear that the Serbs would completely dominate the successor state. Having shown restraint and conducted a popular referendum on independence, Macedonia had at least as much right to international recognition as Slovenia, Croatia, and Bosnia. But neighboring Greece voiced the specious objection that Macedonia wanted to seize Greek territory and that even using the name "Macedonia" was threatening, because it applied historically to northern Greece. Although most Greek officials and politicians knew that tiny, poor, weak Macedonia posed no threat to Greece, a member of NATO and the European Community, they could not summon the political courage to resist frenzied popular sentiment against Macedonia.

Similarly, while Western governments all thought the Greek position was without merit, none could defy it. Greece threatened to veto any European Community move to recognize Macedonia. It also handcuffed the Bush administration, which was put on notice by the powerful Greek-American lobby that it would work against the president's reelection if the United States recognized Macedonia. The leverage and determination of this lobby are all the more evident in the fact that neither Bush after losing to Clinton nor Clinton after defeating Bush was prepared to recognize Macedonia, even though international law and the strong U.S. interest in containing the Balkan war argued for such a step. Fortunately, restraint on the part of both the Macedonian leadership and the country's large Albanian minority prevented a repetition there of the violence that wracked Bosnia. But Macedonia remained a crisis-in-waiting.

Greek policy in general toward the former Yugoslavia was problematic for the West, whether under the moderate Constantine Mitsotakis before 1993 or the mercurial Andreas Papandreou subsequently. Greece exhibited a tilt toward coreligionist Serbia. It consistently violated the trade embargo. And Greece generally was suspected of seeking a chance to divide and share Macedonia with the Serbs. While the strategic importance of Greece to the West has declined with the disappearance of the Soviet Mediterranean presence, its ability to exert leverage by blocking Western consensus remained unabated. No Greek politician appreciated that more than Papandreou.

The chief American strategic concern during the Bush administration and later under Clinton was to keep the Yugoslav conflict from spreading southward, where its flames could leap into the Atlantic alliance. Therefore, while the Bush administration was not convinced of the need to intervene in Bosnia, it took a markedly different attitude toward Kosovo. Washington feared that a Serbian assault against the Albanian

Kosovars would consume the entire southern Balkan region in a conflagration that would pit one NATO ally against another. Hostilities in
Kosovo would probably spill into Albania proper. This in turn could incite the large Albanian minority in Macedonia and lead to Serbian or
Greek intervention there. Bulgaria and Turkey would then feel pressure
to act in order to prevent Greek control of Macedonia. Whereas the
Bosnian war could be contained, conflict in Kosovo most likely could
not.

Concerned that Belgrade might think that the example of U.S. restraint in Bosnia would apply as well in Kosovo, Bush sent Milosevic a
terse warning on Christmas Day 1992: Serbia itself would face attack if
the Serbs used force in Kosovo. Washington was so certain that this
threat was necessary that it made it despite misgivings among its U.N.
Security Council partners. The warning worked: indications of a Serbian offensive against the Kosovars faded. Of course, the subliminal
message, embedded in the very fact that such an explicit threat was necessary, was that Bosnia, unlike Kosovo, was fair game for the Serbs. As
its last act in the Yugoslav conflict, the Bush administration found it necessary to assert through this focus on Kosovo and Macedonia that its
failure to stop aggression in Bosnia should not be misinterpreted.

Clinton Temporizes

The Clinton administration's "lift and strike" initiative of February 1993
accentuated transatlantic discord, highlighted defects in the Vance-
Owen plan that could not be remedied, demonstrated the inability of
the United States to lead, raised the hopes of the Bosnian Muslims that
the West would intervene after all, and committed the United States to
join in the enforcement of a dubious peace agreement. It also signaled
to the Serbs that a large NATO force would be inserted in Bosnia not if
the fighting continued, but only if it stopped! Not surprisingly, the new
administration hastily retreated into the same public posture that its
predecessor had employed when stymied, portraying the Bosnian conflict, inaccurately, as a hopelessly complicated civil war in which all parties were at fault and in which no American interests were at stake.

While the chief beneficiaries of the failure of the new American policy were the Serbs, the collapse of "lift and strike" also gratified the west
European allies, whose unspoken aim it was to deprive the Bosnian
Muslims of any reasonable hope of rescue so that they would accept defeat and agree to a settlement. The efforts of U.S. officials, in turn, to pin
the blame for the failure of their initiative on America's closest allies
suggest that they wrongly believed that this transparent tactic might
somehow reduce the damage to American prestige and interests.

In trying to fulfill his campaign promise to stand up to the Serbs, the new president strayed from two of his predecessor's basic rules: do not make the United States responsible for a problem it cannot solve and make no threat that the United States cannot execute. (It must be said that George Bush's more cautious stewardship of the nation's credibility in the Yugoslav conflict—keeping his distance as his "new world order" perished in Bosnia—was hardly a success.) Now the United States was on the hook both to join in the quest for a peace agreement that would unavoidably codify Serbian conquests and to send American ground troops to enforce it.

There U.S. policy rested, uneasily, until February 1994, when a Serbian mortar shell hit Sarajevo's marketplace on market day—an obscene act, but no worse than other atrocities committed routinely in Bosnia. Public reaction to the gruesome television footage prompted Washington to insist on a NATO ultimatum threatening air strikes if the Serbs failed to pull their heavy weapons out of range of Sarajevo. When the threat worked, American advocates of air strikes proclaimed that they had been right all along to refute the view that hitting the Serbs would simply get their backs up and endanger U.N. peacekeepers on the ground. But within a few weeks, defiant Serbs were shelling the "safe" city of Gorazde, firing on NATO aircraft, and detaining U.N. peacekeepers, thus casting doubt on the theory that if NATO even bared its teeth, the Serbs would turn tail.

It took the NATO bombing campaign of August–September 1995 to demonstrate what was required to produce more than pallid results in Bosnia. Clearly, force impressed the Serbs more than other forms of coercion, such as economic sanctions. But doses of force too small to alter military outcomes did not lead them to alter their behavior strategically. The belief of some in 1992–94 that once hurt, the Serbs would become reasonable overlooked the fact that the Serbs had been given to understand that the selective use of force was not a prelude to, but rather a substitute for, significant intervention. Indeed, the failure until 1995 of the United States and its allies to use air power in a truly punishing way, combined with the advertised fears of U.N. authorities that force would endanger relief personnel and operations, created a classic situation of "escalation dominance" favoring the (objectively weaker) Serbs.

The Promise of Bombing

The dramatic results of the NATO bombing campaign of August–September 1995 begs the question as to whether robust air strikes earlier might have altered fundamentally the course of the Bosnian conflict. Several good opportunities were missed in 1993–94 to test the physical and psychological effects of bombing. Had the United States and its allies chosen not to give the Serbs the benefit of the doubt when the latter failed to comply completely with NATO demands to pull back from the safe haven of Gorazde, they might have attacked Serbian forces on a scale large enough to change the military situation on the ground, if not the strategic calculus of the Serbs. But until August 1995 the allies did not choose this path. So eager were they to avoid escalation that they settled for partial and temporary results, thus reinforcing the Serbs' belief that they would see no worse than "patty-cake" bombing. Thus U.S. air power, as constrained by the allies and the United Nations, was having precisely the opposite of its intended effect.

Serious, unhesitating air strikes like those of August–September 1995—the earlier the better—might have deterred the Serbs from attacking other Muslim safe havens. They might even have caused Milosevic to intensify pressure on the Bosnian Serbs to negotiate more flexibly in order to reach an overall political statement. But by 1994 nothing less than strategic bombing—heavy, wide-ranging, relentless, and targeted on infrastructure, including that within Serbia proper—would have caused the Serbs to give back most of the land they had already taken from the Muslims. Only massive use of air power could have undone the results of two years of Serbian aggression and Western inaction.

Ironically, the time when limited air strikes *might* have caused the Serbs to stop their aggression coincided with the incumbency of an American administration that took a dim view of military action short of the use of "decisive force." In view of its well-earned credibility, the Bush administration might have caused the Serbs to rethink their entire strategy if it had confronted them early on with even limited use of U.S. military power; but the risk of having to escalate to large-scale intervention was deemed too high. In contrast, President Clinton decided to conduct selective air strikes after it was too late for such limited means to change fundamentally the results of successful Serbian aggression. But in attempting to demonstrate the will to use force, the Clinton administration demonstrated instead how sharply limited any use of force would be, which is why the Serbs merely licked their wounds and went on with their basic strategy after Gorazde and other instances of selective use of Western air power.

Thus, the cumulative effect of four years of failed policies was that the West found itself working toward the same outcome as Milosevic himself: carve up Bosnia and stop the fighting. The NATO allies, particularly the Europeans, were willing to partition Bosnia and relax economic sanctions in order to end the violence. Flawed Western policy from 1992 to mid-1995 virtually guaranteed that continued war would not rectify the situation in Bosnia nor lay the groundwork for a decent peace agreement. U.N. peacekeepers in fact became the hostages that London and Paris feared, largely because these governments openly admitted to having such fears.

What Went Wrong?

While the violent breakup of Yugoslavia may have been unavoidable, irrespective of Western policy, it took bad policy—on top of bad policy—to bring us to such a tragic juncture.

Stronger and more consistent American leadership might have made a difference. When the United States did exhibit leadership, the results were usually positive, if limited or transitory. For example, economic sanctions were imposed on Serbia in 1992 and subsequently strengthened as a result of U.S. initiative and insistence. The inspiration for and implementation of the humanitarian relief effort came largely from the United States, as did enforcement of the flight ban, protection of safe havens, and stationing of monitors to contain the conflict. The occasional presence of U.S. leadership has been enough to demonstrate what might have been possible if it had been steady and strong.

Why was such leadership not forthcoming from the seasoned, interventionist, Atlanticist, Bush administration—from the same people who built the coalition and sent the force that crushed Iraq? This was not a case of a breakdown in the ability of the U.S. government to read and act on the warning signs, for no such breakdown occurred. Rather, George Bush and his lieutenants studied the facts and concluded that such leadership in this particular crisis would have major drawbacks for the United States. So soon after the Gulf War, it would mean that the United States was assuming the role of international policeman, that it would take responsibility even in an area of more immediate importance to America's rich European partners. With its military preponderance, this would have established that the United States was prepared to confront aggression even where it had no vital interests. That the United States under Bush did not seize the lead, rally the West, and take strong action to stop the Serbs in Croatia in 1991 or Bosnia in 1992 is proof (for those who need it) that the liberation of Kuwait was not about international law and order but about oil.

Of course, unlike the Iraqi invasion of Kuwait, the breakup of Yugoslavia was a problem with no good, feasible solutions. Only massive Western intervention would have been sure to stop and reverse Serbian aggression. The larger the military task, the greater the American role, the greater the American burden and casualties, and the greater the need for resolute public support. Desert Storm had taught the American people, wrongly, that vital interests could be defended with a handful of casualties in a video-game war. Whatever popular backing for the use of force in Yugoslavia there might have been at the outset would have quickly evaporated, even though a commitment lasting years could be needed. Lacking solutions, the Bush administration had no incentive to wrest leadership from the willing if not eager Europeans.

The contrast between the American reaction to Iraq's invasion of Kuwait and its reaction a short time later to Serbian aggression in Bosnia illuminates an acute dilemma of post–Cold War American foreign policy. The end of the bipolar world has placed new and heavy burdens on the United States. Its military capabilities are unrivaled, and its ideals have triumphed. This combination of physical and moral weight together imply responsibilities and prerogatives resembling a Pax Americana. While no serious American leader—least of all the prudent Bush—advocated such a role, neither was it explicitly rejected. Indeed, international expectations of the United States were at a peak just as war erupted in Yugoslavia. The new order, it seemed, required a guardian—an obvious role for the only world power, whose own values (not coincidentally) matched those of the order to be guarded.

At the same time, the end of bipolarity and the collapse of communism unlocked instabilities globally. Old sores were reopened and old scores began to be settled, typically along tribal lines, making violence especially hard to prevent and harder still to stop once started. A dozen such disputes, mainly around the periphery of the former communist bloc, revealed a powerful source of insecurity and conflict in the post-Soviet world. Neither America's military might nor its moral weight provides the means to prevent, stop, or resolve such problems. The same political revolution that left the United States supreme also presented America with international problems too daunting and numerous to solve. Faced with seemingly open-ended responsibilities to keep order and right wrongs globally, the American people and their government are drawn to a much easier—intellectually and physically—line of defense: the United States should use force only when its vital interests are at stake.

Clearly, and correctly, American leaders did not see "vital" national interests imperiled by the Yugoslav conflicts. And while the Bush administration did admit to a moral responsibility to aid the innocent victims of this war, this rationale did not stir the American public to a willingness to risk American casualties. What U.S. leaders did not see—or if they did, they failed to translate their view into public support and purposeful policies—was that the Yugoslav crisis, especially the conflict in Bosnia, was setting the worst possible precedents for the new era. They did not appreciate the importance of defeating this case of malignant nationalism before it metastasized elsewhere in the former communist world.

To be clear, neither the Bush nor Clinton administration could or should have intervened militarily in defiance of a national consensus opposing such a course. The unwavering, bipartisan refusal of elected American leaders to send U.S. troops to fight in Bosnia suggests that responsibility for Yugoslav policy failure is not only presidential but national. But to recognize this is not to accept the excuse made by those same leaders that the attitudes of the American people made good policy impossible. The American people surely would have supported reasonable and helpful steps—inclusion of an American contingent in UNPROFOR, for instance—if they had been given a clear and consistent explanation of the Bosnian war and its effects on American interests.

Instead, the U.S. government under two administrations tuned its public explanations depending on its immediate predicament. When wanting to marshal public support for tough action, Washington spoke of the need to combat naked Serbian aggression, to stop atrocities, to exercise American leadership. When wanting to justify inaction—worse, to cover tracks when backing away from tough threats—U.S. spokesmen described Bosnia as a civil war with fault on all sides, a problem too complicated to understand let alone solve from the outside, and in any case a problem for Europe to solve. As a consequence, the American public was never sure which of these contradictory explanations to credit and was therefore left too ambivalent to support strong and steady policy. Confused, the American public accepted the inaccurate image of a civil war instead of the reality that a largely innocent people were overrun by the murderous soldiers of a fascist regime. The truth about Bosnia requires an admission of failure, which is painful for American leaders to offer and for the American people to accept.

Entangled with American failure is west European failure. Had the Europeans confronted the problem when Washington alerted them to the dangers of the Yugoslav crisis, had they acted more cohesively and been more willing to sacrifice, the United States could have joined them in a strategy of applying concerted Western pressure on the Slovenes, Croats, and Serbs to find a new formula for Yugoslavia peacefully. Under both the Bush and Clinton administrations, the United States was prepared to do more than was done, including the early use of massive air power. But it was not prepared to act alone or over the objections of its allies. Although many British, French, Dutch, Spanish, and other European men and women served courageously in the Yugoslav conflict, Europe itself was a failure. Each of the most powerful members of the EC had its own agenda. This not only helped ensure that the EC would fail to act but reminds us why Europeans still need American involvement in managing their continent's security.

Finally, shortsighted, wrong-minded, and even craven as Western policy has been, we should not forget that it was Yugoslavs who destroyed their multiethnic state and started the ensuing war, and who have fought it in a most heinous fashion. Slovenes seceded unilaterally without regard for what they knew would be tragic consequences for others; Croats gave ethnic Serbs every reason to fear for their safety; Milosevic injected into Serbs the venom of ethnic hatred that had been absent in modern Yugoslavia. The abundance of Balkan villains does not excuse Western failures, yet it does help explain why it has been and remains so difficult to find solutions to the conflict in the former Yugoslavia.

Notes

1. Far from considering a massive economic infusion to save Yugoslavia by supporting its legitimate federal government, the United States, via the Nickles amendment of November 1990, cut off the tiny ($5 million) extant aid program to Yugoslavia over repression of ethnic Albanians in Kosovo. Just the opposite of what Markovic wanted, this action demonstrated the difficulty of isolating and paralyzing Serbian policies while sparing, if not nourishing, the moderate federal government.

2. One of the most interesting what-ifs is whether the Bush administration would have challenged Milosevic, and meant it, had the United States not been preparing for a major war in the Gulf during the critical second half of 1991. The author knows of no explicit U.S. decision to eschew engagement in Yugoslavia due to the Gulf crisis. That said, since policymakers knew that a threat against the Serbs might lead to a second simultaneous major U.S. military engagement, one can conclude that the crisis in the Gulf must have inhibited U.S. policy as Yugoslavia moved toward breakup and war.

3. For example, see *The Economist*, May 11, pp. 45–46, and June 29, 1991, pp. 41–42.

4. This concern about the rights of members of minority groups applied to Albanians, Hungarians, and Muslims in Serbia as well as Serbs in Croatia. Ironically, there was little concern—and little cause for concern—about the rights of Serb and Croat minorities in Bosnia, which was a model of ethnic tolerance. Another facet of the difficulty of finding formulas for addressing the minorities problem in Yugoslavia is that Europe and the United States, while equally committed to human rights, have a basic difference in philosophy and law, the former believing that minority groups have rights and the latter recognizing only individual rights.

5. By mid-1991 the officer corps of the once-multiethnic YPA had become almost entirely Serbian.

6. See *The Economist*, July 6, 1991, pp. 45–46.

7. Ironically, the one European leader with the will to stand up to the Serbs, Margaret Thatcher, was removed from her position by her own party—with no tears shed by her continental counterparts—because of her opposition to European integration and to any EC requirement to have common European policies.

8. Though NATO did not have in mind the possible use of its new "rapid reaction corps" in Yugoslavia, the YPA was not so sure. The Yugoslav defense minister, General Veljko Kadejevic, told the author after the Rome summit that he suspected the alliance of preparing an intervention force.

Chapter 6

U.S. and European Attitudes toward Intervention in the Former Yugoslavia: *Mourir pour la Bosnie?*

RICHARD SOBEL

THE DILEMMAS confronting both the United States and Europe over the question of intervention in the former Yugoslavia are enmeshed in how democratic governments respond to the political opinions of their citizenry on the conduct of foreign policy. This analysis looks at the attitudes toward intervention in Bosnia of both the American public and several European publics. It contrasts relatively strong citizen preferences, particularly for multilateral action, with relatively weak governmental policies even about employing allied forces. It considers the implications of comparatively supportive attitudes for the continuation of outside involvement. Finally, it suggests why the discrepancy between relatively supportive publics and reluctant governments has persisted since the fighting began in the spring of 1992.

While the results of U.S. public opinion surveys about possible intervention began to appear in mid-1992, the results of surveys of west European public opinion began to be published only at the end of that year. The American data derive largely from national polls conducted by the news media (by the ABC, CBS, and NBC networks, for example) and major pollsters (such as the Gallup and Harris organizations). The data for Britain, France, Germany, and Italy derive from both national polls and the cross-national Eurobarometer series.[1] Because of the number of survey organizations involved and because the wording of questions varies from poll to poll, it is difficult to identify trends over time or to make direct comparisons across nations.[2] But in general, the responses reveal strikingly similar attitudes in favor of allied intervention on the part of Americans and Europeans alike and distinct contrasts between public opinion and governmental responses in both the United States and Europe. Among the European publics, in particular, there has been consistent plurality to majority support for intervention in Bosnia, in sharp contrast to the disinclination of national governments or international organizations to take forceful action until summer 1995.

American Attitudes toward Intervention in Bosnia

While the vast majority of Americans have paid attention to the events in Bosnia (Harris, 8/13/93: 84 percent; 6/8/95: 85 percent), until the summer of 1995 only about a third to a half have followed the situation closely (see table 6.1). Very few Americans considered the war in Bosnia to be the most important issue—foreign or domestic—the United States faces (Harris, 1/22/93–5/23/94: 1 percent, except 4/25/93: 4 percent), though a somewhat greater proportion considered it the most important U.S. foreign policy issue (Harris, 4/4/94: 11 percent; PSR, 6/8/95: 18 percent). The large proportions of respondents, especially early on, who did not know how to evaluate the president's handling of the Bosnian situation also suggests that Americans were not very knowledgeable about or focused on the problem (table 6.2). The vast majority of Americans viewed military action as largely a European or a multilateral responsibility (table 6.3), not an American one (table 6.4).

The proportion of Americans who think the United States has a responsibility to act militarily in Bosnia increased substantially into mid-1994, but has since declined (table 6.4). If there were no other way to "get humanitarian aid to civilians" and prevent the "practicing [of] atrocities," 58 percent said that the United States had an "obligation to use military force" (27 percent agreed strongly; *Los Angeles Times*, 1/14/93).[3] But only a plurality of 37 percent believed the main reason the United States should take military action was that it had "a moral responsibility to stop ethnic cleansing" (Gallup, 1/28/93). Although the "post-Vietnam syndrome" is still apparent in the desire expressed by most Americans to stay out of such foreign involvements as the Reagan-era interventions in Central America, 49 percent of Americans thought intervention in Bosnia would be comparable to that which brought swift victory in the Gulf War, whereas 43 percent thought it would end in slow defeat, as in Vietnam (Gallup, 4/6/93).[4]

American attitudes about intervention in Bosnia can be gauged roughly by looking at both general questions concerning the president's handling of the Bosnia crisis (table 6.2) and at specific questions concerning the use of U.S. air and ground forces for humanitarian or military purposes (tables 6.5–6.7). Since August 1992, when George Bush was in office, most polls have shown a plurality, majority, or relatively even split in approval of the president's handling of the Bosnia situation (table 6.2). During times of inaction or vacillation, the public has tended to disapprove more than approve (for example, Gallup, 7/15/94: 31–48 percent).[5] When the president has threatened or participated in direct allied action in Bosnia, a larger proportion of Americans typically approved than disapproved of his handling of the situation: for example, the public approved when President Clinton discussed possible U.S. intervention in spring 1993 (Gallup, 5/6/93: 48–35 percent) and when he issued the ultimatum after the Sarajevo market massacre in early 1994 (ABC, 2/23/94: 48–39 percent).

There have been distinct differences in attitudes among Americans, however, depending on the type of proposed intervention in Bosnia (see table 6.12). Support has been strongest for sending U.N. peacekeepers (Harris, 7/7/92, 80 percent), airdrops of humanitarian relief (Gallup, 2/26/93: 67 percent), air cover for U.N. peacekeeping troops (CBS, 8/2/93: 61 percent), and shooting down Serbian planes violating the October 1992 no-fly zone (Harris, 4/28/93: 61 percent). Support for lifting the September 1991 arms embargo (CBS, 6/21/94: 57 percent), bombing by the North Atlantic Treaty Organization (NATO) to protect safe havens (CBS, 4/16/94: 54 percent), and joint U.S.-U.N. peacekeeping after a settlement (CBS, 6/21/93: 54 percent) has at times ranged above 50 percent. A majority of Americans thinks that any military intervention in Bosnia should be a coordinated effort with west European allies through the United Nations or NATO (Harris, 1/22/93: 62 percent; 4/28/93: 52 percent). In contrast, there has been little enthusiasm for having the United States go it alone. For instance, approval for unilateral American air strikes has ranged from only a fifth to a quarter in the polls (table 6.9).

Although support for allied air strikes against Serbian military forces in Bosnia was initially low (Gallup, 4/22/93: 30 percent), approval rates grew over time (table 6.5). During the summer of 1993, a majority approved of retaliatory strikes in response either to Serbian attacks (Yankelovich, 8/4/93: 54 percent) or to threats against U.N. peacekeepers (ABC, 8/6/93: 85 percent) and to protect humanitarian shipments (Yankelovich, 8/4/93: 69 percent). Ironically, there was at that time less sentiment for strikes to protect the Bosnian Muslims in Sarajevo (Yankelovich, 8/4/93: 50 percent) or to force the Bosnian Serbs out of territory occupied during the war (Yankelovich, 8/4/93: 40 percent). Thus, Americans were more willing to use air power to protect U.N. soldiers providing aid than to save Bosnian civilians or punish the Serbian military. Since then, most Americans became willing to use U.S. air power when either U.N. troops (CBS, 8/2/93: 61 percent) or Bosnians in safe havens (CBS, 4/21/94: 54 percent) were attacked.

Moreover, besides the high approval rates for U.S. planes joining in NATO bombing, there has generally been plurality to majority support for U.N. humanitarian or peacekeeping efforts (table 6.10) even if they were to involve some U.S. ground troops (table 6.8). But only a minority of Americans support the use of U.S. ground troops for combat against the Serbs (table 6.7), although somewhat more approve of the use of allied forces for this purpose (table 6.10). Again, there has typically been more support for protecting U.N. soldiers than Bosnian civilians (compare tables 6.7 and 6.8). In short, for efforts such as airdrops of humanitarian aid for which the justification is compelling or for air strikes where the risk to U.S. soldiers is low and expectations of success relatively high, support has been fairly strong (table 6.12). When the risks to American soldiers increase, approval drops. There has, however, been some public support even for committing U.S. ground forces in allied efforts under appropriate circumstances (table 6.8).

In sum, between 1992 and 1995, there has generally been majority support for U.S. assistance in providing humanitarian aid and protecting peacekeepers (tables 6.6 and 6.8). Most Americans also were willing to use U.S. air power to protect U.N. troops and Bosnians in safe havens. Support grew for active U.S. involvement (table 6.7) and specifically for the use of U.S. combat troops (Gallup, 12/12/92–4/16/94: 26 to 41 percent), though it has still been in the minority (Yankelovich, 6/2/95: 40 percent; except PIPA, 4/5/94: 56 percent overall approval, 31 percent strong approval). There has been somewhat more support for allied military actions in which the United States might participate (tables 6.9 and 6.10), and considerable approval of U.S. soldiers protecting U.N. forces (table 6.8). Yet as the risks grow, support generally drops (see table 6.12).

The fact that a key issue for Americans is whether any intervention is to be unilateral or multilateral is instructive. Only one in four Americans (27 percent) wanted the United States to undertake air strikes alone; this contrasts sharply with the 60 percent who approved allied strikes (compare ABC, 8/6/93 in table 6.9). Yet Americans have been ambivalent about turning U.S. forces over to U.N. or NATO commanders. While most Americans (51 percent) thought the United Nations was doing a good job in general (Harris, 4/28/93) and favored U.N. (39 percent) over NATO (25 percent) command (PIPA, 4/5/94), in September 1993, a month before the Somalia disaster, over two thirds of Americans preferred that American forces remain under U.S. (69 percent) as opposed to U.N. command (25 percent; PSR, 9/3/93). Evidently, Americans think that U.S. soldiers are less at risk when they are commanded by U.S. officers. The reluctance of the United Nations to call in NATO air strikes on Serbian targets in both fall 1994 and spring 1995, moreover, provided the basis for Americans' suspicions of the military effectiveness of the United Nations.

Public opinion is volatile on issues that are not perceived to be of primary importance to U.S. security, as has typically been the case for Bosnia. American attitudes toward Bosnia and the issue of intervention have not crystallized until late, too, because Americans have been buffeted by events and changes in U.S. policy. Contradictory pronouncements from the White House, inconsistent U.N. policies, and the multiple peace proposals, threats, and cease-fires have all contributed to the inconsistency of American public opinion. Because leadership by high U.S. officials, particularly the president, is a central factor in catalyzing American public opinion, when the administration took a clear position against Serbian aggression in May and August 1993, in February 1994, and in August 1995, the public moved in the direction of supporting military action.[6] For instance, during the spring of 1993, when the Clinton administration began talking about possible American intervention, support for military action rose from 23 to 40 percent (table 6.9).[7] Interestingly, in late summer 1993, nearly a majority of Americans thought that Clinton had not been tough enough on the Serbs (Harris, 8/13/93: 47 percent). At the same time, a plurality (44 percent) supported U.S. military intervention, and another 13 percent would have supported earlier action (Yankelovich, 8/4/93).

During the summer of 1993, when the Serbs began attacking U.N. peacekeepers in Sarajevo, and the Clinton administration again threatened air strikes, support for U.S. air attacks to protect U.N. troops grew to 61 percent (CBS, 8/2/93). The American-backed NATO ultimatum on air strikes after the February 1994 Sarajevo market killings not only produced a breakthrough with the Serbian pullback, it also contributed to higher support among Americans for military action (up to 80 percent for air strikes: PIPA, 2/9/94).[8] In short, when the United States or NATO has provided forceful leadership that countered Serb maneuvers to gain dominant military positions, the American public has also responded favorably. In fact, even though when asked in advance only half (48 percent) supported air strikes, two thirds (65 percent) of Americans said they would support air strikes if the president and Congress ordered them (Gallup, 2/7/94). When U.S. and U.N. leadership waffled in response to Serb advances around Bihac in late 1994 and to the renewed attacks on the safe havens in the spring of 1995, support for a U.S. response weakened. Interestingly, approval for lifting the arms embargo was below a majority (PIPA, PSR, ABC, Yankelovich, 4–7/95: 36

to 43 percent) in 1995, around the time the Senate voted to lift the embargo, when it reached 61 percent (table 6.11).

Remarkably, however, there was also high approval during the crises of mid-1995 for possibly sending U.S. troops to protect (61 percent), relocate (66 percent), or rescue (78 percent) U.N. peacekeepers (PSR, 6/1/95). A series of polls conducted in June 1995 (Gallup, NBC, PSR, Yankelovich) all shows similar results. Forty percent of Americans even supported sending U.S. troops to join in NATO efforts "to punish Serb aggression" (Yankelovich, 6/3/95). A plurality (37 percent) would support sending U.S. troops to help the United Nations enforce an agreed-upon cease-fire, even if this meant a hundred American casualties (PIPA, 4/19/95). This challenged the idea given currency by the media and partisan rhetoric that there was absolutely no public support for sending U.S. forces into Bosnia.[9]

Because approval for U.S. intervention in Bosnia was often near to majority levels and responsive to presidential leadership, had the United States became more directly involved militarily, the public would likely have rallied around the president, at least initially.[10] Should direct U.S. intervention have been quick and successful, support would have remained strong. But if costs and casualties rose, leadership weakened, intervention dragged on, and a way out became elusive, support would have dropped and opposition would have increased in both public opinion and the now more partisan Congress.[11] While more would be at stake if U.S. soldiers were in combat, similar dynamics should apply to sending U.S. forces for peacekeeping. At the time of the peace agreement at the end of 1995, however, public support reached a bare majority only for the most general question of sending peacekeepers (Gallup, 9/22/95: 52 percent). Approval stayed in the minority when the public faced the realities of deploying 20,000 Americans to Bosnia (table 6.6).

Support dropped substantially, however, when the American public was confronted with the possibility of U.S. soldiers' actually dying for Bosnia: two thirds (67 percent) would support a U.S. deployment if no American soldiers were killed; only a third (31 percent) continued to approve if a hundred died (Gallup, 9/19/95). Yet there is evidence that perceived success of the action to some extent compensates for the potential sacrifice of lives. A majority felt that if the peacekeeping operation were successful, the United States would have done "the right thing in contributing troops," even if 50 American soldiers were killed (PIPA, 11/22/95: 60 percent). Unfortunately only a quarter (27 percent) of the public thought the NATO force would be "successful in establishing a long-term" peace (Yankelovich, 12/6/95). Yet potential support lay in substantial majorities of Americans who thought that both the realistic concerns for keeping the war from spreading (63 percent) and the humanitarian desire to stop more killing (64 percent) justified the sending of U.S. forces (CBS, 12/9/95).

An awareness of the dynamics of potentially declining public support—a legacy of Vietnam—underlies the demand of those who, with Senator Sam Nunn, have called for an exit strategy before U.S. troops were committed.[12] In the face of both relatively supportive public attitudes, for instance, for air strikes and continuing evidence of Serbian misdeeds, the reluctance of the Clinton administration and the Republican congressional majority to act suggests that the American leadership has been more mired in the post-Vietnam syndrome than the public.[13] While the U.S. administration's willingness to commit troops to withdraw U.N. peacekeepers but not to protect Bosnian Muslims did reflect, to a degree, the public's greater concern for protecting soldiers rather than saving civilians, it also provides a confusing message to the American people.[14] The actual deployment of U.S. peacekeepers after a settlement provided a focus for raising public support.[15] After the settlement but before most of the soldiers reached Bosnia, approval of the deployment rose slightly (for example, CBS, 11/27/95: 33 percent; 12/9/95: 40 percent). However, it did not reach a majority. In short, the American public retained an open, but skeptical, mind about the wisdom of sending American forces to maintain the peace agreement.

European Attitudes toward Intervention in Bosnia

European governments generally have had a stronger base of support for potential action among a citizenry cognizant of the perils of appeasement and willing to undertake even unilateral action to counter Serbian aggression. Since at least late 1992, the publics of France, Britain, Italy, and usually Germany have supported intervention in Bosnia. But the reluctance of European governments and the United Nations to engage directly in military action other than peacekeeping has kept that involvement minimal and restricted direct action against the Bosnian Serbs. Only after the Serb attacks on British and French U.N. peacekeeping forces in August 1993 did the governments of Britain and France become willing to respond forcefully. The deadly mortar shelling of the Sarajevo market in February 1994, which led to NATO air strikes against Serbian positions around Sarajevo and Gorazde, changed the willingness of leaders to intervene. But the vacillating allied and U.N. response to Serbian attacks on Bihac at the end of 1994, and on Srebrenica and Zepa in mid-1995, as well as Britain's and France's threats to pull out the beleaguered peacekeepers did nothing to deter further Serbian aggression. It was the Croatian offensive in late 1995 and robust allied air strikes that pushed the Serbs into a weaker position and, ultimately, a willingness, at least in Belgrade, to agree to a peace settlement.

For the most part, European publics have been more willing than their governments to act against Serbian misconduct. A large plurality (47 percent) across western Europe has held very negative images of the Serbs (Eurobarometer, May 1993), and a majority supported the use of force against them (ORM, 1/27/93). European publics, like the American public, also prefer multilateral action and leadership. Majorities in each European country thought "the United Nations should authorize a multinational force to intervene militarily in the former Yugoslavia" (ORM, 1/18/93). While Americans have tended to look to Europe or the United Nations for leadership (CBS, 11/29/94: 73 percent), Europeans have tended to look to the United States or the United Nations. According to a European poll conducted in early 1993, "a plurality of those who express[ed] an opinion [said] the United States should take the lead" in U.N.-authorized military action (ORM, 1/27/93). Yet European citizens also have been more supportive of direct intervention than Americans in general or European leaders.

In particular, there has been strong support among the citizens of western Europe for the use of force (tables 6.13 and 6.14). In late 1992 and early 1993, pluralities to majorities in France, Britain, Italy, and western Germany supported the authorization of multilateral U.N. intervention in the crisis (Q6: 44 to 70 percent).[16] Large majorities supported humanitarian intervention, particularly by a multilateral force (table 6.13, Q9a: 64 to 92 percent). But majorities supported even unilateral humanitarian intervention by their own governments (table 6.14, Q10a: 64 to 79 percent). And one third to two thirds thought their countries were too little involved in Yugoslavia (Q5). Majorities supported multilateral intervention to enforce a cease-fire (table 6.13, Q9b: 51 to 87 percent), and the French, British, and Italian publics supported cease-fire enforcement by their own troops alone (table 6.14, Q10b: 63 to 77 percent), though initially only a minority of west Germans concurred (42 to 52 percent). Similar majorities supported using force to separate the warring parties multilaterally (table 6.13, Q9c: 52 to 78 percent) or unilaterally (table 6.14, Q10c: 53 to 60 percent; except western Germany, 40 percent).

There has been substantial support for imposing a military solution on Bosnia multilaterally (table 6.13, Q9d: 52 to 79 percent; declining in Germany). Moreover, near majorities in Britain and France have supported imposing a military solution unilaterally (table 6.14, Q10d: 48 to 56 percent); however, only a minority in western Germany (40 percent) has favored imposing a unilateral solution. Overall, "roughly half of the

French (54 percent), British (47 percent), and west German (45 percent) publics supported the use of multinational forces for *all* [proposed] actions," from protecting aid shipments to imposing a solution (ORM, 1/27/93, emphasis in original). French public support for intervention has been widespread but not particularly strong (ORM, 1/6/93).

At the end of 1993, support remained high for intervention even by individual countries. In November 1993, a majority of citizens in each of the four nations surveyed approved of NATO's enforcing a cease-fire (68 to 77 percent) and a majority in each approved of their own troops' participating (52 to 77 percent), with strong support exceeding slight support in Britain (46 percent versus 31 percent) and western Germany (31 percent versus 21 percent). Majorities in Britain, France, and Italy also approved sending NATO troops to help establish peace (59 to 64 percent), while only a minority in Germany approved of doing so (44 percent in western Germany, 28 percent in eastern Germany).[17]

British public support for intervention in Bosnia actually grew over time. From June 1993 to February 1994, approval of British troops' providing humanitarian aid grew from 67 to 74 percent (table 6.15), though it dropped to 62 percent in June 1995. From April 1993 to February 1994, support for sending British troops as a part of an international contingent force to enforce a peace settlement grew from 67 to 75 percent (table 6.15), dropping to 62 percent in June 1995. Nearly half (47 percent) of those surveyed thought that Britain should help to impose a peace settlement if an agreement were not reached (*Gallup Index*, 2/94).[18]

In fact, support for joint European military intervention to establish peace grew from 1993 into 1994 in all four nations (table 6.16; 60 to 65 percent in Britain, 59 to 75 percent in France, 64 to 65 percent in Italy, and 43 to 57 percent in Germany). There has remained majority opposition to withdrawing troops (table 6.17b: 52 to 72 percent) and majority support for fighting to assure that aid convoys get through (table 6.17f: 58 to 90 percent). Majorities in Britain, France, and western Germany have supported air strikes (51 to 57 percent), but only minorities in Italy and eastern Germany (34 to 49 percent) have done so. However, opposition to lifting the arms embargo against the Bosnian Muslims has ranged from 44 to 67 percent; it remained a plurality in Britain in July 1995 (MORI, 7/24/95: 46–37 percent). In early 1994, a majority of Italians favored the participation of Italian troops (DOXA, 2/9/94: 57 percent). In mid-1995, 53 percent of Italians favored allied military intervention (CIRM, 7/17/95), but a plurality opposed direct Italian involvement (47 percent).

In sum, majorities of the French, British, Italian, and western German publics generally have supported the use of multinational forces for actions ranging from protecting aid shipments to imposing a solution on the parties to the conflict. However, German support, especially in the east, has been consistently lower than British or French support. The surprisingly strong approval of European publics for the use of force contrasts sharply with the reluctance of their governments to intervene forcefully. Serbian attacks on allied soldiers in 1993 and on civilians in the Sarajevo marketplace in early 1994 temporarily catalyzed European leaders to respond as their publics were willing to have them do. Despite a French call to arms, the reluctance of the United Nations to act when Bihac was attacked reflected the unwillingness of European governments to put their peacekeeping troops at risk. Yet European publics have largely been opposed to removing their peacekeepers, despite governmental threats to do so. With France's call for action after the safe havens fell in summer 1995, however, Europe moved more aggressively into action. European publics remained supportive of military pressures for a settlement and the redeployment of more forceful peacekeeping.[19]

What These Findings Reveal

When U.S. Secretary of State Warren Christopher visited European capitals in February 1993 to try to gather support for a unified response to Serbian aggression, his arguments fell unheeded, as did the pleas of Bosnian President Alija Izetbegovic since late 1993 for intervention on the side of the Muslims. The governments in question appeared to be unresponsive to either moral imperatives or public attitudes. With the concentrated allied response to the Sarajevo market massacres of 1994 and 1995, however, the complexion of the problem began to change. The strength of interventionist attitudes among European publics, combined with the perceived success of the ultimatum given the Bosnian Serbs, made it easier for the European governments to undertake stronger policies. This appears to have been the case particularly for France, whose early 1994 call for sending NATO troops came with the strong support of the French public. And the French government's switch in late 1994 from threatening to remove its peacekeepers in the face of Serb attacks and U.N. inaction around Bihac to urging again stronger action was bolstered by the continuing desire of the French public to take action in the Bosnia crisis. The weak response of the major European governments, then, reflected unwilling leadership more than public opposition.

In fact, both the American and the European publics had been generally supportive of outside intervention in the Bosnian conflict for over two years. Although the American public has not supported the deployment of U.S. troops on a unilateral basis, preferring indirect involvement through participation in air strikes, Americans generally have approved intervention, with U.S. troops as part of a U.N.- or NATO-led force. Europeans have preferred U.N.- or U.S.-led intervention but also have been fairly supportive even of their own militaries' acting alone. These findings contrast with the impression held by most governments and the media that the American and European publics are unwilling to interfere in the Bosnia conflict. This misperception may explain to some degree the inaction of the American and European governments, which in turn accounts for the indecisiveness of the United Nations.

The overall European and, to a lesser extent, the American publics' preferences for both multilateral action and leadership have continued across the crisis: they appear, in particular, in the support for the deployment of U.N. forces and for NATO air strikes. While most Americans thought that the United Nations was generally doing a good job, they questioned the extent to which the United Nations or NATO is an effective vehicle for multilateral action. And although Americans have been willing for U.S. fliers to carry out NATO air strikes, they have been leery of risking U.S. casualties, especially under U.N. command. There is little sentiment among the European publics or governments for lifting the arms embargo against the former Yugoslavia, despite the stated preference of the U.S. administration to end it, curtailment of U.S. enforcement, and a congressional vote in favor of its lifting. Disagreements between the United Nations and NATO in late 1994 and early 1995 over how to deal with the Serb attack on Bihac and Srebrenica also weakened the allied response, but European publics typically continued to support an ongoing peacekeeping presence. The generally approving opinions in Europe and, less clearly, the United States have provided a basis for undertaking the greater political and military risks of more active intervention and peacekeeping.

Why have the U.S. and European governments typically been unwilling to act militarily? Obviously they have wished to avoid taking risks in a complex and dangerous conflict. Early on, European leaders expressed a concern that intervention would put their peacekeeping troops in harm's way, and they avoided escalation until the peacekeepers were attacked; yet their lack of response to the Serb advances near Bihac, Sarajevo, and Srebrenica, in fact, contributed to the Serbs' taking of U.N. forces as hostages. Americans too have feared that U.S. ground troops would be captured or killed, yet have supported the use of American forces to protect or remove U.N. peacekeepers. Generally unpopular European and American leaders, with their focus on domestic problems, may have felt that the risk of doing nothing was less than the risk of intervening.

Moreover, as other chapters in this volume emphasize, European leaders initially thought, and the Bush administration hoped, that this was "Europe's hour," that the Bosnian problems could be handled by European diplomacy alone. The weaker and less direct linkages between constituent opinion and policymaking action in European parliamentary systems may have led politicians to disregard public attitudes.[20] Despite the public support for intervention indicated in the polls, no government has been close to falling for failure to solve the Bosnia crisis. It is surprising, however, that some opposition politicians have not become more vocal advocates of intervention. By recognizing interventionist attitudes among the public and the failure of current officeholders to respond to their desire, challengers might have cultivated electoral favor through more aggressive rhetoric. The demands of Republicans since the 1994 U.S. elections for stronger action may have resonated with at least part of the American public. And the readiness of the new French president, Jacques Chirac, to send troops to Bosnia and his near demands for allied air and ground action in mid-1995 likewise may be an example of entrepreneurship in the political marketplace of the French public's willingness to take aggressive action. The vote of confidence won by the British prime minister, John Major, in June 1995 also may have provided a stronger basis for British action in Bosnia and for reversing British public dissatisfaction with the handling of the Bosnian situation.

There also has been a problem with collective action among the American and European governments: each government apparently has hoped to be a "free rider" on someone else's willingness to take up the leadership burden, either unilaterally or multilaterally. The relative preference for multilateral action among leaders parallels the publics' preference that other countries act. The American public's support for multilateral action, despite some reluctance to put U.S. forces under U.N. or NATO command, also suggests a preference that others take responsibility. With no government having a special incentive to get involved, and all clearly having disincentives to take risks, European and American leaders long delayed confronting the crisis head-on. The inability of either the United Nations or NATO to act in the face of the Bihac crisis, in particular, reflected the limits of relying on someone else's leadership in order to act in concert. Even the French calls to action were premised on allied involvement. Without allied leadership, Bosnians continued to perish.

European and American leaders also may have looked at the crisis in realpolitik terms, viewing it as self-limiting, believing that a Serbian victory was inevitable. Continental leaders hoped to contain the crisis without direct action. The Sarajevo market bombing and the Muslim-Croat military resurgence in mid-1994, together with Russian and Belgrade Serbian criticism of Bosnian Serbs' intransigence, temporarily changed the perceptions of European leaders as well as the balance of military and diplomatic forces. With publics, particularly in Europe, more aroused and the apparent success of the Muslim-Croat forces in rolling back Serb advances, government policy may have begun to reflect the more interventionist elements of the American and European publics. The Bosnian Serbs' ability to call the bluff of the United Nations on protecting Bihac or Srebrenica, on the other hand, reflected the governmental preference for inaction. While the allies finally agreed on punitive air strikes after another market massacre and the fall of two safe havens, only the Croat offensive rolled back Serb gains. It also destroyed the myth of Serb invincibility.

The Croat advance followed by NATO's bombing campaign proved successful in reversing Serbian gains. With the American and European publics aroused—and military responses in the offing—the balance of forces began to turn against the Bosnian Serbs. Earlier the restricted nature of NATO retaliations and the refusal of the United Nations to lift the arms embargo limited the effectiveness of military action. The late 1994 decisions to renew diplomacy and to keep the U.N. peacekeeping mission alive stabilized the situation through the spring 1995 cease-fire. Yet at its conclusion both sides moved aggressively back into the war, with the Serbs capturing the two safe havens. Unlike earlier uses or threats of force, which led to Serbian retreat, the minimal air strikes after renewed Serb advances around Bihac and Srebrenica in 1995 encouraged further Serbian offensives. The aggressive French rhetoric, the U.S. Senate vote to lift the embargo, the Croatian recapture of lost territory, and the proven allied resolve on air strikes changed the complexion of the situation considerably. This combination lead, first, to a cease-fire, then, to a political settlement, and, finally, to a deployment of 60,000 NATO peacekeepers, including some 20,000 Americans.

The swift Persian Gulf victory and some dissipation of the post-Vietnam syndrome may have led some in the American and European publics to see less risk of another stalemate in Bosnia. Continental citizens, who are closer to the current problems and to experiences of the disastrous consequences of appeasement, have seemed more willing to act than their not very popular leaders. Growing public pressures in response to continuing Serbian misconduct moved European and American leaders to embrace more assertive actions.

During much of the Bosnian war, then, there has been unrecognized support among allied publics for more aggressive multilateral action in Bosnia. The American and European publics have been surprisingly sensible about the need for cooperative action, yet officials have decried much and decreed little. In short, the missing element has been decisive leadership. Whether allied policies and peacekeeping will lead to regional stability is still unclear. But it will, in large measure, depend on how strongly American and European publics support the continuing pursuit of peace and on how carefully their leaders pay attention.

Notes

1. A list of polls consulted, and their abbreviations in the text, are listed below. The U.S. polls are based on representative national samples of about 1,000 respondents. The European polls commissioned by the European Community (EC) or the United States Information Agency (USIA) are representative samples of about 900 to 1,000 (see Standard Eurobarometer Technical Specifications, A3, and ORM, 12/17/93, appendix B.). The Eurobarometer data were supplied by the Central Archives for Empirical and Social Research at the University of Cologne. The USIA data were taken from Opinion Research Memoranda (ORM) and tables. Most of the U.S. polls used here were identified or checked by the Public Opinion Location Library (POLL) of the Roper Center at the University of Connecticut. The tables cited in the text appear in appendix 1, beginning on page 162. Tables 6.1, 6.3, and 6.4 include question wordings. Question wordings for tables 6.2, 6.13, and 6.14 appear in appendix 2, pages 180–81. Because tables 6.5 to 6.12 include items with different, related wordings, topics are provided in titles and headings, but individual wordings do not appear. Those wordings may be checked through POLL.

    Polls Consulted:

    ABC/*Washington Post* Poll (ABC/WP)

    CBS/*New York Times* Poll (CBS/NYT)

    CIRM (Italy)

    DOXA (Italy)

    The Eurobarometer (EC)

    The Gallup Poll (Gallup)

    The Harris Poll (Harris)

    Los Angeles Times Poll (LAT)

    Market and Opinion Research, Incorporated (MORI, Britain)

    NBC/*Wall Street Journal* Poll (NBC/WSJ)

    Opinion Research Memoranda (ORM)

    Politbarometer (EC)

    Princeton Survey Research (PSR)

    Program in International Policy Attitudes (PIPA)

    Yankelovich Partners Surveys (Yan)

2. On the difficulties in following public attitudes about foreign policy and suggested alternatives for improving the polling, see Richard Sobel, "Polling in Foreign Policy Crises: Creating a Standard Set of Questions," *The Public Perspective*, vol. 7, no. 2, (February 1996) pp 13–16.

3. Steven Kull and Clay Ramsay, "U.S. Public Attitudes on U.S. Involvement in Bosnia" (Program on International Policy Attitudes, University of Maryland, College Park, MD, May 4, 1994.)

4. Richard Sobel, "Public Opinion about United States Intervention in El Salvador and Nicaragua," *Public Opinion Quarterly*, vol. 53, (Spring 1989), pp. 114–28.

5. Percentages connected by a dash show first the percentage who approve, and second the percentage who disapprove. In this example, 31 percent approve and 48 percent disapprove. Percentages connected by the word to and preceded by a range of dates (e.g., 4–7/95, 36 to 40 percent) indicate that several polls from different organizations during the specified period found the given range of support. (For example, in April through July 1995, 36 to 40 percent were in support.)

6. Richard Brody, *Assessing the President: The Media, Elite Opinion, and Public Support* (Stanford, CA: Stanford University Press, 1991); and Catherine M. Kelleher, "Security in the New Order: President, Polls and the Use of Force," in Daniel Yankelovich and I. M. Destler, eds., *Beyond the Beltway: Engaging the Public in U.S. Foreign Policy* (New York: Norton, 1994).

7. Richard Morin, "Not Quite Ready Yet for Action in Bosnia: But Support for U.S. Intervention Is Growing," *Washington Post National Weekly*, May 10–16, 1993, p. 37.

8. In part, because the introductions to the questions provide significant background and the respondents tend toward those with more education, the Program in International Policy Attitudes (PIPA) polls (1993, 1994) typically find higher support for U.S. intervention than do other surveys. See Kull and Ramsay, "U.S. Public Attitudes." Moreover, some of the PIPA questions distinguish intensity of support, which usually skews to the more aggressive options. Because most polls besides PIPA and the *Los Angeles Times* do not ask how strongly attitudes are held, it is difficult to gauge intensity of opinion, though consistently higher overall proportions suggest greater intensity. See also the March 1993 surveys conducted by Market Strategies and Greenberg Research, headed by the president's pollster, for information likely to have reached the White House. For example, they found a two-thirds preference for the United States and United Nations to "use military intervention and overwhelming force to defeat the primary aggressors" (3/23/93: 66 percent). Americans Talk Issues, *Global Uncertainties*, no. 21 (Washington, DC: ATI Foundation, 1993).

9. The media have consistently underreported evidence of U.S. public support for intervention in Bosnia. In February 1994, ABC's *Nightline* broadcast a graphic showing 18 percent support for U.S. air strikes, without re-

vealing that 57 percent approved of strikes with allies (see ABC, 2/7/94). Although a June 4, 1995, *Newsweek* press release did note "a surprisingly large reservoir of public support for U.S. ground troops to aid United Nations forces in Bosnia," the text of a related *Newsweek* article (Russel Watsons, "A No-Win War," June 12, 1995, p. 20), located adjacent to a table showing from 61 percent to 78 percent approval for U.S. assistance to U.N. forces, said only that "Bosnia is an unpopular cause; in the latest *Newsweek* Poll, 55 percent of Americans surveyed said Bosnia was not their problem." A *Washington Post National Weekly* column reported a "big [downward] change" in support for U.S. military action from late April, but had not similarly reported the April support when it occurred. (See Richard Morin, "Toning Down The Tough Talk on Bosnia," *Washington Post National Weekly*, June 12–18, 1995, p. 37.) Perhaps the assumption that there is no support for U.S. troop involvement or the mistaking of partisan leadership reaction against deploying U.S. troops for more generally supportive public attitudes has, as in Gresham's law, driven out the search for an accurate presentation of all the evidence. See also Richard Sobel, "What People Really Say about Bosnia," *New York Times*, November 22, 1995, p. A23.

10. John Mueller, *War, Presidents and Public Opinion* (New York: Wiley, 1973); and Brody, *Assessing the President.*

11. See Richard Sobel, "Staying Power in Mideast," *Dallas Morning News*, October 10, 1990, p. A19. Also see Steven Kull, "Answers on Bosnia: A Study of U.S. Public Attitudes" (PIPA, University of Maryland, May 16, 1995).

12. Elaine Sciolino, "Nunn Says He Wants Exit Strategy if U.S. Troops Are Sent to Bosnia," *New York Times*, September 2, 1993, p. 25.

13. Times-Mirror Center for the People and the Press, *America's Place in the World* (Washington, D.C.: Times-Mirror Co., 1993); and John Rielly, ed., *American Public Opinion and U.S. Foreign Policy* (Chicago: Chicago Council on Foreign Relations, 1995).

14. Morin, "Toning Down Tough Talk on Bosnia," p. 35.

15. Sobel, "What People Really Say about Bosnia," p. A23; Richard Morin, "How Do People Really Feel about Bosnia?" *Washington Post National Weekly*, December 4–10, p. 34.

16. Early 1993 data cover western Germany alone; later data include the entire country.

17. In late 1994, when Serbs set up antiaircraft guns around Bihac, the majority of the German public (54 percent) opposed the sending of Tornado aircraft with the capacity to evade Serbian defenses (*Die Woche*, no. 50, December 9, 1994). At the same time, 75 percent of Germans thought the international community should not remove its troops (*Stern*, no. 50, December 8, 1994). By January 1995, a majority (56 percent) supported using the Tornados to protect aid shipments to Bosnia. Between January and

June 1995, support for U.N. "reinforce[ment] of military intervention" grew from 47 percent to 51 percent, but it dropped to 43 percent in July. However, support for employing German soldiers increased from 39 percent to 51 percent between January and July (Politbarometer, 1/95, 6/95, 7/95). By October, 55 percent felt German participation in NATO military action was "right" (Politbarometer, 9/95).

18. In late July 1995, 65 percent of the British public were dissatisfied with the British government's handling of the Bosnian situation, while 52 percent supported upgrading the involvement of British troops in Bosnia from peacekeeping to direct participation (MORI, 7/21/95).

19. Craig R. Whitney, "Europe Has Few Doubts on Bosnia Force," *New York Times*, December 5, 1992, p. 9.

20. On the role of domestic institutions and coalition-building in the relationship between public opinion and foreign policy, especially in Europe, see Thomas Risse-Kappen, "Public Opinion, Domestic Structures, and Foreign Policy in Liberal Democracies," *World Politics*, vol. 43, no. 4 (July 1991) pp. 479–512.

Appendix 1*
U.S. Attitudes toward Intervention in Bosnia

Table 6.1. How Closely Following Bosnian News (in percentages)

Tell me if you happened to follow this news story very closely, fairly closely, not too closely, or not at all closely. . . . the civil war in Bosnia

	9/10 92	1/3 93	2/20	4/29	7/29	9/9	9/24	9/30 93
Very closely	10	15	15	23	19	17	15	13
Fairly closely	27	33	32	34	37	38	32	29
Not too closely	31	30	33	28	25	26	32	35
Not at all closely	31	22	20	13	18	19	20	23
Don't know	1	0	0	2	1	0	1	0
N	1,508	1,216	1,516	1,009	1,203	2,000	1,529	1,200

	10/21 93	12/2 93	1/6 94	1/27	5/12	6/23	9/9	10/6	12/1 94
Very closely	16	15	15	12	18	12	9	13	13
Fairly closely	36	32	38	31	37	28	29	35	37
Not too closely	30	31	30	32	26	37	39	29	32
Not at all closely	17	21	17	25	18	22	23	22	18
Don't know	1	1	0	0	1	1	0	1	0
N	1,200	1,479	1,494	1,207	1,206	1,021	1,500	1,513	1,511

	2/9 95	3/22	6/1	6/2[a]	6/4[b]	6/5[c]	6/8 95
Very closely	8	11	18	22	14	14	22
Fairly closely	33	27	35	53	45	41	42
Not too closely	32	36	29	19	38	28	22
Not at all closely	26	25	17	6	7	17	18
Don't know	1	1	1	0	0	0	1
N	1,209	1,819	751	1,008	1,256	1,005	1,500

	7/23[b] 95	8/17	9/28	11/27[b]	12/9[b] 95
Very closely	12	16	15	14	21
Fairly closely	35	36	40	51	52
Not too closely	42	26	25	31	25
Not at all closely	10	21	19	4	1
Don't know	1	1	1	0	1
N	1,014	1,476	1,519	504	1,111

* See appendix 2 for selected question wordings.
SOURCE: This information is taken from the Princeton Survey Research, unless indicated otherwise.
[a] NBC.
[b] CBS.
[c] Gallup.

Table 6.2. Presidential Handling of Bosnia/Serbia/Yugoslavia Situation* (in percentage)

	8/6 92 Gal	8/11 CBS	8/13 92 Gal	2/10 93 ABC	4/22 PSR	4/22 Gal	4/28 Har	4/29 PSR	5/4 CBS	5/6 Gal	5/20 ABC	5/26 93 PSR
Approve	38	32	43	46	44	43	38	39	35	48	51	39
Disapprove	38	28	33	23	37	38	57	30	35	35	36	40
Don't know	24	40	24	23	19	19	5	31	30	17	13	21
N	930	1,434	946	1,004	750	1,000	1,252	750	834	603	1,005	750

	5/27 93 CBS	6/21 CBS	8/2 CBS	8/6 ABC	8/13 Har	10/21 93 PSR	2/7 94 ABC	2/15 CBS	2/23 ABC	3/3 Yan	3/4 NBC	4/4 94 Har
Approve	38	36	32	48	31	36	41	35	48	45	53	39
Disapprove	35	24	38	39	61	43	46	35	39	36	33	55
Don't know	27	40	30	13	8	21	13	30	13	19	14	5
N	1,184	1,363	870	1,216	1,260	1,200	521	1,193	1,531	600	1,503	1,255

(continued on next page)

Table 6.2 Presidential Handling of Bosnia/Serbia/Yugoslavia Situation* (in percentage) *(continued)*

	2/24 94 ABC	4/15 ABC	4/21 Yan	4/30 NBC	5/4 Yan	6/15 Yan	6/23 ABC	7/15 Gal	8/4 Yan	12/10 94 NBC	6/1 95 PSR	6/2 95 NBC
Approve	48	46	35	54	35	34	40	31	34	41	33	41
Disapprove	34	43	47	41	49	47	47	48	46	43	35	43
Don't know	12	11	18	5	10	19	13	21	20	16	32	16
N	1,531	513	600	1,002	800	800	1,531	100	600	1,000	751	1,008

	6/4 95 CBS	6/5 Gal	6/8 PSR	6/21 Yan	7/14 ABC	9/28 Har	10/18 Yank	11/10 ABC	11/29 ABC	12/1 ABC	12/1 ABC	12/6 Yan	12/9 95 CBS
Approve	33	51	39	36	37	50	38	44	40	42	41	43	42
Disapprove	47	47	46	46	56	42	37	39	50	47	48	43	47
Don't Know	20	3	15	19	7	9	25	17	10	11	11	14	11
N	1,256	1,005	1,500	1,000	1,548	1,005	1,046	1,005	523	612	2,007	1,000	1,111

* See appendix 2 for question wording.

Table 6.3. Before Taking any Military Action in What Used to Be Yugoslavia, Should the United States Insist That Other European Countries Help, or Should That Not Be a Factor? (in percentage)

	8/11/92	1/12/93	5/4/93
Insist other European countries help	81	82	77
Not be a factor	12	13	16
Don't know/No answer	7	5	7
N	1,434	1,179	834

SOURCE: CBS News/*New York Times* polls.

Table 6.4. Do You Think the United States [United Nations] Has a Responsibility to Do Something about the Fighting between Serbs and Bosnians in What Used to Be Yugoslavia, or Doesn't the United States Have This Responsibility? (in percentage)

	1/12/93	5/4	6/21	12/5/93	2/15/94	4/21
U.S. has a responsibility	24	37	37	26	36	41
U.S. has no responsibility	67	52	51	65	53	49
Don't know/No answer	9	11	12	9	11	10
N	1,179	834	1,363	1,289	1,193	1,215

	11/27	12/6	6/4/95	6/8	7/23	10/22	12/9/95*
U.S. has a responsibility	30	28	24	30	29	28	37
U.S. has no responsibility	62	65	69	64	62	65	56
Don't know/No answer	8	7	7	6	9	7	7
N	1,120	1,147	1,256	1,500	1,014	1,269	1,111

	11/27/94	6/4/95
U.N. has a responsibility	73	58
U.N. has no responsibility	20	35
Don't know/No answer	7	7
N	1,120	1,256

* The question was slightly different, asking about a responsibility "to enforce the peace agreement in Bosnia."
SOURCE: CBS News/*New York Times* polls, except for 6/8/95, which was taken from the Princeton Survey Research.

Table 6.5. (U.S.) Air Strikes against Bosnian Serbs (in percentage)

	U.N. 7/31 92 Gal	U.N. 8/6 Gal	8/6 Gal	8/13 92 Gal	1/14 93 LAT	4/22 PSR	4/22 93 Gal
Approve	35	53	50	49	49	39	30
Disapprove	45	33	37	39	34	49	62
Don't know	20	14	13	12	17	12	8
N	1,001	930*	930*	946	1,733	750	1,000

	Hum. 8/2 93 CBS	PK 8/2 CBS	PK 8/4 Yan	Prot. 8/4 Yan	Hum. 8/4 Yan	8/4 Yan	All. 8/6 93 ABC
Approve	45	61	54	50	69	40	60
Disapprove	43	28	35	38	24	45	34
Don't know	12	11	10	12	7	15	6
N	870	870	1,600	1,600	1,600	1,600	1,216

	All. 2/7 94 Gal	2/7 ABC	NATO 2/9 PIPA	NATO 2/10 Yan	NATO 4/16 LAT	PK 4/16 Gal	NATO 4/21 CBS	All. 4/21 94 Yan
Approve	48	17	80	50	46	65	54	35
Disapprove	43	79	16	38	38	28	32	58
Don't know	9	3	4	12	16	8	14	7
N	635	521	700	500	1,682	1,002	1,215	600

Key: All. = with allies; Hum. = protect humanitarian aid; NATO = with NATO; PK = peacekeepers attacked; Prot. = protect civilians or safe havens; U.N. = with United Nations. *Registered voters.

(continued on next page)

Table 6.5 *(continued)*

4/28 93 Yan	All. 4/28 Har	4/29 PSR	5/4 CBS	5/5 PIPA	All. 5/6 ABC	5/6 Gal	U.N./PK 6/21 93 CBS
36	44	40	38	53	65	36	61
52	48	45	51	31	32	55	29
12	7	15	12	16	3	9	10
1,000	1,252	750	834	810	516	603	1,363

PK 8/6 93 ABC	8/6 ABC	NATO 8/8 Gal	Prot. 8/13 Har	PK 9/10 NBC	Prot. 10/18 CBS	12/4 93 LAT	1/15 94 NBC
85	27	51	38	58	26	33	35
13	70	40	50	33	60	48	56
2	3	9	12	5	14	19	9
1,216	1,216	1,003	1,260	1,006	893	1,612	1,009

NATO 4/30 94 NBC	All. 12/7 Yan	All. 12/7 94 Yan	6/1 95 PSR	All. 6/2 NBC	U.N. 6/4 CBS	All. 7/19 Yan	NATO 7/23 CBS	All. 7/29 NBC	NATO 9/5 95 CBS
64	31	27	37	56	71	35	59	61	59
26	62	64	49	33	24	54	30	27	25
10	7	9	14	11	5	11	11	12	16
1,002	800	800	751	1,008	1,256	1,000	1,014	1,005	1,069

Table 6.6. U.S. Troops (Humanitarian/Peacekeeping) (in percentage)

	Humanitarian					
	8/11 92 CBS	8/12 LAT	12/3 Gal	12/4 92 Gal	1/12 93 CBS	1/14 93 PSR
Approve	41	54	42	57	67	55
Disapprove	45	33	45	36	26	41
Don't know	14	13	13	7	7	5
N	1,434	1,460	602	1,005	1,179	750

	Peacekeeping						
	2/10 93 Yan	3/5 NBC	5/4 CBS	5/5 PIPA	5/6 Gal	5/27 CBS	6/21 CBS	9/10 93 NBC
Approve	58	41	48	76	68	44	54	36
Disapprove	32	51	45	12	30	49	38	59
Don't know	10	8	9	11	2	7	8	5
N	1,000	1,503	834	810	603	1,184	1,363	1,006

	Peacekeeping						
	12/10 94 NBC	4/19 95 PIPA	6/1 PSR	9/22 Gal	10/18 Yank	10/18 PSR	10/19 Gal	10/22 95 CBS
Approve	57	52	61	52	42	27	49	39
Disapprove	36	44	32	43	50	59	44	58
Don't know	7	5	7	5	8	14	6	9
N	1,000	1,204	751	1,011	1,046	750	1,229	1,069

	Peacekeeping				
	12/1 95 ABC	12/6 Yank	12/6 Yank	12/9 CBS	12/15 95 Gal
Approve	40	36	38	40	41
Disapprove	56	57	55	55	54
Don't know	5	7	7	5	5
N	612	1,000	1,000	1,111	1,000

(continued on next page)

Table 6.6 (*continued*)

Humanitarian

1/28 93 PSR	4/9 PSR	4/22 93 PSR	5/4 94 PIPA
57	37	40	66
35	46	51	33
8	17	9	2
754	750	750	700

Peacekeeping

9/23 93 Yan	10/6 NBC	10/8 Gall	12/4 93 LAT	2/9 94 PIPA	3/4 NBC	4/21 Yan	5/5 94 PIPA
57	23	40	46	72	53	39	73
36	67	52	47	25	40	56	25
7	10	8	7	3	7	5	26
800	806	1,019	1,612	700	1,503	600	700

Peacekeeping

10/27 95 NBC	11/6 Gal	11/10 ABC	11/22 PIPA	11/27 Gal	11/27 CBS	11/29 ABC	11/30 95 Har
30	47	38	50	46	33	38	29
65	49	58	47	40	58	58	67
5	4	4	4	14	9	3	4
1,465	931	1,005	722	632	504	523	1,004

Table 6.7. U.S. Troops (Active involvement/Peacemaking) (in percentage)

	7/5 92 NBC	7/17 Har	8/10 NBC	8/19 Yan	12/12 92 NBC	1/3 93 PSR	1/14 LAT	1/23 NBC	4/17 NBC	4/22 PSR	4/29 PSR	5/4 CBS	5/6 93 ABC	1/6 94 Gal	2/7 ABC	2/7 94 Gal
Approve	27	30	33	24	26	32	37	34	35	40	27	31	40	28	13	35
Disapprove	65	65	54	66	62	51	47	54	52	51	60	60	58	68	85	7
Don't know	8	5	18	14	12	17	16	12	13	9	13	9	2	4	2	8
N	1,105	1,256	818	1,250	1,004	1,216	1,733	1,009	1,004	750	750	834	516	1,023	521	635

	2/7 94 ABC	2/10 Yan	4/16 Gal	11/27 CBS	12/7 94 Yan	6/2 95 Yan	6/4 CBS	6/8 PSR	6/8 Har	6/8 Har	6/9 LAT	7/14 ABC	7/19 Yan	7/19 Yan	12/6 Yan	12/15 95 Gal
Approve	47	40	41	34	17	40	21	32	36	35	41	40	28	40	36	41
Disapprove	50	50	53	58	78	51	73	61	57	59	50	58	64	48	57	54
Don't know	3	10	6	8	5	9	6	7	7	16	9	3	8	12	7	5
N	521	500	1,002	1,120	800	600	1,256	1,500	1,004	1,104	1,109	1,548	1,000	1,000	1,000	1,000

Table 6.8. U.S. Troops Help U.N. Peacekeepers (in percentage)

	Evac. 12/10 94 NBC	Reloc. 6/1 95 PSR	Rescue 6/1 PSR	Reloc. 6/2 Yan	Rescue 6/2 Yan	W/dr. 6/2 Yan	Reloc. 6/2 NBC	Rescue 6/4 CBS	Protect 6/4 CBS	Reloc. 6/5 95 Gal
Approve	57	66	78	65	62	59	45	57	43	70
Disapprove	36	26	18	31	33	34	46	37	52	28
Don't know	7	8	4	4	5	7	9	6	5	3
N	1,000	751	751	600	600	600	1,008	1,256	1,256	1,005

	W/dr. 6/5 95 Gal	Attacked 6/8 PSR	Reloc. 6/8 PSR	Strng. 6/8 Har	W/dr. 6/8 Har	Evac. 6/9 LAT	W/dr. 7/14 ABC	W/dr. 7/19 Yan	Protect 7/23 95 CBS
Approve	64	71	65	39	68	71	84	53	31
Disapprove	31	22	29	56	27	21	15	41	61
Don't know	5	7	6	6	5	8	1	6	8
N	1,005	1,500	1,500	1,004	1,004	1,109	1,548	1,000	1,014

Key: Evac. = evacuate U.N. troops; Reloc. = Relocate U.N. troops; W/dr. = withdraw U.N. troops; Strng. = strengthen.

Table 6.9 U.S. Military Activity (in percentage)

	Military Action						Air Strikes						Ground troops	
	Alone	Alone	Alone		Alone	Allies	Alone	Allies	Alone	Allies	Alone	Allies	Alone	Allies
	1/13	1/14	2/25	4/23	5/20	5/20	5/6	5/6	8/6	8/6	2/7	2/7	2/7	2/7
	93			93	93		93			93	94		94	94
	ABC	ABC	ABC	ABC	ABC	ABC	ABC	ABC	ABC	ABC	ABC	ABC	ABC	ABC
Approve	27	31	23	40	14	45	12	61	27	60	17	57	13	47
Disapprove	51	51	68	54	84	50	86	36	70	34	79	37	85	50
Don't know	23	18	3	6	2	5	1	3	3	6	3	5	2	3
N	513	1,510	1,216	1,507	1,005	1,005	516	516	1,216	1,216	521	521	521	521

Key: Alone = U.S. acting alone; Allies = acting with allies.

Table 6.10 U.N./NATO/Allied Troops (peacekeeping/Military) (in percentage)

Peacekeeping

	PK 7/17 92 Har	Hum. 12/4 92 Gal	U.S. 5/5 93 PIPA	U.S./U.N. 5/5 PIPA	U.S./U.N. 5/6 Gal	U.S. 5/27 CBS	U.S. 6/21 CBS	U.S. 10/8 93 Gal	U.S. 2/9 94 PIPA	U.S. 3/4 NBC	U.S. 4/5 94 PIPA	U.N. 4/19 95 PIPA	U.N. 9/22 Gal.	Int'l 10/18 Yan	NATO 10/22 CBS	Int'l 11/6 Gal.	Int'l 11/10 95 ABC
Approve	80	57	76	67	68	44	54	40	72	53	63	87	52	42	37	47	38
Disapprove	18	36	12	21	30	49	38	52	25	40	34	9	43	50	57	49	58
Don't know	3	7	11	11	2	7	8	8	3	7	3	3	5	8	6	4	4
N	1,256	1,005	810	810	603	1,184	1,363	1,019	700	1,503	700	1,204	1,011	600	1,077	931	1,005

Military

	U.N. 7/17 92 Har	U.N./U.S. 1/13 93 Yan	U.N./U.S. 1/22 Har	U.S. 4/28 Har	U.N./U.S. 5/5 PIPA	U.N. 5/6 93 ABC	U.S./NATO 1/6 94 LAT	U.S./All 2/7 Gal	U.S./NATO 2/10 Yan	U.N./U.S. 4/5 PIPA	U.S./Eur. 4/16 94 Gal	U.N. 4/19 95 PIPA
Approve	50	68	62	52	59	56	28	35	40	56	41	64
Disapprove	44	22	32	42	26	40	68	57	50	39	53	26
Don't know	6	10	6	6	15	4	4	8	10	5	6	10
N	1,256	1,000	1,255	1,252	810	516	1,023	635	500	700	1,002	1,204

Table 6.11. Lift Arms Embargo/Arm Muslims (in percentage)

	5/4 93 CBS	5/5 PIPA	5/6 93 ABC	6/21 94 CBS	4/19 95 PIPA	6/1 PSR	7/14 ABC	7/19 Yan	7/23 95 CBS
Lift	50	58	41	57	40	39	43	36	61
Keep	31	26	54	22	51	46	50	50	24
DK/NA	19	17	5	21	10	15	7	14	15
N	834	810	516	1,215	1,204	751	1,548	1,000	1,014

	Sell 4/21 94 Yan	Sell 12/7 94 Yan	Provide 4/19 95 PIPA	Sell 5/5 Gal	Sell 7/29 95 NBC
Weapons	20	13	40	16	43
No weapons	76	80	54	80	47
DK	4	7	5	4	10
N	600	800	1,204	1,005	1,005

Key: DK = don't know; NA = no answer; Sell = sell arms to Muslims; Provide = provide arms to Muslims.

Table 6.12. Comparison of Options in Bosnia (in percentage)

	U.S. Troops	U.S. Milit. Action	U.S. Respon.	U.S. PK	Air Strikes Protect	U.S./U.N. Troops PK	U.S. Lift Embargo	Protect Relief PK	Air Strikes PK	No Fly PK	Air-drops	U.N. PK
	5/4	4/23	4/21	11/6	4/16	6/21	6/21	6/1	8/2	4/28	2/26	7/7
	93	93	94	95	94	93	94	95	93	93	93	92
	CBS	ABC	CBS	Gal	CBS	CBS	CBS	PSR	CBS	Har	Gal	Har
Approve	31	40	41	47	54	54	57	61	61	61	67	80
Disapprove	60	54	49	49	32	38	22	32	28	31	28	18
DK/No opin.	9	6	10	4	14	8	21	7	11	8	4	3
N	834	1,507	1,215	931	1,215	1,363	1,215	751	870	1,252	1,005	1,256

Key: PK = peacekeepers.

Table 6.13. Use of Multilateral Military Force to . . . (Q9)*

United Kingdom			France				Western Germany			Italy	
	1/ 93	3/ 93		11/ 92	1/ 93	3/ 93		1/ 93	3/ 93		3/ 93
9a) Protect humanitarian aid											
Favor	83	84	Favor	76	84	86	Favor	77	64	Favor	92
Oppose	11	10	Oppose	16	11	10	Oppose	21	27	Oppose	4
DK	5	6	DK	8	4	4	DK	3	9	DK	4
9b) Enforce ceasefire											
Favor	69	73	Favor	70	81	85	Favor	60	51	Favor	87
Oppose	24	19	Oppose	21	15	11	Oppose	36	39	Oppose	9
DK	7	8	DK	9	4	5	DK	4	10	DK	5
9c) Separate warring parties											
Favor	67	66	Favor	61	72	70	Favor	56	52	Favor	78
Oppose	24	22	Oppose	27	21	19	Oppose	39	37	Oppose	14
DK	10	12	DK	12	7	12	DK	6	11	DK	9
9d) Impose solution											
Favor	58	58	Favor	52	61	65	Favor	57	52	Favor	79
Oppose	32	32	Oppose	38	34	27	Oppose	39	38	Oppose	13
DK	10	10	DK	10	5	8	DK	4	10	DK	7
9e) Achieve all of above objectives											
Favor	47				54				45		

*See Appendix 2 for question wording.

SOURCE: United States Information Agency, Opinion Research Memoranda (USIA, ORM) for January 6, 1993; January 18, 1993; January 27, 1993; and December 7, 1993, and tables. See ORM for sample sizes (about 900–1,000).

Table 6.14. Use of Military Force to . . . (Own Country) (Q.10)*

United Kingdom		France			Western Germany	
	1/		11/	1/		1/
	93		92	93		93
10a) Protect humanitarian aid						
Favor	79	Favor	71	73	Favor	64
Oppose	18	Oppose	22	33	Oppose	34
DK	3	DK	7	4	DK	3
10b) Enforce cease-fire						
Favor	63	Favor	64	66	Favor	42
Oppose	32	Oppose	27	31	Oppose	56
DK	5	DK	9	4	DK	3
10c) Separate warring parties						
Favor	60	Favor	53	57	Favor	40
Oppose	35	Oppose	27	37	Oppose	57
DK	6	DK	10	6	DK	3
10d) Impose solution						
Favor	56	Favor	48	52	Favor	40
Oppose	38	Oppose	42	43	Oppose	58
DK	6	DK	10	6	DK	3

*See Appendix 2 for question wording.
SOURCE: USIA, ORM for January 6, 1993; January 18, 1993; December 17, 1993, and tables. See ORM for sample sizes (about 900–1,000).

Table 6.15. British Attitudes toward Intervention in Bosnia (in percentage)

B1.1

Do you approve or disapprove of the use of British troops in Bosnia to protect humanitarian aid convoys?

	4/93	6/93	9/93	2/94	6/1/94	6/8/94	10/12/95
Approve	72	67	73	74	62	64	72
Disapprove	20	25	21	21	27	26	20
Don't know	8	7	7	6	11	10	9

B1.2

If the British troops protecting the aid convoys suffered serious casualties, should we pull them out, continue to limit them to fighting back only when they are attacked or take steps to reinforce them?

	4/93	6/93	9/93	2/94	6/1/94	6/8/94	10/12/95
Pull them out	32	39	36	32	38	39	30
Limit	17	17	16	16	16	14	15
Reinforce	43	34	41	43	35	38	43
Don't know	8	10	6	8	11	9	11

B1.3

If an international force were trying to enforce a peace settlement in Bosnia, would you personally like to see British troops forming part of that force or not?

	4/93	6/93	9/93	2/94	6/95
Yes	67	64	68	75	62
No	22	25	21	17	24
Don't know	11	11	10	8	14

SOURCE: *Gallup Political and Economic Index*, Report 402, February 1994; Report 423, November 1995. N = 1,000.

Table 6.16. Should Intervene Militarily to Establish Peace? (in percentage)

	UK		France		Germany		Italy	
	3/4/93	2/25/94	3/93	2/94	3/93	2/94	3/93	2/94
For	60.3	64.8	58.5	75.0	43.5	56.6	64.3	64.6
Oppose	24.2	25.6	24.6	20.2	38.4	40.8	21.4	22.0
Don't know	15.2	9.7	16.9	4.7	13.4	2.6	4.4	13.5
N	1,073	500	1,019	497	2,000	1,576	1,039	505

SOURCE: Eurobarometer 39 (3/4/93); Flash Eurobarometer 24 (2/25/94).

Table 6.17. European Attitudes toward Intervention in Bosnia, 1994

	Britain 2/25/94	Britain 3/25/94	Britain 6/29/94	France 2/25/94	France 3/25/94	France 6/29/94	Germany 2/25/94	Germany 3/25/94	Germany 6/29/94	Italy 2/25/94	Italy 3/25/94	Italy 6/29/94
a) Let things continue												
Favor	11.5	28.4	15.7	8.0	14.5	11.0	20.0	17.1	20.3	6.1	6.5	8.6
Oppose	80.3	65.6	78.3	89.3	79.9	84.6	78.8	77.4	71.8	90.5	89.6	85.5
DK	8.2	6.0	5.0	2.7	5.6	4.4	1.3	5.5	7.9	3.4	3.9	6.0
N	506	507	501	497	502	502	1,576	1,580	1,573	505	510	502
b) Withdraw all troops												
Favor	24.7	26.7	28.3	23.5	26.8	30.7	27.7	25.0	27.1	33.7	32.9	36.5
Oppose	67.1	68.4	65.7	71.9	67.5	62.0	70.5	70.8	65.5	59.0	57.3	52.4
DK	8.1	4.9	5.9	4.6	5.8	7.3	1.7	4.2	7.5	7.3	9.8	11.2
N	506	507	501	497	502	502	1,576	1,580	1,573	505	510	502
e) Lift Bosnia embargo												
Favor	28.2	26.4	25.6	32.1	29.9	35.5	30.1	30.0	33.9	40.8	35.7	37.1
Oppose	55.5	58.9	58.1	57.6	58.7	53.8	67.2	62.9	57.8	44.4	46.5	43.8
DK	16.3	14.7	16.3	10.3	11.4	10.7	2.8	7.2	8.4	14.9	17.8	19.1
N	506	507	501	497	502	502	1,576	1,580	1,573	505	510	502
f) Fight to get convoys through												
Favor	84.4	83.5	77.6	90.2	89.2	85.1	59.4	64.8	57.8	79.8	75.7	67.9
Oppose	11.8	10.3	17.1	7.1	7.0	9.9	39.4	30.1	36.1	11.9	16.9	22.7
DK	3.8	6.3	5.3	2.8	3.9	4.9	1.2	5.0	6.2	8.3	7.5	9.4
N	506	507	501	497	502	502	1,576	1,580	1,573	505	510	502
g) Launch air attacks												
Favor	38.9	55.2	43.0	53.1	58.4	48.3	43.2	49.5	39.8	30.1	37.3	30.7
Oppose	51.7	37.3	47.3	40.6	33.4	45.8	55.5	44.8	50.4	58.4	48.8	55.8
DK	9.4	7.5	9.7	6.4	8.2	5.9	1.4	5.7	9.9	11.5	13.9	14.5
N	506	507	501	497	502	502	1,576	1,580	1,573	505	510	502

SOURCE: Flash Eurobarometers 24: 2/25/94; 25: 3/25/94; 29: 6/29/94. (Options c and d omitted.)

Appendix 2
Selected Question Wording

Table 6.2: Presidential Approval Questions

(ABC/WP) Do you approve or disapprove of the way President Bill Clinton is handling the situation involving the former Yugoslavian Republics of Serbia and Bosnia?

(CBS/NYT) Do you approve or disapprove of the way (President) George Bush/Bill Clinton is [has been] handling the situation in what used to be Yugoslavia [Bosnia]?

(Gallup/PSR; registered voters) Do you approve or disapprove of the way George Bush/Bill Clinton is handling the situation in [the former Yugoslavian Republic of] Bosnia?

(Harris) Overall, how would you rate President Clinton's handling of the situation in Yugoslavia/the war in Bosnia? Excellent, pretty good, only fair, poor?

(NBC/WSJ) In general, do you approve or disapprove of the job (President) Bill Clinton is doing in handling the situation in Bosnia?

(Yankelovich) Do you think President [Bill] Clinton is doing a good job or a poor job . . . of handling the situation in Bosnia?

Tables 6.13 and 6.14: European Opinion Questions

9. Concerning the situation in the former Yugoslavia, are you personally in favor or opposed to the use of military force to . . . (Is that strongly or somewhat?) (10/92, 1/93, 3/93)
   a) Protect the delivery of humanitarian aid in the former Yugoslavia
   b) Enforce a cease-fire
   c) Separate the warring parties
   d) Impose a solution

10. Are you personally in favor or opposed to [own country] using its military forces to . . . (Is that strongly or somewhat?) (10/92, 1/93)
   a) Protect the delivery of humanitarian aid in the former Yugoslavia
   b) Enforce a cease-fire
   c) Separate the warring parties
   d) Impose a solution

21. NATO's role in peacekeeping is being discussed, particularly in Bosnia. If the warring parties come to an agreement there, would you favor NATO sending peacekeeping troops to Bosnia? Or would you oppose NATO taking this role? Is that strongly or somewhat? (10–11/93)

22. And would you favor or oppose [own country] troops participating in NATO sponsored peacekeeping in Bosnia? Is that strongly or somewhat? (10–11/93)

23. What if the warring parties in Bosnia are unable to reach an agreement and the fighting continues, should NATO send forces to help establish peace? Or should NATO not become involved? (10–11/93)

Chapter 7

Dangerous Liaisons: Moscow, the Former Yugoslavia, and the West

PAUL A. GOBLE

Regular contacts between Moscow and Belgrade seem to be enabling Russia to play the role of a mediator between the West and the Serbs as well to show to the opposition at home its international influence. We must admit that "special relations," "historical links," and Moscow's "strong influence" on the Serbian leadership could have been more rewarding. Unfortunately, one can speak now not only about Moscow influencing Belgrade but also about Belgrade and Pale manipulating Moscow's politicians for their own ends. The attitude to Russia is also modified by the historical tradition of rivalry between Russia and Serbia in the Balkans (their being "allies from the start" is a historical-political myth), and the undeniable weakening of the positions of Russia, whose power and influence cannot be compared with those of the Russian Empire or the USSR.
—Kommersant-Daily (Moscow), July 29, 1995

SINCE THE COLLAPSE of the Soviet Union, three factors have defined Russian policy toward the conflicts in the former Yugoslav republics: Moscow's desire to exploit its historic cultural linkages without suffering from the consequences likely to flow if other states draw analogies between the two systems, Moscow's interest in becoming a good international citizen in the post–Cold War environment, and Moscow's need to reproject Russian power both to generate domestic political support and to regenerate Russian influence in Europe and more broadly. Most analyses of Russian involvement in the former Yugoslavia have focused on only one of these three factors and extrapolated sweeping conclusions from it, but Russian policy, in all its twists and turns, reflects the playing out of all three, and only by considering them together can one begin to understand why Moscow has done what it has done and why its actions there and the reasons behind them have such profound consequences for Moscow, the former Yugoslavia, and the post–Cold War international system.

This chapter is divided into three parts: the first examines each of these factors in some detail; the second considers how these various influences have affected the three periods of post-Soviet Russian policy in the former Yugoslavia; and the third points to three lessons of this policy for the West and its efforts to construct a new international system in Europe. Obviously, given the shifts in both Russian and Western policy toward Bosnia and Serbia over the last five years, this discussion must be more like algebra than arithmetic—that is, the specific values of the various elements may change at any time—but an understanding of the algebra here may nonetheless be useful as a guide to both further research and future action.

Three Competing Influences

The first influence on Russian policymaking regarding the former Yugoslavia involves the perceived or asserted cultural and historical linkages between Russia and Serbia, two fraternal Slav peoples—as Russian and Western commentaries almost never fail to point out. But if this influence is the one mentioned most often, it is probably the most overrated and the least understood as a factor in Russian concerns and calculations. That is because the Russian leadership fears the linkage perhaps as much as it welcomes it, first, because Western governments may decide that what happens in one country presages what will happen in the other; and second, because of Russia's need to engage in a new and more open politics in the formation of foreign policy.

Prior to the collapse of Yugoslavia and the Soviet Union, Western scholars routinely pointed to the similarities of these two systems. During the collapse of these two multinational states, Western political leaders routinely warned that developments in one indicated the likely course of development in the other. Soviet and then Russian politicians and commentators shared their concerns. For example, there were oft-repeated suggestions that a disintegrating Soviet Union could form a giant series of "Bosnias" or that what we were seeing was the "Yugoslavization" of the Soviet space. And more recently, Western policy analysts and the Russian press have noted the extent to which political developments in Serbia's neighborhood are reflected in the Russian nationalist movement in Moscow and with the new assertiveness in Russian foreign policy.[1]

In discussing the linkages between Russia and Serbia, Western students point to the following similarities:

1. Both the Soviet Union and Yugoslavia were organized by their communist rulers according to a specific ethnonational policy, one that exploited ethnicity by politicizing, territorializing, and arranging in a hierarchy all ethnic groups—to rule by dividing and conquering the population and, by thus creating or exacerbating social tensions, to generate broader support for authoritarian political arrangements from populations fearful of the consequences of unrestrained ethnic tensions on their own lives. As a result, both countries fragmented along ethnic lines when the costs of authoritarianism could no longer be paid.[2]

2. The two largest successor states—Russia and Serbia—have significant numbers of their titular nationality outside their borders and view the previously established internal borders as fundamentally unjust. The war in Bosnia is, of course, about Serbs outside Serbia, and the fact that 25.4 million ethnic Russians live outside Russia is often cited as a cause for Russian concern—even though fewer than 250,000 of them are actually citizens of the Russian Federation. (In both cases other successor states also have significant numbers of coethnics abroad, but for various reasons—in particular their relative weakness—they have been less able or eager to raise the question of the fate of their coethnics abroad.) Moreover, leaders in both Serbia and Russia see this as an important "bridge" issue, one that links all elements of their populations and helps to generate political support at home during the difficult transitions both states are experiencing.

3. Russia and Serbia both see Islamic groups as threats to their power and even their territorial integrity, an issue that they have discovered has resonance abroad and tends to undercut Western interest in getting involved in any conflicts they provoke. Curiously and significantly, some political actors in both Russia and Serbia see Islam as a force so powerful that it must be co-opted rather than simply opposed. Vladimir V. Zhirinovsky, the extreme nationalist leader of the outrageously misnamed Liberal Democratic Party of Russia, is the classic example; but there are Serbian Zhirinovskys as well. Not surprisingly, this particular twist sometimes gives an unexpected quality to debates within and between Moscow and Belgrade, with presumed allies turning into actual opponents on particular policy issues.

4. Russia and Serbia, having disowned policies of their predecessor states—those of the Soviet government in the former case

and those of the Yugoslav communist regime in the latter—are both seeking to define their places in the world in terms of an earlier and in some instances mythical history. This denial of the past is often described under the rubric "pan-Slavism," but it involves more than that. First, it is an important part of the national redefinition that each of these states must go through. Second, it means that participants often ignore facts—past Russian betrayals of Serbia, for instance—that get in the way of their arguments. And third, it gives the debate an emotional gloss even as leaders on both sides manipulate the historical record.

5. Both of these states are going through a radical transformation in terms of the number of actors involved in the formulation of foreign policy. Prior to the collapse of the Soviet Union and Yugoslavia, foreign policy was exclusively the province of the elite. Now it is being "democratized": not only are more groups involved in the formulation of policy, but the elites must find support for their policies by reaching out to these broader groups. Thus, populist justifications are both demanded and supplied for each particular policy.

6. In both countries, many of the new participants in political life see foreign policy as a means to push domestic agendas. The Russian nationalist agenda has been much commented upon in this regard. A more interesting, if neglected, case is the way in which other, more liberal groups, such as the Armenian community in Moscow, engage in similar behavior.[3]

7. Both Russia and Serbia are interested in becoming part of the West but not at the cost of sacrificing their self-respect. As a result, they see the reassertion of their traditional dominance of their neighbors as a major part of this recovery of national self-confidence.

8. Because of these similarities, each of these countries calculate that whatever one can get away with, the other will be allowed to get away with too, and what the West will not permit in one case, it will not permit in the other.

9. Because of these similarities, both are fearful that developments in one—whether internal or imposed from abroad—will be disastrous for the other. Indeed, such fears rather than the actual facts often seem to drive the analysis on all sides.[4]

10. Last, because of these similarities, many of Russia's and Serbia's immediate neighbors often fall into the trap of responding more to developments of the other former empire than to those in their own. Many Ukrainians, for example, view what happens to Bosnia as a prelude to what may happen not only to themselves but to all other post-Soviet states in Europe.[5]

The problems with these analogies—which routinely are invoked by Russians, Serbians, and many in the United States—are threefold: First, the analogies are not precise. The role of Russia in the former Soviet Union, for example, was fundamentally different from the role of Serbia in the former Yugoslavia, however much the Serbs would like to think otherwise.[6] Moreover, by virtue of its size and power, the position of Russia in the world is so different from that of Serbia that no action against the latter would necessarily have an impact on the former. Second, all three players in this particular game have their own ideas about each of these assumed similarities. While many in Russia emphasize pan-Slavdom, others do not believe it at all, seeing it simply as cover for actions driven by crass political calculations.[7] Many in Serbia think of Russia as something other than a benign elder Slavic brother. And many in the West—even those who accept a view of conflicts that Pushkin once described as "a domestic quarrel among Slavs"—see the analogy as breaking down in the particulars and thus are willing to either support or oppose Russian involvement in the Bosnian crisis. And third, all three groups—the Russians, the Serbs, and Western governments—are increasingly internally divided, with some people in each adopting positions that are at variance with these generalizations both because they are making broader calculations and because they in fact disagree with the consensus just outlined.

That Serbia should look to Russia for assistance and expect to find it in both Russian nationalist pretensions and Moscow's desires to resume a major role on the world stage is no surprise. Russia has a veto at the United Nations, enormous potential power in the region, and the wish to demonstrate that it is still a great power. But that Russia should look to help the Serbs is perhaps less obvious to those who thought the initial Atlanticism of Foreign Minister Andrei V. Kozyrev and President Boris N. Yeltsin was sustainable. Although Serbia is obviously the weaker party, it may in some respects be more useful to Russia than Russia is to it. This is because the international discussions about the future of the former Yugoslavia provide Moscow with a valuable opportunity to advance its own position in the world more generally— but only at the possible cost of entrapping the Russians in a "lose-lose" situation vis-à-vis both the West and its own population.

Given these limitations in the analogies so often drawn between the two countries and the concerns of the Russian elite about the implications of their being drawn at all, one needs to ask why the Russian authorities both in the parliament and in the executive branch nonetheless continue to talk about Slavic ties. A more rational Russian policy would seem to require that such discussions be carefully limited. But the reason for the current and perhaps even increasing dominance of Slavdom as a factor in Russian policy lies in the opening up of the foreign policy process in Moscow. Under the Soviets, foreign policy was made by a small group of men—usually smaller in number than the entire Politburo—and implemented with little regard as to what the population or even the broader political elite thought. Now that has changed.

Foreign policy choices, like choices in every other sphere, must now be justified to ever broader groups. There is a serious foreign relations committee in the Duma, foreign policy commentators in every major paper, and politicians prepared to use foreign policy as a means to advance their own careers—in short, there is a messy foreign policymaking environment in which the senior elite must justify what it is doing in terms that the population can understand and support. Nor is it surprising that the most extravagant statements in support of Serbia and the Serbs have come from the legislature rather than the executive. In Russia today, references to a pan-Slav mission elicit a positive response from a broad section of the political spectrum.

The reasons for this lie in the special difficulties Russia found itself in after the collapse of the Soviet Union. Alone among the 15 former Soviet republics, the Russian Federation felt the trauma of loss rather than the ebullience of victory; and alone among the governments of these states, the Russian authorities could not resort to nationalism to generate support for themselves at a time when their ability to deliver the goods was at an all-time low. That is because Russian nationalism, unlike that of most of the other successor states, is almost invariably inherently revisionist with regard to the existing international system— that is, it seeks to recover something that has been lost rather than to glory in what has been achieved. When things go bad in one of the other successor states, the national elites can use nationalism virtually with impunity, but for the Russian government to do so risks negative reaction from both Russia's immediate neighbors, who remain deeply suspicious of Moscow's intentions, and Russia's potential partners and competitiors farther away. Thus, discussions about the Serbs who live farther away are really a means for talking about the 25.4 million ethnic Russians who live in the 14 other former Soviet republics. Such discussions are thus simultaneously a sop to Russian sensitivities and a test of Western reaction.

An apparently countervailing factor in Russian calculations is somewhat less complicated: the desire of Russian elites to become "good international citizens," either out of a genuine belief that such behavior is good in itself or because of a conviction that such behavior is the price of extracting resources from the West while Russia recovers. Despite their behavior, Russians have tended to be obsessed by what others, and especially Westerners, think of them. To the extent that the West makes clear its views when it is in a position of strength, Russians may be more inclined to go along than might be expected. When the West, and especially the United States, has made clear the linkages between specific behavior and specific rewards, Russian elites in recent years have seldom had any option but to go along. But whenever the West has been divided on a particular question or has been uncertain of what to do, many in Moscow have concluded that Russia can get away with more while retaining its standing as a good international citizen.

Divisions and uncertainties in the West make it more rather than less likely that Moscow will respond to domestic political pressures. Indeed, with Western governments reluctant to take any action in this first post–Cold War crisis in Europe, Moscow generally has been able to win points for being a good citizen simply by arguing that more talks are always preferable to the use of force. Moreover, the very nature of the West as an entity is in doubt in the absence of a clearly defined East; as a result, by siding with the European states against the Atlantic alliance and the Americans in the name of "good citizenship," Moscow has been able, despite its weakness, to open the door to a redefinition of the geopolitical map of Europe.

This brings us to the third factor that has been operative in defining Moscow's approach to the crisis in the former Yugoslavia: the desire to build authority at home and to promote geopolitical interests abroad. For the reasons cited, many in the Russian government see support for Serbia as useful in generating domestic political authority. Obviously, many—such as Kozyrev—who have been charged with being too deferential to the West are anxious to prove that they can be just as tough as anyone in promoting Russian interests abroad. As one right-winger put it in *Pravda* at a time when Russia seemed unprepared to act in defense of ethnic Russians abroad, "Thank God that in contrast to Yeltsin's Russia, Serbia has not left these Serbs [beyond the borders of Serbia] in the lurch."[8] It is noteworthy that Russian right-wing commentators continued to state views like these even after Croatia occupied the Krajina in the summer of 1995 and expelled most of its Serbian population. The same was true for the Dayton accords the following November. Milosevic, they argued, had done the best he could. Indeed, a broad range of politicians, from right-wing extremists such as Zhirinovsky to "liberal reformers" such as Kozyrev and Yeltsin, seem to believe that, given Western divisions and uncertainty, the crisis in the former Yugoslavia represents an important chance to reassert Russian power in its traditional domain, to signal that Moscow is not prepared to adopt a permanently subordinate position to the West, and not unimportantly, to gain Western approval for Moscow's own self-defined "peacekeeping" activities in the Commonwealth of Independent States.

But the government and the parliamentary opposition are very much divided on three other questions: the relative importance of maintaining ties with the West as opposed to reasserting Russian power; the impact of supporting Serbian nationalism on Russian nationalism; and the importance of the Serbian-Bosnian model for Russia's relationships with the so-called near abroad.

While Russia looms very large for Serbia, the reverse is certainly not true. Serbia represents both an opportunity and a problem for Moscow, but the Russian authorities—and especially the Yeltsin government—always will view Serbia in the context of a much larger game. Russia's relations with Europe as a whole, with the United States, and even with its immediate neighbors are part of Moscow's calculus. Consequently, Russian policy toward Serbia has been and will remain inconsistent.

Although no one knows for certain what the consequences of the interaction between Russian nationalism and Serbian nationalism will be, some on the right of the Russian political spectrum hope that Serbian successes will embolden Russian nationalists; some on the left are afraid that this will be the case. Both groups have been affected by developments in Bosnia, with the right becoming more assertive with Serbian successes and the left less able to resist playing the Russian nationalist card.

Both liberals and conservatives in Moscow see in the Yugoslav case implications for Russia's relationships with what many Russians call the "near abroad," the former Soviet republics that are now independent countries. Some on the right believe that Serbia by its support and use of Serbians in Bosnia has shown the path Moscow should follow; some on the left fear that if Moscow were to follow Belgrade's lead, this would isolate Russia internationally and ultimately destroy its prospects for a successful transition to democracy and a market economy.

As a result of such differences as well as of the broader geopolitical situation, Russia's approach to Serbia is likely to end up being very different from what the Serbs expect. It is entirely possible that Russian support for Serbia will turn out to have been a feint, a move intended to allow the Russian government to insist on Western recognition of its claimed special rights in the so-called near abroad. That is certainly where Kozyrev, until Yeltsin dismissed him as foreign minister, and now Yevgeny M. Primakov, his successor, appear to have been heading—unless, of course, they can get even more. In the end, the Serbs may be left up the proverbial creek, precisely because they have tended to ignore the fact that Russia has a broader agenda than they do.

Three Stages in the Evolution of a Policy

The history of the Russian-Serbian relationship over the last five years reflects the interplay of these three factors.[9] At first, Russia's desire to be a good citizen led Moscow to be deferential toward Western opinion on what to do or what not to do in the former Yugoslavia, even as some Russian politicians worried about linkages between Serbia and Russia while others saw the conflict as an opportunity for building domestic authority. Later Russia saw the conflict as an opportunity to ratify its desire to be accepted as a good citizen on the world stage while pursuing its geopolitical interest in dividing Europe from the United States and projecting power once again in those regions that many Russians assume are properly their own. Later still Russia faced the prospect that it would be marginalized by a newly united West unless it was willing to lend its good offices to the West's plan for solving the Yugoslav crisis. In the face of sharpening criticism from the Russian right, the Yeltsin government occasionally adopted even tougher anti-Western rhetoric, even as it sought to find a continuing, albeit reduced role in international regulation of the situation in the former Yugoslavia.

Prior to the collapse of the Soviet Union in August 1991, Moscow dealt with Yugoslavia as an East-West issue rather than as a question that was likely to have an impact on Russian domestic developments. Mikhail S. Gorbachev occasionally talked about the disintegration of Yugoslavia in terms of the possible breakup of the Soviet Union, but in general he discussed developments there as if there were no such connection. That is not to say that all Russians, or even all Soviets, felt that way: the Soviet military and several rightist groups took advantage of *glasnost* to argue that Moscow had a special responsibility in Yugoslavia, out of both Slavic solidarity and self-interest. But this was not the dominant motif of the discussions.

In the period from August 1991 to February 1992, Moscow did not have a well-developed policy with respect to the former Yugoslavia. The scope and rapidity of change in Russia itself meant that even Russian diplomats had little time to discuss the equally dramatic changes taking place in Yugoslavia. In general, the Russian government, and especially Foreign Minister Kozyrev, simply echoed Western statements, primarily because of their self-absorption with domestic affairs, but also because of a desire to register Russia as a good partner with the West. Indeed, throughout this period Kozyrev repeatedly suggested that the development of the Moscow-Washington relationship in the post-Soviet era meant that Moscow could not hold on to its shibboleths about policy.

Not surprisingly, as conditions stabilized in Russia, many in the Russian political elite concluded that a more assertive Russian policy in the former Yugoslavia would pay handsome dividends at home, and that past concessions to the West had been unnecessary and even counterproductive. The turning point came in June and July 1992 during a full-dress parliamentary debate on Russian policy toward the former Yugoslavia. Various parliamentarians attacked the government for going along with U.N. sanctions on Serbia and condemned Kozyrev's "kowtowing" to the West on this and other issues. In response, Kozyrev and the Foreign Ministry began to revise Moscow's hitherto accommodationist stance, seeking modifications in the September 1992 U.N. resolutions and agreeing to support the West's position only after the West modified its original proposal on sanctions. But this was not enough for the Russian right—including many in the Foreign Ministry apparatus itself. Smelling blood, they pressed their case throughout the fall and winter.

This pattern repeated itself in early 1993, with Kozyrev and the Russian government seeking to solidify the East-West relationship even at the price of "selling out" the Slavic Serbs while the Russian right in the parliament, among the public, and within the regime pressed for and achieved modifications in Kozyrev's rhetoric and, ultimately, in Moscow's policies. A major shift came in April and May 1993, one marking a new approach to the crisis by Moscow. This approach reflected a calculation by Yeltsin and his allies that the crisis in the former Yugoslavia represented an opportunity for Russia at home and abroad and that Moscow need not fear that what was happening in the former Yugoslavia would occur in Russia itself. At that time the Russian Supreme Soviet insisted, and Yeltsin agreed, that Moscow had a special role to play in the Balkans, one that could not be ceded to the United Nations or the West generally, and that Moscow should adopt a position more supportive of Serbia to counter the West's perceived pro-Muslim position. Indeed, the Yeltsin government showed signs that it believed that it could have it both ways, introducing Russian troops under U.N. cover as blue helmets to show that it was cooperating with the West, but allowing these troops to act in symbolic ways that pleased both Russian nationalists at home and their friends in Serbia.

The formation of the five-country contact group in 1993 provided Russia with several new opportunities. By participating in the first place and then pushing itself forward as the only possible mediator with Serbia, Russia had its status as a great power publicly reaffirmed. By playing off the Americans, who felt something had to be done, and the west Europeans—and especially the Germans and British—who opposed taking any step that might lead to a wider war, Moscow could advance its broader geopolitical agenda. And by keeping the talks going and demanding that the international community avoid any use of force, Moscow provided the Serbs with the opportunity to expand their gains.

While Russian diplomats might bemoan this at contact group meetings, Russian politicians and some groups in the Russian population saw this as a major victory for their fellow Slavs. During this period Yeltsin and Kozyrev also successfully insisted that the West not blame Belgrade for the behavior of the Bosnian Serbs. This was a first step toward satisfying a demand heard ever more frequently in the Russian parliament in 1994 and 1995: that the international community lift its sanctions against Belgrade and that the West readmit Serbia into the community of nations.

But precisely at this time, both Kozyrev and Yeltsin themselves again began to draw an explicit comparison between developments in Yugoslavia and those in Russia, a linkage that others in the Russian political milieu had been drawing from the beginning. This appeared both to signal Yeltsin's realization that he could make this case without sacrificing his ties to the West and especially to Washington—which had now invested in the Russian president personally, just as it had with Gorbachev before him—and to point to an ever harder Russian line within both the contact group and the U.N. Security Council. Even if it were argued that Russia was simply being a good international citizen, it must be conceded that the results of Russian policy, whatever it was intended to do, were in that period precisely those desired by the Russian right wing.

After Yeltsin dispersed the parliament in October 1993, many in the West were hopeful that he would move toward a more balanced approach, retreating from the increasingly nationalist line that the old parliament had insisted upon. In fact, there was no time for that hope to be realized, for in December 1993 the parliamentary elections revealed both strong support for the Russian right, including for Zhirinovsky, who openly advocated Russian intervention on behalf of the Serbs, and the weakness of those parties that had pushed for a more Atlanticist position, one stressing cooperation with the United States even at the possible cost of support for traditional allies. In light of these developments and also because he calculated that Washington was not prepared to use force in the former Yugoslavia, Yeltsin toughened his position still further, thereby winning on both counts, at least for a time. In the contact group, Kozyrev protected Serbian interests by attacking ever more vociferously the Bosnian Muslims—undoubtedly having realized how effective such attacks on Islam and especially Islamic "fundamentalists" could be in paralyzing American and west European policymakers.

Moscow's support for the Serbs began to backfire in late 1994 and early 1995. At first the shift was not dramatic, but it has had significant consequences: after the Serbian government agreed and the Bosnian Serbs rejected the contact group's proposed partition of Bosnia, and after the west Europeans demonstrated that they were not willing to use force to defend either the split or the safe havens set up for Bosnian Muslims, Yeltsin and his government sought to force Washington and the West to adopt a more evenhanded policy regarding Belgrade. From the Russian president's point of view, he could kill two birds with one stone—he could appease the still-strong nationalists at home and he could reaffirm his status as an international good citizen in the eyes of the West. Such a calculation, along with Russian concerns about the enlargement of the North Atlantic Treaty Organization (NATO), helps to explain Yeltsin's sharp criticism in August 1995 of the West's continuing tilt toward Bosnia.[10]

But continuing Bosnian Serb intransigence and aggression, the entry of Croatian forces into Bosnia, and the strengthening of the Bosnian Muslim army relative to its opponents combined to create a situation in which Moscow was ever more trapped. At the same time, these factors opened the door for a tougher American approach, one that largely excluded Russia by using NATO rather than U.N. forces. Whether Washington and the West more generally will stay the new course remains to be seen, however, and if the West retreats at any point, past Russian complaints about the possible use of Western power in Yugoslavia could ultimately work to Moscow's advantage if the use of force fails—as it might—to achieve its ends.

Throughout the Yugoslav crisis, Yeltsin and Kozyrev shifted their policies in response to both domestic and foreign pressures, but they also seemed to learn by observation one fact that is profoundly disturbing: namely, that although Washington seeks to deny it, sphere of influence politics is back.[11] While the phrase cannot be said, the concept has, in fact, been acknowledged. That is perhaps the most frightening implication of the West's mishandling of the Bosnian crisis

Three Lessons for the Future

Despite the hopes of many in the West, the end of the Cold War did not herald the end of history or repeal the imperatives of geography. Indeed, as with virtually all other conflicts that the United States has been engaged in, Americans have redefined the nature of the conflict both to ennoble their past actions and to ease the transition to peaceful cooperation with former opponents. Thus, the Cold War, which was in fact about containing Moscow's expansionism in Europe, is now said to have been about ending communism. (If that is the standard for declaring victory, the continued existence of communist China suggests that the war is far from over.) This shift in perspective, however, has had an enormous impact on NATO and on the Western alliance's response to the tragedy of Bosnia in particular, as well as on Russian perceptions of what the post–Cold War international system will tolerate and what it will not.

It has been observed that NATO was designed to keep Russia out of Europe, America involved in Europe, and Germany contained within Europe. Those tasks are important still, especially in view of the fact that Moscow's involvement in the former Soviet Union has changed, but it has not been completely transformed. Moreover, in some ways, Moscow is a far less predictable participant in international affairs than it was during the Cold War. The opening up of Russian politics forces Russian elites to pay more attention to popular attitudes and parliamentary pressures—just as in the West—inclining them to be far less cooperative and rational than they might otherwise be. The good thing about such an opening up, of course, is that the public and the politicians may like the rhetoric of expansion, but they may not be prepared to bear its probable costs. Neither group is likely to be quite as willing to see Moscow change course 180 degrees overnight, as frequently happens in more authoritarian political systems. Thus, the widely shared assumption that a more democratic Russia will inevitably be more likely to cooperate with the West in every case does not hold true. With regard to Bosnia, Russian politicians and the Russian people have on occasion imposed serious constraints on the ability of the Russian foreign minister and the Russian president to cooperate with the West— assuming, that is, that these men do not already share many of the attitudes they are "forced" to manifest.

Nor has the geopolitical situation changed.[12] Russian elites are interested in projecting power into the Balkans both to advance their own interest in dominating the region or—at the least—to deny others influence and to win the support of an apathetic and suspicious Russian public. Russia has very real interests in eastern Europe; the issue is how it will advance its interests and whether the projection of Russian power will take place at the cost of the integration of the states of the region and of Russia itself into the democratic and free-market West. Moreover, Russia has an interest in preventing the "Yugoslavization" of the Russian Federation and its immediate neighbors. Ethnic Russians in northern Kazakhstan and Ukraine's Crimea certainly have been encouraged by what has happened in Bosnia to believe that Moscow ultimately will find a way to support them, and Moscow certainly was able to move against Chechnya far more brutally because it was able to tap into continuing Western opposition to any change in international boundaries, fears that help explain why Washington has made the integrity of Bosnia a major goal.[13]

The tragedy of the former Yugoslavia suggests that NATO's original purpose of containing Russian expansionism remains just as valid as it was earlier despite all the changes in Europe since 1989. As the major institutional link between western Europe and the United States, NATO institutionalizes a countervailing role for Washington in Europe. In the absence of American involvement in Europe, no European country or even concert of countries will be able to protect itself from Russia as it recovers its position, and west Europeans will remain both divided and inactive and thus that much more susceptible to Russian influence. Clearly, it is in Moscow's geopolitical interest to promote divisions between Washington and western Europe, to play on European concerns about too much American power in Europe, and so on. Despite its shifts in tone, Moscow has continued to harp on that fundamental theme in most of its statements on the former Yugoslavia. But Washington will not stay engaged in Europe unless it perceives a threat, and at the moment, it does not want to perceive one. Thus Washington must either dismiss the Bosnian disaster as marginal to its concerns—or change its tune and admit that the stakes in Bosnia for the credibility of the West and as an indication of what will and will not be tolerated in Europe are far greater than many want to believe.

Twice before in this century, the United States and the west Europeans concluded that conflicts in eastern Europe need not have broader consequences for themselves: first with regard to the Balkan wars of 1908 to 1912 and then in the 1920s, when many assumed, in Churchill's oft-quoted words, that "the war of the giants has ended [and] the quarrels of the pygmies have begun." In both cases, those making these assumptions proved to be wrong, and the world slid toward larger conflicts from which the great powers could not remain aloof. Bosnia represents the latest version of such a "quarrel." It will be a tragedy if those who want to believe that it has no broader implications for the region, for Russia, and for ourselves, carry the day.

Notes

1. See Paul A. Goble, "Serbians' Success Echoes in Russia," *New York Times,* August 23, 1992; ——,"Russia's Extreme Right," *The National Interest,* vol. 20 (Fall 1993), pp. 93–96; Frank Umbach, "The Consequences of Western Policy Towards the Yugoslav Conflict and Its Impact upon the Former Soviet Union," *European Security,* vol. 2 (Summer 1993), pp. 244–70; S. P. Ramet, "The Bosnian War and the Diplomacy of Accommodation," *Current History,* vol. 94 (November 1994), pp. 380–85; and S. K. Pavlowitch, "Who Is 'Balkanizing' Whom?" *Daedalus,* vol. 111 (Spring 1994), pp. 203–23.

2. For a discussion of this use of ethnicity, see Paul A. Goble, "A New Age of Nationalism," in Bruce Seymore, ed., *ACCESS Guide to Ethnic Conflicts in*

Europe and the Former Soviet Union (Washington, DC: ACCESS, 1994), pp. 3–4. On the origins of this system, see ————, "Rozhdeniye stalinskoi natsional'noi politiki," in P. Goble and G. Bordyugov, eds., *Mezhnatsional'nyye otnosheniya v Rossii I SNG* (Moscow: 1994), pp. 14–20; and A. N. Nenarokov, "Sem'desyat let nazad: natsional'nyi vopros na XII s"ezde RKP(b)," *Otechestvennaya istoriya* vol. 3, no. 6, 1993, pp. 111–24, and no. 1, 1994, pp. 106–17.

3. For a fascinating discussion of this conjunction of reactionaries and liberals in Moscow, see Marina Pavlova-Silvanskaya's account of the ways in which Armenian activists have collaborated with the Serbs, *Obshchaya gazeta*, no. 5, August 20–26, 1993, p. 9.

4. For an unintended example of this phenomenon, see the roundtable of Russian experts in *Novoye vremya*, no. 31, August 1994, pp. 34–35.

5. For a useful discussion of this use of a distant, if imperfect, mirror in the case of Ukraine, see J. F. Dunn, *Ukrainian Attitudes to the Crisis in the Former Yugoslavia*, RMA CSRC Occasional Paper, no. 21, 1993.

6. See, for example, Pavlo Rudyakov's comments in *Politichna dumka*, no. 3, 1994, pp. 219–23.

7. Yeltsin adviser Sergei Karaganov remarked that "almost nobody is interested in Serbia here, but the opposition is playing it up to make things more difficult for the administration and the administration has to bow to that." Cited in *Financial Times*, April 20, 1993.

8. *Pravda*, January 13, 1992, p. 4.

9. The following discussion draws on the most comprehensive collection of documents and analyses of the Russian involvement in the Yugoslav crisis: *Iugoslavskiy krzis I Rossiya* (Moscow, 1993–), multiple volumes. I am indebted to academician Vladimir Volkov for making these studies available to me. In addition, see Albert Wohlstetter, "Creating a Greater Serbia," *New Republic*, August 1, 1994, pp. 22–27; Michael Ignatieff, "Homage to Bosnia," *New York Review of Books*, April 21, 1994, pp. 3–4; Misha Glenny, "Heading Off War in the Southern Balkans," *Foreign Affairs*, vol. 74 (May / June 1995), pp. 98–108; and Steven Greenhouse, "Year's Effort by 5-Nation Group Accomplishes Little in Bosnia," *New York Times*, March 22, 1995, p.1.

10. On the shift and Russia's isolation as a result, see David Hoffman, "Attack on Bosnia Shows Russia's Drift from West," *Washington Post*, September 16, 1995, p. A20. On this general pattern in Russian foreign policy, see Alexander Rahr and Joachim Krause, *Russia's New Foreign Policy* (Bonn: Research Institute of the German Society for Foreign Affairs, 1995), especially: "Russia's policy will collide with Western policy in several areas in the years to come. This does not necessarily mean, however, that a new strategic competition is about to begin. Russia is too weak for a new strategic competition with the West and would expose itself to new weaknesses," p. 41.

11. See Paul A. Goble, "And Unfortunately [Yeltsin] May Get It," *Wall Street Journal Europe*, September 28, 1994, p. 15.

12. To say this is not to fall into either an extension of Cold War thought or historical determinism. See the brilliant essay by David Hooson, "The Return of Geography," in Ian Bremmer and Norman Naimark, eds., *Soviet Nationalities Problems* (Stanford, CA: Stanford University Press, 1990), pp. 61–68.

13. See Paul A. Goble, "Back to Biafra? Defending Borders and Defending Human Rights in the Post–Cold War Environment," *Fordham International Law Journal*, vol. 18 (May 1995), pp. 1679–84.

Chapter 8

After the End

ABRAM CHAYES AND ANTONIA HANDLER CHAYES

WRITING THE HISTORY of the future is a dangerous enterprise. As we were completing this chapter, first, warplanes from the North Atlantic Treaty Organization (NATO) struck Bosnian Serb targets with a seriousness and persistence that seemed impossible earlier; then what appeared to be end-game negotiations began under American leadership; and a tentative cease-fire was secured and then turned into a fragile peace by the General Framework Agreement initialed at Dayton, Ohio, on November 21, 1995.[1]

Even so, some of the basic contours of the situation remain the same. None of the parties to the conflict emerges from it with the military capability to achieve a decisive victory over the others. And the outside powers, despite their newfound energy and purpose, still remain unprepared to commit the ground forces for the time period necessary to impose a settlement if the Dayton accords break down.

Ever since the end of the first winter of stalemated siege warfare, it was apparent that the fighting in Bosnia would be brought to an end only by a peace agreement, brokered by the major powers and the United Nations in some combination, and accepted, however grudgingly, by the three Bosnian communities. Even then it was not too early to think about picking up the pieces and charting the painful return to normal life—which eventually would mean healing the wounds of communal hatred. Now it would be negligence not to think beyond the end of hostilities.

Just as outside intervention ultimately was necessary to bring about the Dayton accords, there will be a continuing and substantial role for the international community in the aftermath. Despite real temptations to turn away through sheer exhaustion, the international community will have a strong interest in maintaining some sort of peace. Among the central tasks that must be assigned in whole or in part to international bodies in postwar Bosnia are peacekeeping (in its original sense of monitoring and supervising an agreed settlement); economic and social rehabilitation and reconstruction (including resettlement and reintegration of refugees); and the treatment of war crimes and other crimes against humanitarian law.

The way in which such tasks are approached is heavily conditioned by the kind of settlement that is ultimately implemented as the provisions of the Dayton accords are implemented and then modified through practice. In principle, the settlement could, at one extreme, have been imposed on the parties by outside force or, at the other, be freely accepted by the parties. It is apparent that all three of the tasks would look very different under each of these polar outcomes. Under an imposed settlement, the military aspects would look much like an occupation; an external authority would bear major responsibility for reconstruction activities; and what would be in essence the governing military power could assure the apprehension of war criminals and their prosecution before the U.N. War Crimes Tribunal. Under a voluntary settlement, on the other hand, only more traditional peacekeeping procedures could be undertaken, reconstruction might be more easily left to local and nongovernmental processes, and the prosecution of war criminals would be much more difficult.

Of course, the Dayton accords and their implementaion were not at either of these extremes. International force sufficient to end all acts of war and establish control over the territory has not been deployed, and it seems equally clear that the parties will not resolve the issues underlying their conflict without considerable outside prodding. We cannot predict where developments will fall on the range between coercion and genuine agreement. Nor can we predict with what degree of commitment the parties will enter into or outsiders enforce the final settlement beyond the end of the first year, when most NATO units are scheduled to depart. Yet the characteristics of a postwar regime will vary as the settlement approaches one or the other pole. Thus, it may be useful to spell out at greater length the manifold implications of international involvement in postwar Bosnia.

Postwar Peacekeeping

In mid-1994, the United Nations Protection Force (UNPROFOR) in the former Yugoslavia comprised 37,000 military personnel and police officers (primarily British, French, and Canadian troops), most of them in Bosnia. UNPROFOR was originally established under chapter VI of the

U.N. Charter to implement the Geneva Agreement between the parties to the war in Croatia and was conceived as a relatively standard peacekeeping operation, though it ran into difficulties even in that role.

The force first entered Bosnia in the spring of 1992 in the form of a small contingent of military observers dispatched to Mostar as the situation there worsened. In June, after agreement was reached on handing the Sarajevo airport over to UNPROFOR, more substantial elements were deployed to "supervise" the withdrawal of heavy weapons and antiaircraft emplacements to agreed locations and later "to secure the security and functioning of Sarajevo airport and the delivery of humanitarian assistance."[2]

The Security Council invoked its chapter VII powers for the first time in August, when it authorized "all measures necessary to facilitate . . . the delivery . . . of humanitarian assistance to Sarajevo and wherever needed in other parts of Yugoslavia."[3] The resolution was directed to member states, not the peacekeeping force, but in September the Council decided to turn over the job of protecting humanitarian assistance to UNPROFOR.[4] The force was enlarged for this purpose, but the limits on its authority to use force were not expanded.

This initial mission of securing the delivery of humanitarian aid to the civil population during an ongoing war was a comparatively novel use of U.N. forces, rather different in its demands from the monitoring of cease-fires and peace accords or the interposing of troops between opposing forces that were the staples of many years of U.N. peacekeeping experience. Operational requirements, and particularly the potential need for limited use of force, were not well understood. UNPROFOR was lightly armed and not large enough to undertake combat operations on any significant scale. Its rules of engagement confined it to the use of force only in "self-defense." In practice, the political and military leadership adopted a very narrow construction of self-defense, and although there seems to have been some variation among national contingents, for the most part, UNPROFOR troops did not fire even when fired upon. Indeed, in late 1994 and again in May–June 1995, hundreds of U.N. troops were taken hostage by the Bosnian Serbs without offering resistance.

In October 1992 the Security Council invoked chapter VII in resolution 781 to establish a "no-fly zone" over Bosnia and yet again to proclaim "safe havens" in Sarajevo and half a dozen Bosnian Muslim villages, an important innovation that significantly expanded the UNPROFOR mission.[5] By that time, the practice as to the use of force was already established and, in the absence of a specific decision by the Security Council, remained unchanged. It was contemplated that UNPROFOR might call on NATO air power to enforce these Security Council mandates, but although intimations and threats of air strikes were frequent, mostly from U.S. quarters, the attempts to enforce the Security Council decisions had little immediate effect. Until the large-scale air strikes in September 1995, more than two years after the resolutions were passed, they had been backed up by little more than symbolic action.

Among the most frustrating aspects of the conflict in the former Yugoslavia was the apparent ineffectiveness of the peacekeeping forces. It is true that the United Nations never undertook the tasks of imposing a settlement or punishing the Bosnian Serbs for "aggression" or other offenses. UNPROFOR's mission was first limited to ensuring the delivery of humanitarian aid and later to policing the no-fly zone and then the very difficult task of protecting the safe havens proclaimed by the Security Council with inadequate forces. These distinctions were not always clearly drawn even by political leaders, much less by the media and the general public. Indeed, they were sometimes deliberately obfuscated. As UNPROFOR proved itself impotent in the face of repeated refusals by the Bosnian Serbs to comply with Security Council decisions, the United Nations itself was increasingly humiliated and discredited. Yet despite the general disappointment with the performance of the United Nations, it will still play a major role in the implementation of the civil police agreement, primarily in connection with refugees, humanitarian efforts, and the many tasks of rebuilding a shattered society. The NATO Implementation Force (IFOR) has the critical action on the military side, although the withdrawal of the Serbs from eastern Slavonia remains a U.N. responsibility. The ongoing division of labor among the different organizations and their ability to coordinate their efforts is uncertain, but the requirements to do so inevitably complicate the management of any peacekeeping effort.

The military provisions of the Dayton accords, which condition the requirements for the peacekeeping force, contemplate some force reductions, at least for the Serbs and Croats. They do not call for demobilization and disarmament of the opposing forces. Indeed, given the territorial division, each side can be expected to continue to insist on its right to maintain its own military establishment. The Dayton agreement does require all parties to withdraw military personnel and redeploy heavy weapons to zones away from territorial borders. But experience—in Cambodia, in Somalia, and on the scene in the Krajina—suggests that it will be very difficult for a peacekeeping force to carry out such provisions without recourse to more coercive power than it is likely to have or be permitted to use.

Thus, there will be regular military units and armed irregulars on all sides. In such circumstances, the most likely mission for a peacekeeping force is what has come to be called classical peacekeeping: patrolling the newly assigned territorial boundaries to keep the regular armed forces apart and trying to suppress any continued fighting by actual or alleged irregulars. A good deal of effort has gone into planning the size, composition, and rules of engagement of the peacekeeping force, but a number of difficult issues have not received much public attention.

Size and Composition

IFOR, the NATO peacekeeping force, is on the order of 60,000 troops, one third of them American. The Clinton administration had argued forcefully that the force should have a significant U.S. component, if for no other reason than to preserve the European alliance. One of the many grounds on which Britain and France resisted U.S. efforts to induce UN-PROFOR to adopt more aggressive and, thus more risky, tactics was that the United States had been categorically unwilling to expose its own ground troops. The serious problems of command and control, and some U.S. domestic concerns, are now met by the NATO mantle. But it has elevated issues of legitimacy abroad, and particularly exacerbated the tensions between the West and Russia. A major potential problem was resolved by the quick agreement for the participation of a substantial Russian component under U.S., not NATO, command. Military command-and-control arrangements in Bosnia are not likely to suffer from the deficiencies and contradictions of U.N. operations in Cambodia (UNTAC) or Somalia (UNOSOM). But the necessity for the United Nations and other international entities, including nongovernmental organizations (NGOs), to carry out a broad range of social and economic functions whose activities will have to be coordinated with and protected by the military complicates the broader issue of command and control. If some form of American military training of Bosnian Muslims is also going on simultaneously even through private groups, the military problems facing a peacekeeping force may increase. A comprehensive plan that anticipates unpleasant turns must be well developed, well understood, and supported by the relevant members of the Security Council and their domestic constituents, if earlier command-and-control mishaps are to be avoided.

Use of Force

IFOR has been deployed pursuant to a resolution of the Security Council authorizing it under chapter VII to employ "all necessary means including the use of force" to carry out its mission. Nevertheless, it is very doubtful that the countries supplying troops, having failed to do so heretofore, will permit them to be used in large-scale offensive missions on the ground to "enforce" the provisions of the peace settlement. The wisdom of such a course is equally doubtful. Somalia is an object lesson in the difficulties and dangers of shifting from peacekeeping to peace enforcement against armed and locally supported irregular units, even when the peacekeeping force commands significantly more powerful formations.

NATO authorities have made it quite clear that the peacekeeping force will not be bound by the rules of engagement as heretofore interpreted in Bosnia. The principal traditional limits on peacekeeping forces are that they act with the *consent* of the parties and that they use force only in *self-defense*. But these are not self-defining terms, and in the past they have provided considerable leeway for energetic action by U.N. forces.

Consent to the deployment of the force and to its mission was, of course, given by the central authorities of the Bosnian Muslim-Croat and Serb "entities" when they accepted the Dayton accords. That consent, once given, should continue to operate at least until someone at a similar level is prepared to take public responsibility for withdrawing it. In the past, the principle of operation by consent did not require the specific agreement of local civil or military authorities on the scene, much less of irregular forces, to every action of the U.N. forces carrying out their mission.

Similarly, "self-defense" need not be limited to instances in which a passive peacekeeping unit is fired on by attacking forces. The following excerpts from communications of the U.N. secretary-general defining the limits of self-defense for the force in Cyprus (UNFICYP), a chapter VI operation, give some sense of the scope of the term in past U.N. practice:

> Examples of situations in which troops may be authorized [to use force] are:
> (a) Attempts by force to compel them to withdraw from a position which they occupy under orders from their commanders, or to infiltrate or envelop such positions as are deemed necessary by their commanders for them to hold, thus jeopardizing their safety.
> (b) Attempts by force to disarm them.
> (c) Attempts by force to prevent them from carrying out their responsibilities as ordered by their commanders.
> (d) Violation by force of U.N. premises and attempts to arrest or abduct U.N. personnel, civil or military.[6]

The secretary-general later reported that he "intend[ed] to proceed on certain assumptions and to instruct the force accordingly":

> (a) That in establishing the force and defining its important function, the Security Council realized that the force could not discharge that function unless it had complete freedom of movement in Cyprus, which could only mean such unrestricted freedom of movement as may be

considered essential by the force commander to the implementation of the mandates of the force.

(b) That the force, in carrying out its mandate to prevent the recurrence of fighting, is reasonably entitled to remove positions and fortified installations where these endanger the peace, and to take necessary measures in self-defence if attacked in the performance of this duty.

(c) That in seeking to prevent a recurrence of fighting, it may be demanded by the commander that the opposing armed forces be separated to reasonable distances in order to create buffer zones in which armed forces would be prohibited.[7]

There was no objection to these "assumptions" from the Security Council, so they continued to define the activities for the effectuation of which UNFICYP could use force in self-defense. These provisions and understandings, which provided significantly greater latitude for the use of force than has been exercised by UNPROFOR, were carried over into subsequent peacekeeping operations, for example, UNEF II (the U.N. Emergency Force) in 1973.

The judicious use of such expanded interpretations of consent and self-defense would permit a Bosnian peacekeeping force to adopt a much more aggressive posture than UNPROFOR when necessary, without moving to large-scale combat. It is true that such a policy is not without the risk of incurring some casualties, though if the Cyprus experience is any guide, the long-term casualty rate would not be very high. UNFICYP, originally interposed between two warring communities, has kept the peace for 30 years, during which time the hostility, ethnic and otherwise, between Greek and Turkish Cypriots has not faded. Although UNFICYP has been deployed much longer than anyone thought likely, the costs of continued hostilities or superpower intervention would surely have been greater.

In Bosnia, despite NATO's newfound assertiveness, the forces of the parties to the cease-fire or, more likely, "irregulars" might be inclined to test any new U.N. attitudes about the use of force on the ground, particularly after UNPROFOR's cautious interpretations of its rules of engagement. This might result in more serious casualties than prior peacekeeping operations, at least at the outset. But certainly the cost would be many times smaller than that of imposing a peace. If the contributors of troops are not willing to accept even this risk, probably it would be better not to undertake the enterprise in the first place.

Rehabilitation

Two major tasks fall under this heading: repatriation and resettlement of refugees, and reconstruction of the basic infrastructure and economy of the country. The outlines of these tasks have begun to emerge.

Refugees

As of mid-1995, the total number of refugees and displaced persons produced by the wars in the former Yugoslavia was reported at over 4.6 million, or one out of every five of the prewar population of 22 million. Less than 1 million had found asylum abroad. The remaining 3.7 million were displaced within the former territory of the country, most of them in Bosnia.

The office of the United Nations High Commissioner for Refugees (UNHCR) is responsible for the care and protection of refugees worldwide, and the magnitude of its task in the former Yugoslavia dwarfs all others. Out of a total budget of over $1.3 billion in 1994, the UNHCR spent about $300 million in the former Yugoslavia. (Afghanistan, the next largest client, was budgeted at about a fifth of this figure.) By May 1994, 860 UNHCR personnel, or about 15 percent of its staff, were in the former Yugoslavia, where they constituted by far the largest nonmilitary presence. The agency established a network of more than 25 offices, a dozen warehouses, and a large trucking fleet, mostly in Bosnia and Croatia. This network is likely to grow further.

Because of the size and centrality of its mission, the secretary-general designated the UNHCR as the "lead agency" in the area. The UNHCR had never performed this role before, and the concept itself was poorly defined. Although it implied some obligation for coordinating the activities of the civilian U.N. agencies in the field, neither the authority nor the responsibility was ever fully spelled out. The UNHCR's writ did not extend even nominally to the other government and intergovernmental aid activities or to the many nongovernmental organizations involved in the assistance effort. It is widely agreed that, as a result, the overall effort was not fully coordinated at both the policy and the operational levels, dominated by ad hoc responses to current crises, and lacking in comprehensive strategic planning, even though relations with UNPROFOR apparently went relatively well.

Those charged with the postwar task of resettling and reintegrating the refugees will inherit both assets and liabilities from the wartime experience. On the one hand, there will be a large and experienced agency on the ground, with extensive knowledge of local conditions and needs, as well as a well-developed operating network of facilities. Moreover, the UNHCR will be able to build on its record of remarkable success in Cambodia, where it resettled over 360,000 refugees from the camps along the Thai border, and many more internally displaced persons. On the other hand, the legacy of poor overall planning and coordination for Bosnia has not been improved by the appointment of a High Representative whose task it is to coordinate all agencies and organizations, but whose budget has not reflected the enormous scope of the job. Neither the High Representative nor the United Nations were in a position to do planning, even if they had the capacity, since there was no designation of responsibility before the Dayton agreement.

The peculiarly vicious character of the Bosnian war already has vastly complicated the work of the UNHCR. One aspect of "ethnic cleansing" was the deliberate creation of refugees and displaced persons as an objective of military action. Since the failure of the Vance-Owen peace plan, moreover, it seemed likely that any negotiated settlement would divide Bosnia into ethnically defined territories more or less consistent with the situation on the ground at the end of the fighting. That is roughly what happened. Its effect was to convert a simple battle for all territory into a battle for territory in which the occupying force is ethnically dominant, again putting a premium on displacing minority groups.

The UNHCR has had to cope not only with the extraordinary size of the refugee population but with a special moral dilemma that emerged in what is ordinarily thought of as a straightforward humanitarian mission. The UNHCR often was faced with the agonizing choice of moving people from their homes—and thus, in practice, assisting in the ethnic cleansing—or leaving them to death, rape, or torture at the hands of the prevailing party. As time went on, the UNHCR became readier to move its charges to protect their lives and to accept the risk of the taint of complicity with ethnic cleansing.

The issue has been reprised in only slightly different form after the war. Since the settlement divides Bosnia into relatively self-governing territories, each with a dominant ethnic population, resettlement policy will have to deal with the ethnic pattern existing at the time of the cease-fire. Many of the displaced will not be able to return to their former homes, even if they are prepared to accept the risk of doing so. The civilian organizations, including the UNHCR, will find themselves uncomfortably implicated in the division of people along ethnic lines. (In Cambodia, although refugees were given the option of returning to their original homes, many found their lands or villages occupied by others when they arrived.) There seems to be no escape from this dilemma, but it is one that requires continuing thought and planning so that gross injustices can be kept to a minimum.

Reconstruction

In the past, U.N. peacekeeping missions have paid little attention to the problems of political and social reconstruction after national or internal disputes have been settled and the fighting has stopped. In many instances, even if peacekeepers continued to patrol cease-fire lines, civilians serving as election observers, human rights monitors, and humanitarian workers went home soon after peace was declared. Large-scale economic assistance never seems to arrive.

In recent cases, however, it has been increasingly understood that without some significant effort at rebuilding social and economic infrastructure, any peace is likely to be precarious, especially in internal and intercommunal situations where the bitterness and intensity of conflict is highest and neighbor is set against neighbor. Shortly after the peace agreement between the Palestine Liberation Organization and Israel was signed, in September 1993, the World Bank announced a comprehensive $1.2 billion economic program for the Gaza Strip and Jericho to support the agreement, which was to be funded by a consortium of 40 donor nations. By December, when widespread rioting broke out in the Gaza Strip, little or none of the promised assistance had been delivered.

Cambodia marked the first full-scale U.N. effort at postwar reconstruction. One of the major components of the plan prepared by the secretary-general and approved by the Security Council for the U.N. Transitional Authority in Cambodia (UNTAC) was "rehabilitation." It targeted food, security, health, housing, training and education, the transportation network, and the restoration of Cambodia's basic infrastructure. The budget of $595 million, as estimated by the World Bank, was to be covered by voluntary contributions. In fact, a ministerial conference in Tokyo in June 1992 generated $880 million in pledges.

Despite these promising beginnings and the initiation of a number of useful projects, the overall results in Cambodia have been disappointing. The appalling macroeconomic situation and the devastation of the 25-year war overwhelmed the U.N. effort. The pledged amounts were never collected in full, and much of the total was fulfilled by repackaging earlier commitments. Persisting hostility among Cambodian political factions frustrated decision-making and disrupted operations. There were the usual difficulties with U.N. coordination and management.

All these problems are likely to reappear in some guise in a Bosnian reconstruction effort. The physical and psychological devastation of the war is enormous. While the economic viability of an intact Bosnia had by no means been assured, that of the ministates that are likely to emerge is even more problematic. And they will share in full measure the woes of economic transition of their east European neighbors.

The distribution of the benefits also will raise problems, many of which were foreshadowed by the UNHCR's experience during the war. Its duty is to all civilian displaced persons, whatever community they come from, and many of the displaced persons in Bosnia are Serbs. The UNHCR has therefore been faced with the difficult problem of dividing supplies and assistance between the groups that had been chiefly victimized by the war and the compatriots of the chief victimizers. Moreover, distribution of humanitarian aid has depended on the cooperation of the military forces on the ground, which were in many instances Serbian. Frequently, cooperation was forthcoming only if the distribution formula was skewed in favor of their community. The United States and other Western states are not likely to be enthusiastic about contributing scarce economic resources to the reconstruction of the Serbian areas of Bosnia, since they regard the Bosnian Serbs as the "aggressors" and the principal perpetrators of ethnic cleansing and other violations of basic humanitarian norms.

On the other hand, unlike Cambodia, many Bosnians are educated and trained in the requirements of contemporary political and economic institutions. It should be easier to generate the economic resources for reconstruction than it was to assemble the military forces to intervene effectively in the fighting. But it remains to be seen whether significant economic assistance will be forthcoming. Foreign assistance of all kinds is declining, and national responses to the periodic calls of the secretary-general for funds to support humanitarian assistance have been falling off.

One counter to this decline in national contributions as well as to the bureaucratic deficiencies of the United Nations would be for the major international financial institutions to take a stronger role. Although in the cases of Cambodia and the West Bank, studies by the World Bank formed the basis for the secretary-general's call for funds, the appeal was addressed to individual national donors. Neither the bank nor the International Monetary Fund (IMF) committed major resources. The Balkans, however, present a somewhat different case. The former Yugoslavia was a major client of the international financial institutions. At the time of its disintegration, it was the sixth largest user of IMF funds. Croatia is currently a member of the bank and the IMF, and it appears that the resources of both institutions were deployed in support of the Croat-Muslim federation formed under the Washington accords of April 1994. Shortly thereafter, the bank approved a $128 million loan to Croatia, and the IMF was considering a $250 million standby credit. Bosnia is also a member of both institutions and thus will presumably be eligible for assistance from them. The European Union pledged 125 million ECUs plus funds for Sarajevo and Mostar immediately, and considerably more since then, as has the World Bank.

These more or less haphazard beginnings could be brought together in an integrated plan of targeted interventions to support Dayton's agreed settlement of the Bosnian war. One important precedent is the involvement of the World Bank and IMF in the democratic transition in South Africa. In July 1993, almost a year before the elections that brought Nelson Mandela to power, the World Bank announced its intention to lend South Africa $1 billion a year for five years once a democratically elected government was in place, and two months later, after the Transitional Council was organized, the IMF approved a drawing of $850 million for debt repayment. In the former Yugoslavia, the two global financial institutions could be joined by the European Bank for Reconstruction and Development (EBRD), which, unlike the others, is explicitly mandated by its charter to foster the development of multiparty democracy, pluralism, and market economics and has several projects in the Balkans. Croatia is a member; Bosnia is not. But that can be rectified with little difficulty once a peace accord is in place.

The concerted efforts of these institutions could be a powerful incentive to keep the peace. They could be directed not only toward the reconstruction and reintegration of Bosnia and its economic system but toward reestablishing economic connections with surrounding countries—both within and outside the former Yugoslavia—on which Bosnia's ultimate survival will depend. Assistance could be deployed in ways that encourage renewed contacts among the three main Bosnian communities and discourage continued ethnic conflict. A postwar Bosnia could become a test case for a new policy of "strategic" lending and investment, which has been urged on the financial institutions from a number of quarters.[8]

Binding the Wounds

Activities and programs mounted by formal international organizations will be a necessary part of any effort to rebuild Bosnia. But they are not the only, and perhaps not even the most important, part. Restoring the integument of that society will require more than the resettlement of refugees and money for reconstruction. Picking up the threads of normal life is something that the people concerned must do for themselves. But Bosnia was an advanced case of social breakdown: the ties of community were shattered; trust evaporated; there remains no real communication among different parties; positions were polarized; moderate elements were cowed and silenced. None of this will be ended by the signing of a settlement agreement. In the theory and practice of conflict resolution, such cases call for intermediation by outside parties.

Formal mediation efforts were part of the Bosnian effort, but success was painfully slow. Agreements and plans worked out by distinguished emissaries of the United Nations and the European Union, whether for local cease-fires or for a more comprehensive settlement, were repeatedly rejected or undermined by the parties. In part, this was because of the essential ambiguity as to the purposes of the international intervention. While the mediators placed primary emphasis on bringing the fighting to an end, the Security Council and other important actors condemned the Bosnian Serbs and sought to roll back Serbian military gains by diplomatic pressures. However morally correct the anti-Serbian policy may have been, its effect was to compromise the necessary neutrality of the mediators' position. Even so, meditative efforts on a smaller scale chalked up tangible accomplishments, especially in providing minimal levels of food and necessities to besieged communities. The U.S. mediation, following the first robust NATO air strikes to protect safe areas and the Croatian ground attack that drove the Serbs from the Krajina, finally brought about a fragile settlement.

Now that the fighting has stopped and the parties have entered into a more permanent agreement as to their future relations, intermediation will have a very different role. No matter what the agreed-upon map, it will not be possible to establish ethnically "pure" territories. There will inevitably be ethnic minorities in all the newly established regions. The settlement provides formal protections for these minority communities. The trick is to make these protections a reality in daily life. Issues will arise over access to jobs, housing, education, and public services. The new minorities are unlikely to have much confidence in formal legal procedures controlled by members of a majority who were only recently their deadly enemies, as became clear in the Serb flight from the suburbs of Sarajevo in early 1996. There will still be work for senior diplomats operating on the level of the national governments. But more important will be an array of informal processes at all levels, down to the village, the neighborhood, and even the schoolyard, in which all affected parties—majority and minority—can participate. It will be hard to get these processes going without the help of some form of third-party intermediation.

Successful intermediation at any level will require the restoration of a degree of openness and cooperation by all parties. This in turn will depend on building enough trust and confidence so that the parties will be prepared to disclose their interests and aspirations to the mediator. Where feelings and emotions are high and communications have broken down, as in Bosnia, an intermediary can help defuse the situation and get the parties talking again. If they will not talk directly to each other, each may talk to the mediator, knowing that the message will be conveyed to the other side. A long history of mutual suspicion and hostility may mean that every phrase is subject to distortion and may require a process of emotional translation before progress can be made. These are the classic functions of shuttle diplomacy. Ultimately, it may be possible to restore face-to-face dialogue to address the management of ongoing issues.

The office of High Commissioner on National Minorities (HCNM) of the Organization for Security and Cooperation in Europe (OSCE) has had considerable success with these techniques in potentially explosive situations in eastern Europe and the former Soviet Union. Beginning in the earliest stages of interethnic friction, the commissioner, Max van der Stoel, has been able to employ quiet, low-key tactics, first developing the facts of the situation and making contact with the relevant parties in an exploratory vein to develop their confidence in his impartiality and in the potential for intermediation. The HCNM worked to resolve ethnic tensions in the Baltic states (particularly Estonia), between Slovakia and Hungary, and in Romania, Macedonia, and Albania. In each case, Ambassador van der Stoel made several visits, not only to the capital, but to regions in which ethnic tensions were severe. He has had ready access to the highest levels of government and has made significant recommendations on legislation and policy dealing with ethnic minorities, many of which have been adopted. In most of these countries he successfully encouraged the establishment of official commissions on ethnic relations or ethnic roundtables at which representatives of the affected groups maintain a continuing dialogue with government officials. In the case of Slovakia and Hungary, he secured the assent of both sides to the creation of an unofficial expert group that visits both countries at stated intervals to advise on the implementation of his recommendations and on further steps to be taken. A key to the success of these interventions is that the high commissioner did not focus on the substantive elements of the issues in dispute, much less on assigning blame. Instead his emphasis was on devising and activating processes by which the parties could work out their own solutions.

The Dayton agreement permits, but does not require, the establishment of an entity with a similar mandate for postsettlement Bosnia. Or the HCNM's charge could be extended to cover that situation. Whether this is done or not, a major share of the required intermediation, especially at local levels, will be accomplished by nongovernmental organizations and people who happen to be in the area on a variety of missions connected with reconstruction. Despite the notion that mediation is an art that cannot be taught, there is now a body of a theory and practical experience that provides a basis for training people who are likely to find themselves in such situations. An important function of any postsettlement international effort will be to ensure that official personnel are given such training and that it is available to others, including members of the local population, who will be working in the area.

However, security guarantees of some kind are also likely to be needed.[9] The international community will not accept a permanent peacekeeping operation—a repetition of Cyprus is unthinkable, given the financial crisis of the United Nations and the costs that the former Yugoslavia has already imposed. Nor will continuing problems be settled by training and equipping the Bosnian Muslims to strengthen the deterrent effect of their military forces. A standard criticism of international intervention—Cambodia, for example—is that the international community withdraws too quickly for settlement to adhere. Planning for some form of security guarantee, although unpopular domestically, will require ongoing effort.

War Crimes and War Criminals

The war in Bosnia produced the most heinous crimes against the laws of war, human rights, and human dignity since World War II, at least in Europe. Television brought the horror home to people everywhere. Although it is said that atrocities were committed by all sides, and although reports of Croatian behavior have been very disturbing too, U.N. and Western observers uniformly report that the transgressions of the Bosnian Serbs far outweigh those of others. In view of the developments in international human rights law over the past four decades, demands that the perpetrators be punished were inevitable.

The United Nations already has invested substantial political capital in the effort to assure that those responsible for crimes against humanity are brought to justice. Security Council resolutions 808 and 827 established the International Tribunal for the Prosecution of Persons Responsible for Serious Violations of International Humanitarian Law Committed in the Territory of the Former Yugoslavia since 1991. Resolution 808, adopted under chapter VII of the U.N. Charter, "decided that all states shall take all measures necessary under their domestic law to implement the provisions of the present resolution and the statute, including the obligation of states to comply with requests for assistance or orders issued by a trial chamber [for the arrest, detention, or surrender of persons accused]."[10] The Statute of the Tribunal, resolution 827, adopted at the same time, stipulates that the seat of the tribunal is at The Hague and that it will consist of six trial and five appellate judges, a registrar, and a prosecutorial arm. Its budget for the first four years is more than $30 million. Legal experts and constitutional lawyers have drafted rules of fair procedure for what is a new and difficult forum. The chief prosecutor, appointed after some delay, has been Judge Richard Goldstone of South Africa, a man of impeccable professional and moral credentials who made an energentic start.

Punishing war criminals has a strong moral and political appeal. Unlike military intervention, it enjoys almost universal approval. Some, perhaps cynically, have suggested that it was the only way to "do something" about the Bosnian tragedy on which U.S. and European leaders could agree. But it is unclear, as a practical matter, how the war crimes enterprise will relate to peacekeeping in postwar Bosnia. The powers of the peacekeeping force, plus the activities of human rights monitors attached to it, may well be sufficient to prevent human rights abuses in the future. But what about past war crimes?

The peace settlement permits, but does not require the peacekeeping force to arrest and surrender suspects pursuant to the statute of the new tribunal. Radovan Karadzic, the political leader of the Bosnian Serbs, and General Ratko Mladic, their military commander, have already been indicted for war crimes. Croatians in similar positions, and even some Muslim leaders, also may be vulnerable to criminal proceedings. In the 1985 agreement in Uruguay between the military junta and the opposition for a return to civilian rule after more than a decade of dictatorship marked by horrific human rights violations, the question of amnesty or punishment was purposely not considered because touching on this subject may have meant that possibly no agreement could have been reached. Although the Dayton agreement is not wholly silent on the issue of war crimes, its provisions are highly ambiguous. In theory, even in the absence of an agreement between the parties, the Security Council could direct the peacekeeping force to execute the orders of the tribunal for the detention and surrender of suspects, but such a resolution might face opposition from the Russians, given their historical and political ties to the Serbs, and from China, which is congenitally opposed to Security Council coercion.

The secretary-general or the NATO force commander, under the terms of the Security Council resolution just quoted, might be empowered to order such action on his own initiative. Yet even if the legal basis for such an order were unassailable, there are strong considerations arguing against it. To enter the territory of Serbian Bosnia or Croatia (which is also within the tribunal's jurisdiction) to execute such an order might require a force of a size and armament comparable to that which would have been needed to impose a peace. It is unlikely, not to say unseemly, that states unwilling to commit the troops to prevent the outrages from occurring in the first place would do so to punish the perpetrators after the event. In any case, the effort would complicate immeasurably the already daunting mission of the force guaranteeing a peace agreement. The attempt to arrest General Farah Aidid after the Security Council declared him an outlaw, it will be recalled, marked the beginning of the disintegration of the U.S. and the U.N. operation in Somalia. Moreover, any such effort in Bosnia would undermine the conditions for Russian participation in the peacekeeping force, without which the chances for long-term success would be much diminished.

It might be thought that, at a minimum, the peacekeeping force should be able to act as custodian for suspects arrested by each of the Bosnian authorities in its own territory and to surrender them on the call of the tribunal. But this too raises problems. Serbs, Croats, and Muslims are not likely to arrest very many of their own compatriots, although a few may be turned over as tokens of "cooperation." The arrangement would thus set majority communities against minorities in each territory, creating a climate for continuing violence. Moreover, it would create incentives for irregular forces to cross borders to kidnap suspects for return to their own territories where the authorities could turn them over to the U.N. force. This is hardly a prescription for a cease-fire, much less a lasting peace.

The U.N. War Crimes Tribunal faces practical difficulties apart from the problems it poses for any peacekeeping operation. Although the legal basis for the Security Council resolution has been certified by the U.N. legal office, it is not unassailable. Arrests made under it will no doubt be challenged in national courts, with results that are by no means certain. For example, an order of the international tribunal, based on the Security Council resolution, may not be sufficient for an arrest to withstand a habeas corpus challenge in a U.S. court. As with extradition, a specific treaty or an act of Congress may be necessary. More important, it cannot be assumed that all states called upon to take action under the resolution will do so. It is not only Serbia that will hold back, although many of the suspects are likely to be found there. There is talk of economic or even military sanctions against states that refuse to co-operate with the tribunal, but again, Serbia's long-standing relationship with Russia might lead Moscow to raise obstacles in the Security Council. Moreover, the record of economic sanctions in compelling state behavior, either in the former Yugoslavia or elsewhere, is not impressive.

On the other hand, it is simply not possible for the United Nations, or the world in general, to wash its hands of the abominations that took place in Bosnia. Apart from the abstract requirements of law, the demands of the victims for justice and reparation cannot be ignored. The tribunal is in place, and the prosecutor's office is proceeding apace with aggressive and painstaking investigations. The first indictment was lodged in absentia in November 1994 against a Bosnian Serb camp commander, and German officials were asked to detain another, who had originally been arrested to answer for his war crimes under German law. A trial was begun in Germany against an indicted defendant arrested there. The indictments of Karadzic and Mladic have already been mentioned. Undoubtedly a number of other indictments will be brought and additional trials will take place. But even under the most favorable circumstances, given the time and resources available, it will not be possible to try more than a very small proportion of those who are thought to have committed such crimes.

This rather limited outlook for the War Crimes Tribunal is not necessarily all bad. It is not prudence alone that counsels a more cautious approach to U.N. policy on war crimes. The historical and moral position for retribution is not as unassailable as it may at first appear. The Nuremberg trials often are cited as precedent for the current measures, but they remain the only instance in which war crimes were punished by an international tribunal. The distinguishing feature of that episode was that World War II ended in unconditional surrender. The victors did not have to gain the assent of the vanquished to the postwar regime. Agreed settlements of civil wars, by contrast, and other transfers of power between authoritarian and democratic regimes generally have forgone punishment for crimes committed on either side. Neither Pol Pot or Saddam Hussein, Idi Amin or Augusto Pinochet, or the Argentine generals (save briefly for a few of the very highest), or the Sandinistas or the Contras in Nicaragua, or the leaders of the FMLN or ARENA in El Salvador have had to face criminal punishment. In Uruguay, where it is estimated that one in five persons was arrested and tortured by the military junta, a mobilized public gathered the needed 500,000 signatures (in a country of three million) for a referendum to overturn the amnesty law that was passed by the newly elected democratic Congress under pressure from the former military rulers. But in the referendum, 53 percent voted to sustain the law.

In other such situations, a way has been found between impracticable punishment and unacceptable amnesia—by no means a perfect way—but one that permits the parties to get on with their lives. The answer the Latin Americans seem to have found is exposure to the truth. Truth-telling by official investigations, in the naming of names, in identifying criminal acts and victims puts the perpetrators on public record. In Argentina and Chile, following the downfall of the dictators, such reports, both entitled *Nunca Mas* (Never Again), were published by the new democratic governments. The Argentine report led to the trial and conviction of a few members of the military government, already discredited by the Falklands/Malvinas disaster. In late 1986, a law imposed a 60-day limit on initiating prosecutions for human rights offenses committed during the period of the junta, and in June 1987, legislation effectively voided the prosecutions of most of the lower-ranking officers, who had been the actual torturers. Although "everyone knew" what had happened without having to be told by the investigating commissions, the official acknowledgment of the acts and of the identities of the perpetrators seems to have had a cathartic effect.

In El Salvador, the peace accord between the FMLN and the government brokered by the United Nations provided for an investigation by the three-person Commission of Truth, appointed by Secretary-General Boutros Boutros-Ghali. After an investigation of 18 months, the commission released a detailed 270-page report charging numerous high-ranking military officers with murder and other gross abuses of human rights. Some rebel leaders also were named in the report, but on a lesser scale. Thomas Buergenthal, one of the members of the commission, said, "I don't think you can ever have reconciliation and a democratic state in El Salvador in which the rule of law prevails unless there is a statement of what happened." Buergenthal also argued that the most serious offenders should be prohibited from holding public office for at least ten years. "The way to end impunity is to make these people pay a price and they must be seen to be paying a price." In the event, the rightist ARENA-controlled National Assembly passed an amnesty law over the objections of the left and center oppositions, despite which the ruling party won a comfortable victory at the first elections held after the peace agreement. Thereafter, although there were no criminal prosecutions, President Alfredo Cristiani dismissed at least 15 of the top army officers named in the report. The Dayton agreement specifically prohibits Radovan Karadzic and General Ratko Mladic, the civilian and military leaders of the Bosnian Serbs, from holding office in the new government, but beyond that it is silent. In South Africa, President Nelson Mandela initially favored, but has been unable to sustain, the total amnesty approach. Instead he is proposing a program of official investigation to provide a public record of the factual details of the criminal activities of the secret police and other government officials in enforcing apartheid.

The "truth commission" approach, with or without the sanction of the settlement agreement, should be considered for Bosnia. It would expose, if not punish, the worst offenders and lay a basis for future reparations to the victims. Indeed, the War Crimes Tribunal, by bringing indictments even if the defendants cannot be brought to trial, may be performing these functions. Moreover, under its rules of procedure, the tribunal is empowered to hold public hearings to present the evidence when it cannot bring an accused to trial. Identifying the perpetrators and holding them up to public shame may not be as satisfying an answer to our justifiable feelings of moral outrage as the quest for punishment. But it may be the only way to permit the healing process to go forward. Prosecutions by national authorities may come later. After the conviction, 50 years after the event, of Paul Touvier for the execution of seven Jews by the Vichy militia in Lyon, Michel Zaoui, one of the prosecutors, concluded: "Fifty years were necessary to break the silence, to emerge from the shame, to look Vichy in the face—to speak without hate and without fear. Only with the third generation can justice be done, in all serenity."[11]

Even this preliminary sketch demonstrates that the problems facing a postwar Bosnia in every dimension—military, economic, and humanitarian—will be enormously complex, difficult, and demanding. The only visible preparation for facing these problems early on was in the war crimes area, and the proposed plan has the limitations just discussed, even though its ultimate impact may be closer to a truth commission than to the Nuremburg trials. The overwhelming need for an immediate, serious, and comprehensive planning effort was realized rather late, and then it focused primarily on military tasks. Only time will tell whether it was adequate to the task. It is perhaps understandable that the nations of the world were unable to mount a military operation to end the horrors of the Bosnian war. It will be unforgivable if they fail to summon the material, intellectual, and moral resources to deal with its aftermath.

Notes

1. The text of the General Framework Agreement for Peace in Bosnia and Herzegovina may be found on the World Wide Web under the heading http://dosfan.lib.uic.edu/www/current/bosnia/daytable.html. Its many annexes can be accessed through the same site.

2. U.N. S.C. Res. 758, June 8, 1992.

3. U.N. S.C. Res. 770, August 13, 1992.

4. U.N. S.C. Res. 776, September 14, 1992.

5. U.N. S.C. Res. 781, October 9, 1992; S.C. Res. 816, March 31, 1993; S.C. Res. 824, May 6, 1993; S.C. Res. 836, June 4, 1993.

6. *Note by the Secretary-General Concerning Certain Aspects of the Function and Operation of the United Nations Peacekeeping Force in Cyprus*, April 11, 1964, 19 U.N. SCOR, Supp. April–June 1964 at 12, U.N. Doc. S/5653 (1964).

7. *Report of the Secretary-General to the Security Council on the United Nations Operation in Cyprus*, Sept. 10, 1964, 19 U.N. SCOR, July–Sept. 1964 at 280, U.N. Doc. S/5950 (1964). The force was already authorized to interpose "where specific arrangements accepted by both communities have been, or in the opinion of the commander on the spot are about to be, violated, thus risking a recurrence of the fighting or endangering law and order" (*Note by the Secretary-General*, n. 1).

8. See Wolfgang H. Reinicke, "Can International Financial Institutions Prevent Internal Violence? The Sources of Ethnic Conflict in Transitional Societies," in Abram Chayes and Antonia H. Chayes, eds., *Preventing Conflict in the Post-Communist World: Mobilizing International and Regional Organizations* (Washington, DC: Brookings Institution, 1995).

9. Barbara Walters argues in her study of 41 civil wars over 50 years that civil wars have not been resolved by even the most skillful mediation. Security guarantees by third parties are required in order to provide the reassurance necessary for disarmament or integration of the military. Unlike transnational conflict, parties cannot retreat behind borders. Bosnia represents a hybrid example. "The Resolution of Civil Wars: Why Negotiations Fail," unpublished manuscript, Columbia University, Institute of War and Peace, 1995.

10. Article 25 of the Charter provides that members "agree to accept and carry out the decisions of the Security Council."

11. Sarah Chayes, "French Justice Struggles with War Crime Issues," *Christian Science Monitor*, April 27, 1994.

Index

About the Authors

Abram Chayes, a former legal adviser, U.S. Department of State, is Felix Frankfurter Professor of Law emeritus at the Harvard Law School. Among his recent works are *The New Sovereignty: Compliance with International Regulatory Agreements* (coauthor, with Antonia Handler Chayes, 1996) and *Preventing Conflict in the Post-Communist World: Mobilizing International and Regional Organizations* (coeditor, with Antonia Handler Chayes, 1996).

Antonia Handler Chayes, a former under secretary of the U.S. Air Force, is senior adviser to the Conflict Management Group and lecturer in the John F. Kennedy School of Government at Harvard University, and a director of United Technologies Corporation. Among her recent works are *Peace Operations: Developing an American Strategy* (coeditor, with George T. Raach, 1995), *The New Sovereignty: Compliance with International Regulatory Agreements* (coauthor, with Abram Chayes, 1996) and *Preventing Conflict in the Post-Communist World: Mobilizing International and Regional Organizations* (coeditor, with Abram Chayes, 1996).

Paul A. Goble, senior fellow at the Potomac Foundation, was an analyst of and special adviser regarding Soviet nationality problems in the U.S. Department of State (1982–89, 1991–92). He was director of research at Radio Liberty (1989–90) and senior associate at the Carnegie Endowment for International Peace (1992–95). He is the editor of four books and the author of many articles on ethnic and nationality problems in the former Soviet Union.

David C. Gompert is vice president, National Security Research Division, of the RAND Corporation. His policymaking positions in government include special assistant to the president for national security affairs (1990–93), deputy assistant secretary of state for European affairs (1981–82), and special assistant to the secretary of state (1973–75). When not in government he has held a variety of high-level positions in the telecommunications and computer industries. He is the author of many articles on issues of international security.

Stanley Hoffmann is the Douglas Dillon Professor of the Civilization of France at Harvard University and was chairman of the Minda de

Gunzburg Center for European Studies at Harvard from 1969 to 1995. His latest book is *The European Sisyphus* (1994).

Jean E. Manas is an associate in investment banking at JP Morgan, Inc. He wrote this chapter in the course of a one-year fellowship at the European Law Research Center of the Harvard Law School.

Richard Sobel is lecturer in history and faculty associate at the Center of International Studies at Princeton University, and research associate at the Roper Center for Public Opinion Research at the University of Connecticut. He edited and coauthored *Public Opinion in U.S. Foreign Policy: The Controversy over Contra Aid* (1993) and is currently at work on a study of public opinion and military intervention.

Richard H. Ullman is David K. E. Bruce Professor of International Affairs at Princeton University. His most recent book is *Securing Europe* (1991).

Thomas G. Weiss is associate director of Brown University's Watson Institute for International Studies and executive director of the Academic Council on the United Nations System. He has written extensively on aspects of development, peacekeeping, humanitarian relief, and international organization. His most recent books are *The United Nations and Civil Wars* (1995); *Mercy Under Fire and Humanitarian Politics* (1995, with Larry Minear); *NGOs, the UN, and Global Governance* (1996, with Leon Gordenker); and *From Massacres to Genocide* (1996, with Robert I. Rotberg).